Military Divorce Tips

Military Divorce Tips

*Health Care, CHCBP,
Uniformed Services Former Spouses'
Protection Act (USFSPA),
Survivor Benefit Plan (SBP),
Retirement Benefits, and Law Answers for
Service Members and Former Spouses*

OR

*Money and Medical Answers for
Service Members, Former Spouses, and Lawyers*

TRACY FOOTE
TracyTrends
New York, USA

This book is sold with the understanding that you will not hold the author or publisher liable for any losses, damages, or alleged losses or damages attributed from the information within and that you will seek professional assistance appropriate to your unique circumstances.

First printing
Printed in the United States of America
Copyright © 2010 by Tracy Foote
Published by TracyTrends
www.TracyTrends.com

All rights reserved. No part of this book may be reproduced, copied or utilized in any form or by any means, electronic or mechanical, including photocopying, recording or by any information storage or retrieval system, without written permission from the Publisher. Making copies of any part of this book for any purpose other than your own personal use is a violation of United States copyright laws.

Please send all inquiries to:
TracyTrends
c/o T. Foote
27 West 86 Street, Suite 17B
New York, NY 10024
tracytrends@aol.com

ISBN: 978-0-9814737-2-7
Library of Congress Control Number: 2010924414
Law/Divorce & Separation
Military/Life and Institutions

To make suggestions for future editions, visit:
http://www.militarydivorcetips.com
To view updates not included in this printing, visit:
http://www.militarydivorcetips.com/updates.html

No Substitute
For Professional Guidance

This book is to be used as a starting point to understanding the unique circumstances involved in a military divorce.

Every effort has been made to ensure that all statements contain references current as of the printing date. Constant changes are being made concerning military divorce. Information in this book is not a substitute for informed professional guidance on tax, legal, investment, accounting, or any other type of specialized advice.

The intention here is not to provide legal advice but to establish a foundation upon which to better communicate for negotiations and litigation.

It is sold with the understanding that you will not hold the author or publisher liable for any losses or damages attributed directly or indirectly to contents within and that you will seek professional assistance appropriate to your own circumstances. One should understand the difference between information and advice, with the latter being a recommendation for actions to take after considering one's particular situation. This book is intended for informational entertainment purposes only.

Contents

Preface vii

Introduction ix
    Terminology x

The Companion Book xi

Abbreviations xii

Organize and Plan Ahead 1
    File or Binder Method 1
    Divorce Notification Checklist 1
    Acknowledgement of Understanding 2
    Lawyer Interview Checklist 2
    Checklist of Reasons to (or not to) Delay Divorce 5
    Divorce Process Checklist 6
    Discovery Checklist for Retired Pay Division 7
    Divorce Decree Checklist for Military Finances 8
    Remarriage Checklist 8

Health Care 9
    Dental Coverage 10
    Health Care for the Children 10
    Military Married to a Military Spouse 11
    Prior Military (Veteran) Dependent Spouse 13
    Non-Veteran Dependent Spouse 16
    The 20/20/20 Rule for TRICARE Health Care 16
    Valuing the Loss of Full Military Health Care 17
    The 20/20/15 Rule for TRICARE Health Care 17

> CHCBP Coverage for 36 Months.. 18
> Extending to Unlimited CHCBP Coverage 23
> Health Care for the Spouse of the Reservist 27
> Health Care Letters and Forms 28

Copies of Court Orders 40
> Legal Fees 40

Military Benefits 41
> Which State to Divorce In? 41
> Jurisdiction 42
> Saving/Losing the Retired Pay Division 43
> Servicemembers Civil Relief Act (SCRA) 44
> Military Spouses Residency Relief Act (MSRRA) 44
> Moving Expenses - Travel and Transportation 45
> Accrued Leave 46
> Thrift Savings Plan (TSP) 46
> Commissary and Exchange Benefits 46
> Last Will and Testament 47
> Military Spouse Preference Program 47

Preserving USAA Membership 48

Garnishments 50
> Alimony 50
> Child Support 51

Life Insurance 52

Post 9/11 GI Bill for Education 53

VA Home Loan 56
> Veteran Spouse 58

Designated Agents 59
  Preparation Checklist for Assistance 60
  Waiver of Privacy Act 61

Retirement Pay Overview 63
  Vested Retirement Pay 64
  Disposable Retired Pay 65
  Retroactive or "Back Pay" 65
  Retirement Pension and Death Beneficiaries 66
  Remarriage 66

Uniformed Services Former Spouses' Protection Act 67
  10/10 Rule for the Agent (not Division) 68
  50 Percent Limit Rule for the Agent 69
  65 Percent Limit Rule for the Agent 70
  Abused Spouses 70
  Order of Priority of Payments 71
  Timely Account Set Up & Payments 72
  Indemnification Statement - Civil Service Employment 72

Computing the Division of Pay 73
  Cost of Living Adjustments (COLAs) 74
  Disability Pay 78
  Indemnification Language - Disability Waiver 79
  Example A: Disability Pay Indemnification and Tax Benefits .. 84
  Concurrent Retirement Disability Pay (CRDP) 87
  Retirement Pay and Social Security 88
  State Percentage to the Former Spouse (a) 89
  Marital Share (b) 90
  Marital Share for Reservists 92

    Former Spouse Percentage *94*
    Example B: Divorce after Retirement.. *95*
    Example C: Service Member Not Yet Retired *96*
    Example D: Marital Share as of Date of Divorce....................... *97*
    Retirement Pay Figure (c) *98*

Language for Division of Pay **103**
    Example E: Language for Division of Pay *104*
    Fixed Amount or Percentage Language *108*
    Formula Percentage Language *109*
    Hypothetical Formula Language *111*
    Remaining in Service - Avoiding the Award *113*
    Hypothetical Award Amount.. *114*
    Calculations at Retirement Time... *117*
    Summary of Retirement Award Steps Checklist....................... *122*

Military Pay Charts 2002-2010 .... **123**

Former Spouse Award Requirement... **133**
    Retired Pay Application *133*
    DFAS Retired Pay Acknowledgement Letter *136*

Retiree Account (Pay) Statements... **137**
    Retiree Account Statement (RAS) Copies.................................. *137*
    Reading the RAS... *138*
    MYPAY.Gov for the Former Spouse *140*

Survivor Benefit Plan (SBP) & The Reserve Component (RCSBP) **141**
    SBP Comprehension Checklist.. *142*
    SBP Eligibility Requirements.. *143*
    SBP and Remarriage... *143*
    SBP Base and Annuity Amounts *144*

    SBP Premium Cost 146
    SBP Tax Benefit 147
    SBP or Life Insurance 148
    SBP Premium Responsibility 150
    Calculating SBP Premium Reimbursement 153
    Reserve Component Survivor Benefit Plan (RCSBP) 158
    Awarding the Former Spouse SBP 159
    Former Spouse Deemed Election 159
    DFAS Deemed Election Acknowledgement Letter 163
    Service Member SBP Election 164
    SBP Processed Incorrectly 166
    Decree Language Awarding SBP 168

Taxes Incident to Divorce and IRS Form 1099-R 169

Forms 171
    Form W-4P Withholding Certificate for Pension or Annuity Payments 171
    DD Form 149, Application for Correction of Military Record under the Provisions of Title 10 172
    DD Form 2293, Application for Former Spouse Payments from Retired Pay 174
    DD Form 2656, Data for Payment of Retired Personnel 176
    DD Form 2656-1, Survivor Benefit Plan Election Statement for Former Spouse Coverage 180
    DD Form 2656-10, Survivor Benefit Plan (SBP)/Reserve Component (RC) SBP Request for Deemed Election 182

Contacts 184

Further Reading 184

Internet Resources 184

Index 185

Preface

While it takes two decisions to marry, it only takes one decision to divorce. This book is intended to provide a little more control in an uncontrollable situation.

Having spent almost twenty years associated with the military (over nine in service and ten more as a dependent spouse) I have a familiarity with both viewpoints in a military divorce. Having experienced the military divorce process first hand, I've also dealt with the future consequences and errors that might transpire during retirement.

Accurate comprehensible information pertaining to military divorce is not readily available. Internet searches on this subject can be overwhelming and time consuming, and often, only bits and pieces of issues are covered. The consolidated information included here provides essential grounding upon which to ask questions or read further.

This book will guide you down correct paths, ensuring the right questions are asked, and providing direct references for use in discussions with both customer service personnel and attorneys. The overall goal here is to facilitate a positive outcome for both parties during divorce and thereafter.

As you gain awareness of the complexities of the U.S. Codes, and become familiar with the applicable rules and regulations, I encourage you to have patience. Some topics, by their nature, often require several readings to obtain a full understanding. It is inevitable that you will encounter misleading, contradictory, and perhaps incorrect (due to inexperience or lack of knowledge) advice from various sources. Use the enclosed information and references to steer your divorce down the most beneficial path.

Military divorce issues are constantly changing. My goal is to share accurate information both within this book and on the website. Feedback, comments, and documented updates are welcomed, will be considered for future editions or online articles, and can be emailed to militarydivorcetips@gmail.com.

If you would recommend this book to others, please consider writing a five star review on Amazon.com. Your valuable time and comments are appreciated.

Introduction

This efficient reference tool provides quick insight to military divorce complexities without delving too heavily into the U.S. Codes themselves. At the same time, attorneys are able to use the numerous footnotes when sources are needed for litigation. The history, logic, and reasoning behind the Congressional laws are not covered, but instead, the focus is on the applications of the current laws as written.

The main audience is military members (who entered service after September 7, 1980) and their spouses who are currently considering or facing divorce. This book can also provide limited guidance for service members with earlier entry dates and divorces already finalized. Service members and former spouses in those categories should obtain further consultation to be aware of the different exceptions that may apply to them.

The personnel office, finance office, SBP counselor, judges, lawyers, and clients, are just a few involved at both divorce and retirement time. They will all express their knowledge and opinions concerning how an issue should be addressed or how a form should be completed. When one takes into account all the participants, codes, and regulations involved, it is understandable (but undesirable) that an error might be made either during the writing, interpreting, or processing of the paperwork enforcing a final divorce decree.

The goal is to "get it right the first time," thus avoiding appeals and modifications through either the court system or the military Board of Corrections. This is the principal purpose of this book.

It is difficult to compare military divorces. Each decree includes a unique mixture of personal complexities and application of laws exclusive to the particular state. Due to the complex information involved, sections of this book may require several readings for full comprehension.

It is important to take time to understand these areas to avoid pricey mistakes. A mistake of $100 a month costs $1,200 a year. In 45 years, this would result in a $54,000 error, and this loss is even greater considering the investment potential. Suddenly, the seemingly small error is a very costly mistake.

As this books educates and increases one's knowledge and understanding of the laws applied, it should be easier to set aside some of the emotions involved in a divorce.

This book is a tool for finding advantageous angles in a military divorce, as well as setting expectations and follow-up actions for the future. Detailed checklists are provided up front as a preview of forthcoming sections. After reading the final chapters, they should be referred to and re-read.

The content here is intended as an introduction to complex topics. Further detailed information can be found through the many links provided on http://www.militarydivorcetips.com.

Terminology

Former Spouse: The terms spouse and former spouse are used interchangeably to refer to the current dependent spouse of the service member (possibly a soon-to-be former spouse) as well as those who are already former spouses (ex-spouses).

Gross Retired Pay: The service member's pay before deductions.

Retired Pay: The terms military pension, retired/retirement pay, disposable retired pay, disposable pay, and retainer pay are often but not always used interchangeably. Technically the terms pension and retired pay are incorrect, as the military pay after retirement is a retainer pay, a reduced pay for reduced service. Nevertheless, there are instances in the regulations referring to the pay as "retired pay." This is the term generally used throughout this book. In this context, when any of the above terms are mentioned, they are all referring to the *disposable retired pay* of the service member as defined by law to be divisible by states as marital property. (Usually the concerns and emotions surrounding terminology arise when discussing the logic and legality of the laws themselves, which is not addressed in this book.)

Present Value Offset: This method of marital asset division refers to waiving the right to retired pay in exchange for some other asset. It requires the services of an accountant to compute the retired pay present value. It is not covered in this book but links to this topic are at http://www.militarydivorcetips.com/present-value-offset.html.

The Companion Book

Family Divorce Tips

Financial Impact of Divorce Decisions Concerning Children, Taxes, and College

Seemingly small divorce decisions often result in unexpected consequences. While *Military Divorce Tips* focuses on issues in a military divorce, the forthcoming companion book, *Family Divorce Tips*, addresses financial issues often overlooked in divorces involving children.

It covers specific financial issues affecting parents, such as:

— Taxes: custody and dependency exemption consequences

— Child Investments: education accounts, EE Bonds, etc.

— College: financial aid strategies for divorced parents

— Child Support: jurisdiction issues when relocating

— Parent Relocation Restrictions: due to child visitation

— Passports: considerations for obtaining and/or travel

While most divorce books focus on the present day division of property, *Family Divorce Tips* focuses on the future consequences of these financial decisions. It includes a unique mixture of financial considerations associated with children and divorce. It also contains explanations for one of the most overlooked and sometimes forgotten issue in a divorce — the long term financial impact of decisions surrounding the U.S. tax laws.

Family Divorce Tips will not only help strengthen the financial areas surrounding children in a divorce decree, but it will assist in ensuring one understands the long term consequences behind the signed document. Military families should own both books prior to finalizing a divorce decree.

Abbreviations

CHCBP: Continued Health Care Benefit Program
COLA: Cost of Living Adjustment
CRDP: Concurrent Retirement and Disability Pay
CRSC: Combat Related Special Compensation
DEERS: Defense Enrollment Eligibility Reporting System
DFAS: Defense Finance and Accounting Service
DRO: Domestic Relations Order
DRP: Disposable Retired Pay
DVA: Department of Veterans Affairs
HMO: Health Maintenance Organization
JAG: Judge Advocate General
LAA: Legal Assistance Attorney
MCO: Military Court Order (military version of QDRO)
MMTF: Military Medical Treatment Facility
MSRRA: Military Spouses Residency Relief Act
PCS: Permanent Change of Station
PCA: Permanent Change of Assignment (on the same base)
QDRO: Qualified Domestic Relations Order
RCSBP: Reserve Component Survivor Benefit Plan
RSFPP: Retired Serviceman's Family Protection Plan
SBP: Survivor Benefit Plan
RAS: Retiree Account Statement
RSO: Retirement Service Office
SCRA: Servicemembers Civil Relief Act
SGLI: Servicemembers' Group Life Insurance
TAP: Transition Assistance Program
TAMP: Transitional Assistance Management Program
TSP: Thrift Savings Plan
USAA: United Services Automobile Association
USFSPA: Uniformed Services Former Spouses' Protection Act
VGLI: Veterans' Group Life Insurance

Organize and Plan Ahead

File or Binder Method

Getting organized should be the first step in planning for an upcoming divorce. A binder or file box works well and should contain folders or divisions for the following:

- Original documents: court orders, letters, etc.

- Time-line, calendar, or journal annotating meeting dates and times, names of persons spoken with, topics discussed, actions taken or to be taken, and the next follow-up date.

- A list of all expenses divided into categories such as legal, household, child living costs (food, clothing, and shelter), child extracurricular (music, athletics, art), vacation, etc.

- A list of current assets and debts, including amounts

Divorce Notification Checklist

Upon first mention of possible divorce, consider the following:

- Take inventory of all financial assets, including current debts, account balances, and personal property.

- Change the life insurance beneficiary.

- Separate all joint credit cards, but try to preserve current credit card limits by explaining the household income is the same and only the name is to be removed.

- Update your Last Will and Testament.

- Be cautious of all communications, including phone calls and text messages.

Acknowledgement of Understanding

Clients expect their lawyers to educate them, protect them, and take actions to ensure their best possible future. It is not uncommon for lawyers to also wish to protect themselves by avoiding any state bar grievances, malpractice allegations, or negligent claims. Lawyers may ask clients to sign an acknowledgement of understanding of specific items discussed. Occasionally this statement itself will shed even more light on a complex topic. For a sample of such a statement see the American Bar Association's Summer 2008 Newsletter to the Military Committee, Appendix 2.[1]

Lawyer Interview Checklist

The initial interview questions should be designed to determine the knowledge and experience of the lawyer as well as assessing personality and attitude.

One should look for a lawyer licensed in the applicable state and specialized in family law, domestic relations, and if possible, military divorce. By asking the right questions and carefully listening to the lawyer's responses, one can determine the overall approach the lawyer will be using throughout the divorce and then decide if this working relationship will be well-matched.

Interview questions should be designed to obtain distinct new information. If one already knows the answer to a question, it should not be asked. This is not a time to test the lawyer. Instead, take advantage of the opportunity (usually free) to learn more. Try rephrasing a question to gain some new knowledge, such as asking how the issue has been handled in the applicable state.

The questions recommended in this checklist assume at the time of interview, the potential client has read this book entirely and is well educated in the core issues behind each question.

---

1. Wm. John Camp, "The Continuation of Health Care Benefits Program (CHCBP) as a Long-Term Health Care Option for Former Military Spouses," *Roll Call*, Newsletter of the Military Committee, ABA Family Law Section, Vol. 2008-1 Summer 2008, Appendix 2. http://meetings.abanet.org/webupload/commupload/FL115277/newsletterpubs/rc_sum08.pdf.

Try to obtain these answers by phone, at no charge, prior to the interview, perhaps from the lawyer's paralegal or assistant:

1. How long can a military divorce case take?
2. Can this lawyer represent me for the entire case?
3. How many years has this lawyer practiced?
4. What is the educational background of this lawyer?
5. What is the usual rate per hour? Is there a minimum charge for each contact (phone calls, etc.) with this lawyer?
6. What additional charges might be incurred such as phone calls, voice mails, faxes, staff time, hours spent obtaining copies of court documents, etc.?
7. Will this lawyer accept after hour phone calls to his or her home or cell phone?
8. What tasks might be performed by assistants?
9. Is a retainer required or can payment wait until the completion of the divorce? What happens if a retainer is used up? If we decide not to proceed, what happens to unused portions of the retainer?
10. Will the billing statement show a description of how time was spent and for how long?
11. Are clients permitted to pay a set amount per month as opposed to paying a bill in full?
12. What happens if I fall behind on my payments?

Consider these questions for the initial lawyer interview:

13. In how many military divorce cases did you represent the service member and in how many the former spouse?
14. How long ago did these cases take place?
15. Could you explain an issue in one of these cases that was not ruled (or unable to reach a negotiation) in your favor?
16. How many of these cases have you taken to trial?
17. How many appeals have you handled?

18. Will I review drafts of all documents, letters, and orders prior to transfer to the opposing lawyer?
19. What states have jurisdiction over the issues in my case?
20. What is the formula used by this state in awarding the division of retirement pay to the former spouse?
21. Does this state use the *date of divorce*, date of separation, or another date as the date for division of retirement pay?
22. How has this state handled requests for the opposing party to pay all legal fees and relating costs?
23. What are the percentages (50/50, 40/60, etc.) used by this state to divide assets? Does this change if the former spouse has been out of the workforce for several years?
24. What is the alimony amount and duration permitted in this state and is it affected by remarriage?
25. What is the child support amount and duration permitted in this state? Are there automatic increases for inflation?
26. How does this state treat the various pays received by the service member when calculating child support and alimony?
    a. Does the state consider all pay figures from the Leave and Earnings Statement or only the taxable figures?
    b. If the state includes the nontaxable figures, will they be adjusted upward to reflect their true value as if taxes had been paid?
    c. If the service member lives on base, does this state assign the income the service member would receive if living off base?
27. Has this state ever considered the spouse's potential future military health care benefits as part of the marital assets?
28. Does this state consider the service member's accrued leave when dividing assets?
29. How has this state handled the responsibility for payment of the Survivor Benefit Plan premiums?

30. If the service member continues active duty beyond the year eligible for retirement, does this state order former spouse retirement payments to begin anyway?

Pitfalls

— *Clients are not the lawyer's teacher:* If a client is spending time educating the lawyer, a request should be made for reduced billing.

— *Story hours cost clients money:* Lawyers should not be the client's therapist. Some lawyers will listen to all the venting a client wishes to express. Others, recognizing this tendency, will steer conversations down more professional paths.

— *Focus on the big picture:* When negotiating for possession of a $15 vase, don't end up with a $770 bill (from four $5 faxes and three $250 discussion hours). Decide ahead of time the items and issues worth pursuing during negotiations. With legal issues, time really is money. Every fax, phone call, and meeting contributes toward increased fees.

Checklist of Reasons to (or not to) Delay Divorce

Consider the following issues when deciding on the date to finalize a divorce *(see* details in applicable sections):

- ✓ Better jurisdiction options
- ✓ Military commitment (Servicemembers Civil Relief Act)
- ✓ Upcoming line numbers, promotions, and bonuses
- ✓ Dual-military to dependent spouse for CHCBP health care
- ✓ 15 and 20 year marriage mark for health care
- ✓ 20 year mark for commissary and exchange benefits
- ✓ Owning a USAA policy for lifetime benefits
- ✓ Travel and Transportation Entitlements, relocation of the former spouse and household goods
- ✓ Use of the Spouse Preference Program for employment
- ✓ VA Benefits: Home Loan and GI Bill options

Divorce Process Checklist

The checklist below is a general overview of what might need to be accomplished in a military divorce (actual order may vary):

1. Hire lawyers and decide the possible states of jurisdiction; then choose a state for litigation.
2. Petition for divorce and/or file Respondent answers.
3. Complete the discovery process by obtaining income documents, Leave and Earnings Statements (LESs), and other information listed on the Discovery Checklist.
4. Discuss and draft provisions for all items in the Divorce Decree Checklist for Military Finances.
5. Draft the Military Retirement Pay Division Order including SBP, alimony, and child support (if applicable), and after considering pay increases based on service entry date anniversaries, line numbers, promotions, and bonuses.
6. Finalize all drafts through negotiations.
7. Obtain copies of court orders as well as a copy on disk.
8. Establish or change life insurance policy beneficiaries.
9. If there are children, send one decree copy to TRICARE.
10. If desiring CHCBP, the former spouse applies and receives health care approval within 60 days following divorce.
11. If awarded a retirement pay award, the former spouse submits the Form 2293 application within 90 days.
12. If awarded SBP, the former spouse submits the DD Form 2656-10, deemed election, within one year of divorce (but preferably, within 90 days).
13. If applicable, the former spouse receives written acknowledgement from the designated agent of the retirement pay award application and receipt of SBP coverage.
14. If so ordered, (at retirement or immediately if the service member is already retired), the service member completes the DD Form, 2656 and DD Form 2656-1 electing the former spouse as the SBP beneficiary.

15. Review respective Forms W-4, Employees Withholding Allowance Certificate or W-4P, Withholding Certificate for Pension and Annuity Payments for necessary adjustments.
16. After 36 months, if participating in CHCBP, the former spouse might apply for unlimited CHCBP health care.
17. If so ordered, the service member sets up allotments for child support, alimony, former spouse retirement pay, disability indemnification and SBP reimbursement.
18. If so ordered, the former spouse sets up an allotment for reimbursement of SBP premiums.
19. The service member and former spouse check retirement pay figures computed by the designated agent.
20. The service member and former spouse sign up online to monitor monthly pay through http://www.mypay.gov.

Discovery Checklist for Retired Pay Division

The following information should be obtained in the discovery process for computation of a division of retired pay:

— Marriage date

— Copies of past income tax forms

— Service member's service entry date

— Disclosure of any current disabilities

— Predicted divorced date and predicted rank on this date

— Length of service (creditable years) at time of divorce

— Rank during the 36 months prior to divorce, including any promotion dates

— Copies of Leave and Earnings Statements (LES) or Retiree Account Statements (RAS) for the last 36 months

— Disclosure of any bonuses received or upcoming

— For a reservist, a copy of the Statement of Retirement Points, also called a Point Summary, or Points Record

— If already retired, retirement rank and date, and a copy of the retirement orders and the DD Form 214, *Certificate of Release or Discharge from Active Duty*

Divorce Decree Checklist for Military Finances

Discuss and include the following in a divorce decree if desired:
- ✓ Waiver of Privacy Act
- ✓ Garnishment for alimony, child support, retirement pay
- ✓ SBP election, base amount, and premium responsibility
- ✓ TSP, accrued leave, relocation expenses, legal fees
- ✓ Indemnification statement, in general or specific for federal employment, Disability Pay, CRDP, CRSC, etc.
- ✓ Sharing health care premiums and cost of decree copies
- ✓ Eligibility for VA home loan and/or USAA membership

Remarriage Checklist

Upon remarriage, consider the following:

* **Health Care for the Former Spouse:** The 20/20/20, 20/20/15, and 36 Month health care options all stop upon remarriage. It is unclear if CHCBP Unlimited Care continues when remarriage occurs after age 55.

* **Commissary and exchange privileges:** Privileges are suspended upon remarriage but can be reinstated.

* **Former Spouse Retirement Award:** The award (pay) continues after remarriage. *Exception:* If the former spouse is receiving an award under the rules of an *abused former spouse*, upon remarriage, payments are suspended but may later resume in the case of annulment, divorce, or death of the new spouse.

* **SBP (Premiums, Annuity, Beneficiary):**
  — If a former spouse remarries before age 55, the SBP premium is suspended (but can later resume in the case of death, annulment, or divorce; as the right to coverage is not lost). SBP annuity payments follow the same rules.
  — In general, when a service member remarries, the SBP beneficiary remains the former spouse.

* **Social Security:** Upon remarriage, one can no longer claim Social Security based on an ex-spouse's salary.

* **Last Will and Testament:** Update after remarriage.

Health Care

Health care for the service member is usually not a concern in a military divorce, because the service member's health care will continue to be covered by the military.

The former spouse has several health care options which are set by federal law. These plans are not negotiable items in a divorce. The sources for information on former spouse health care are:

1. U.S. Code § 1078a. Continued Health Benefits Coverage[2]

2. Department of Defense Regulation Title 32 Code of Federal Regulations (C.F.R.) § 199.20 Continued Health Care Benefit Program (CHCBP)[3]

3. Humana Military Healthcare Services *Continued Health Care Benefit Program (CHCBP) Handbook*[4]

4. The *TRICARE Standard Handbook* which contains the rules followed by CHCBP [5]

---

2. U.S. Code Title 10 > Subtitle A > Part II > Chapter 55 > § 1078a. *Continued Health Benefits Coverage,* Jan. 5, 2009, http://www.law.cornell.edu/uscode/10/usc_sec_10_00001078---a000-.html.

3. Title 32 C.F.R. § 199.20 *Continued Health Care Benefit Program (CHCBP),* http://law.justia.com/us/cfr/title32/32-2.1.1.1.7.0.1.20.html.

4. Humana Military Healthcare Services, "Continued Health Care Benefit Program," *CHCBP Handbook,* http://www.humana-military.com/library/pdf/chcbp-handbook.pdf.

5. TRICARE Standard Handbook, http://www.TRICARE.mil/mybenefit/download/forms/Standard_Handbook_06.pdf

Dental Coverage

Dental Coverage is not offered under any of the military health care benefit program options, so a former spouse must obtain outside private dental insurance, a dental discount plan, or a dental plan connected to civilian employment.

Health Care for the Children

Dependent children will retain their *dependent status* and will still qualify for use of TRICARE, the health care program provided to service members and their families. This includes health care for the children at military facilities.

The former spouse can apply for an escort letter which will permit access to military facilities for the purpose of bringing the children to medical appointments.

Each child will continue to have a dependent ID card. These ID cards are either obtained by the service member or the service member can provide a copy of the DD Form 1172, *Application for Uniformed Services Identification Card DEERS Enrollment*, to the former spouse, who can apply for the cards. The dependent ID cards should be kept by the custodial parent.

An entire copy of the divorce decree must be sent to establish custody in the medical records when all of the following occur:

- The former spouse is the custodial parent of the children,
- The children still use TRICARE for their health care, and
- The parent wishes access to the TRICARE medical records.

An entire copy of the divorce decree must be sent to:

PGBA, LLC,
Attn: Priority Department
P.O. Box 870146
Surfside Beach, SC 29587

Military Married to a Military Spouse

In the case of a service member divorcing another service member (dual-military spouses), both service members will continue to be covered under the TRICARE military health care program.

If a full military career is planned for both parties, health care coverage should not be a concern at divorce time.

In other cases, one military spouse may have never intended a full military career, but instead, expected to separate from the military, remain married, and receive lifelong health care coverage as a dependent spouse.

> **Example:** Sgt. Alyssa Finch is divorcing Sgt. Jack Finch. Alyssa always wanted a military career, so she intends to stay in service where her health care will continue. Their original plan was for Jack to finish his remaining two years, separate from the military, and become a dependent husband. Jack looks at the situation and wants to know what his health care choices are after divorce and after separating from the service.

This divorcing (expecting to separate) service member has several choices, (each discussed in their applicable sections):

1. If possible, consider re-enlisting and perhaps reconsider a military career which would continue TRICARE.

2. Check if eligible for the 20/20/20 or 20/20/15 former spouse medical rules.

3. Check for eligibility upon separation to participate in the Department of Veterans Affairs (VA) health care program.

4. Check for eligibility upon separation, to enroll in Continued Health Care Benefit Program (CHCBP) which will be limited to 18 months coverage (based on active duty or full time National Guard status).[6]

---

6. Humana Military Healthcare Services, "CHCBP Policy, Section E. Period of Coverage" *CHCBP Handbook*, p. 22, 1 a (1), http://www.humana-military.com/library/pdf/chcbp-handbook.pdf

5. Consider a delay of divorce, long enough to become a dependent spouse enrolled in DEERS and TRICARE, to meet the dependency requirement for qualifying for the 36 month CHCBP program offered to *dependent* former spouses and then later, to possibly transition from the 36 month CHCBP coverage to the unlimited coverage.[7]

6. Find another type of insurance such as purchasing private insurance or that connected to new employment.

Delaying A Dual-Military Divorce for Health Care

If a divorce is close to a possible separation date, lawyers should evaluate the benefits of delaying long enough for the separating military spouse to become a *dependent* spouse enrolled in the Defense Enrollment Eligibility Reporting System (DEERS). This may enable the spouse exiting service to transition from the 36 month CHCBP coverage to the unlimited coverage where dependency is a criteria. Consider the modified scenario.

> **Example:** Sgt. Alyssa Finch is divorcing Sgt. Jack Finch. Alyssa will stay in service with continued health care. The original plan was for Jack to *separate next month* and become her dependent spouse. With divorce pending, Jack wants to know his choices concerning health care.

If the final divorce date is delayed until after Jack separates, Jack can become a dependent enrolled in DEERS, opening up the options for the 36 month CHCBP health care and possible later transition to the unlimited CHCBP health care. Dependency is one of the requirements for both periods of coverage.[8]

---

7. Humana Military Healthcare Services, "CHCBP Policy, Section A Eligibility, *CHCBP Handbook*, p. 15, 3b, http://www.humana-military.com/library/pdf/chcbp-handbook.pdf

8. Humana Military Healthcare Services, "CHCBP Policy, Section E. Period of Coverage, Unremarried Former Spouse," *CHCBP Handbook*, p. 24, E. 1c (2)b, http://www.humana-military.com/library/pdf/chcbp-handbook.pdf.

Prior Military (Veteran) Dependent Spouse

When a service member married another service member (dual-military couple), and later, one spouse separates from service, this spouse is a dependent Veteran spouse.

> **Example:** Captain Joe married Captain Sue. After serving for five years, Captain Sue honorably separated from the service, became Captain Joe's dependent wife, and used the military TRICARE program for her health care. After 7 years of marriage things fell apart and a divorce is pending. Sue wants to know what her options are concerning health care after divorce.

This dependent Veteran former spouse has four health care possibilities, (each discussed in their applicable sections):

1. Check if eligible upon discharge to participate in the Department of Veterans Affairs (VA) health care program.
2. Check if eligible for the 20/20/20 or 20/20/15 former spouse health care rules.
3. Check if eligible to enroll in the 36 month Continued Health Care Benefit Program (CHCBP) with possible transition into the unlimited coverage program.
4. Find another type of insurance such as purchasing private insurance or that connected to new employment.

Department of Veterans Affairs Health Care

Veterans, who were released under conditions other than dishonorable, may be able to participate in the Department of Veterans Affairs (VA) health care program. To be eligible for the VA health care program, Veterans must meet required enlistment dates and restrictions, and have served 24 continuous months or the full period for which they were called to active duty.[9]

---

9. Department of Veterans Affairs, "Basic Eligibility," *Federal Benefits for Veterans, Dependents & Survivors Handbook,* 2009 Edition, p. 1. http://www1.va.gov/opa/vadocs/FedBen.pdf.

VA health care is often overlooked as Veterans either believe they will not qualify, believe the health care program does not have the capability to handle women's health care, or are misinformed in some other manner.

All Veterans should apply for VA health care to determine if they qualify. VA health care benefits can be used even if one participates in Medicare, Medicaid, TRICARE or private health insurance. To apply, Veterans obtain a copy of their DD Form 214, *Certificate of Release or Discharge from Active Duty*, received at discharge and complete the VA Form 10-10EZ, *Application for Health Benefits* (found online at https://www.1010ez.med.va.gov/sec/vha/1010ez/) or obtain one by calling 1-877-222-VETS (8387) to have a form sent by U.S. mail.

The VA health care program is separated into priority groups with a range of category descriptions including disability ratings, war Veterans, Medicaid benefits, income levels, and more. Priority Groups are verified annually and it is possible to move from one Priority Group to another. If the original application was completed online, the annual reconfirmation of status will also be accomplished online. If the original application was mailed, annual reconfirmation will be accomplished by U.S. mail.

Once Veterans qualify for the VA health care program, they may change groups but are never eliminated. The lowest category possible is Priority Group 8, which includes qualifying Veterans with income and/or net worth above both the national and geographical thresholds who agree to the co-pays. Those willing to pay the co-pays, have health care for life.

In the example of Captain Joe and Sue, if Sue was a homemaker with no income, at divorce time she should easily qualify for Priority Group 7, Veterans with income below and/or net worth above the VA national income threshold and income below the geographic income threshold who agree to pay co-pays. Even if she later establishes a high paying job, she should still qualify for Priority Group 8, Veterans with income and/or net worth above the VA national income threshold and the geographic income threshold who agree to pay co-pays.

An income eligibility calculator is found online at http://www4.va.gov/healtheligibility/apps/enrollmentcalculator.

Rules and funding availability frequently change so if denied, Veterans should consider reapplying annually.

The VA enrollment process takes time. After completing the initial application, allow four weeks to receive a reply in writing through the postal system. This letter will confirm enrollment or explain the reason for ineligibility. The confirmation packet also includes directions concerning how to appeal the decision.

Approval letters confirm assignment to a priority group and request the Veteran contact the Enrollment Coordinator at the nearest VA health care facility. The Enrollment Coordinator will either schedule an orientation briefing or provide guidance on how to obtain a VA health care ID card.

At the local VA facility, Veterans should request a copy of:

1) *Department of Veterans Affairs Health Care Overview Brochure Booklet (20 pages)*
2) *Federal Benefits for Veterans, Dependents, & Survivors Handbook (156 pages)*, also found online at: http://www1.va.gov/opa/vadocs/FedBen.pdf
3) *Enrollment Priority Groups Health Care Information sheet*
4) *Financial Income Threshold Information Sheet*
5) *Co-pay Requirements at a Glance Information sheet*
6) Any *Frequently Asked Question Sheets* they may have

Many Veterans understand they meet the definition of a Veteran but do not know they may also qualify for health care benefits after serving only 24 continuous months (or the full period for which they were called to active duty). A former spouse might need to be reminded of his or her existing Veteran status and the health care benefits that come along with it.

The Department of Veterans Affairs should always be considered for health care. It can be used in addition to or instead of the other options of CHCBP, private insurance, or an employer sponsored health insurance program.

Non-Veteran Dependent Spouse

The most common military marriage consists of a service member and a spouse who has no prior affiliation with the military. In these divorce cases, unless the dependent spouse meets all the eligibility requirements of the 20/20/20 Rule, lifetime full military dependent health care privileges will be lost.

Several possible health care options exist for a non-veteran former spouse:

- The 20/20/20 Rule for TRICARE
- The 20/20/15 Rule for TRICARE
- The CHCBP 36 month health care plan
- The CHCBP unlimited health care plan

The 20/20/20 Rule for TRICARE Health Care

Dependency status and full military health care privileges are offered to a former spouse who:

1. Was married 20 years or more to a service member who
2. Served at least 20 years in the armed forces and
3. There is at least a 20 year overlap (there are at least 20 years of marriage while the service member served) and
4. Does not remarry and
5. Has no employer sponsored health care[10]

In cases approaching any of the twenty year deadlines, lawyers might consider possibly delaying the divorce to establish this coverage. There is no monetary cost to the service member and yet the former spouse will gain health care coverage for life.

A "gray area reservist" is the term used for a service member who is retirement eligible but under Reserve rules, must wait until age 60 to draw retirement pay. Former spouses in this category must wait until the service member reaches age 60 for medical benefits to start and thus, there is a gap period of non-coverage.

---

10. U.S. Code Title 10 > Subtitle A > Part II > Chapter 55 > § 1072, *Definitions*, (2)(F), Jan. 5, 2009, http://www.law.cornell.edu/uscode/10/1072.html.

Valuing the Loss of Full Military Health Care

Lawyers representing the former spouse could try to negotiate compensation for the loss of the opportunity for the former spouse to become eligible under the 20/20/20 rules for lifetime health care.

Especially when the service member is the initiator in the divorce, one could argue that due to the service member's actions, the spouse will be unable to meet these 20/20/20 requirements. By filing, the service member has taken this potential privilege away from the former spouse, and therefore, the former spouse deserves some level of compensation.

An accountant specializing in health costs could be hired to place a net present value on this loss. Attorneys could also present arguments for both parties to share responsibility for the former spouse's future health care premiums.

The 20/20/15 Rule for TRICARE Health Care

One year of military health care privileges are offered to a former spouse who:

1. Was married 20 years or more to a service member who
2. Served at least 20 years in the armed forces and
3. There is at least a 15 year overlap (there are 15 years of marriage while the service member served) and
4. Does not remarry and
5. Has no employer sponsored health care [11]

Within 60 days of termination of this one year coverage, the 20/20/15 former spouse can apply to transition to the 36 month CHCBP coverage (discussed next) and then later, possibly transition once again into an unlimited coverage option, (discussed later). At a minimum, the 20/20/15 former spouse should receive four years of health care coverage.

---

11. U.S. Code Tilte 10 > Subtitle A > Part II > Chapter 55 > § 1072 *Definitions*, (2)(G) & (2)(H), Jan. 5, 2009, http://www.law.cornell.edu/uscode/10/1072.html.

CHCBP Coverage for 36 Months

Congress has provided the DoD Continued Health Care Benefit Program (CHCBP) for temporary health care until civilian health care is provided. CHCBP acts like a bridge to transition from one health care program to another. It is offered to service members separating from the military for 18 months of coverage and former spouses for 36 months, (at the end of which it may be possible to transition to unlimited coverage).

Former spouses are often familiar with TRICARE, the military health care program. CHCBP follows most of the rules of TRICARE *Standard* but CHCBP is *not* considered part of TRICARE itself. Former spouses will no longer be enrolled in TRICARE and cannot use military medical facilities or pharmacies.

CHCBP is a government sponsored program and part of the Humana Military Healthcare Services (HMHS) Inc., which uses the same doctors and pharmacies in the TRICARE network and follows *most* of the TRICARE *Standard* rules.

The concern for former spouses at divorce time is learning what health care procedures are covered, eligibility requirements, the cost, and the duration of coverage.

HMHS customer service provides help in understanding what health care procedures are covered and the co-pay costs involved. Former spouses may only elect individual (not family) coverage.[12]

In 2010 the premium cost for an individual plan was $933 per quarter (paid in advance on a quarterly basis). Checks are payable to The United States Treasury. Assuming payments are received timely, the initial length of coverage will last 36 months. Untimely payments result in elimination from the health care program.

CHCBP is easier understood when viewed in two steps:

▶ Qualifying for Eligibility (including enrollment)

▶ Qualifying for Duration

---

12. U.S. Code Title 10 > Subtitle A > Part II > Chapter 55 > § 1078a. *Continued Health Benefits Coverage,* Jan. 5, 2009, (e) Coverage of Dependents http://www.law.cornell.edu/uscode/10/usc_sec_10_00001078---a000-.html.

Eligibility Requirement and Application

The following requirements for eligibility are taken directly from the former spouses' eligibility section in the handbook:

"3. A person who:

a. Is an unremarried former spouse of a member or former member of the uniformed services (for purposes of this program, there is no time requirement regarding the length of time the former spouse was married to the member or former member);

b. On the day before the date of the final decree of divorce, dissolution, or annulment was covered under a health plan under TRICARE or [the Transition Assistance Management Program] TAMP *as a dependent* of the member or former member; and

c. Is not eligible for TRICARE [under 20/20/20 or 20/20/15 rules] as a former spouse of a member or former member."[13]

The 36 month program has no marriage duration requirement which is a sharp contrast to the marriage requirements found in the 20/20/20 and 20/20/15 programs. Theoretically, a marriage of one day would qualify.

For Requirement 3b, the former spouse requests a Certificate of Creditable Coverage *(see* p. 28-29) from the Defense Enrollment Eligibility Reporting System (DEERS) office:

Defense Manpower Data Center (DMDC)
Support Office, Attn: CoCC
400 Gigling Road, Seaside, CA 93955-6771
Phone: 1-800-538-9552, Fax: 1-831-655-8317

---

13. Humana Military Healthcare Services, "CHCBP Policy, Section A. Eligibility," *CHCBP Handbook,* p. 15, Subsection 3, http://www.humana-military.com/library/pdf/chcbp-handbook.pdf

At this point, three different offices (TRICARE, HMHS and DEERS) have become intertwined in the health care process and this is often where mass confusion begins for both former spouses and their lawyers. Be aware that the applicable customer service offices are very patient, with good intentions, but are not always fully knowledgeable.

Applications are sent to HMHS. DEERS assists in the application process by verifying eligibility and correctly coding a former spouse within the DEERS system. TRICARE assists by providing TRICARE Standard network providers and TRICARE rules, *most* of which are followed by HMHS.

Former spouses apply for eligibility by sending HMHS

- The DD Form 2837, *CHCBP Application,*
- Payment for the first three months of premiums, and
- A copy of the *Certificate of Creditable Coverage*

The application must be completed "before the 60 day period beginning on the day after TRICARE coverage for former spouse ends"[14] which in most cases means within 60 days of the divorce date. Forms are found online at www.humana-military.com or by calling (800)444-5445.

> *Note:* If the 60 day window was missed and the former spouse was never notified of the CHCBP option (perhaps the service member processed all paperwork removing the spouse from DEERS, and no one ever actually spoke to the former spouse) there may still be a chance as of enrollment based on lack of notification.[15]

Former spouses should inquire about approval in a timely manner. The responsibility falls on the former spouse (not the administrative office) to ensure timely processing. Paperwork

---

14. Humana Military Healthcare Services, "Election of Coverage, "*CHCBP Handbook,* p. 18, 1 c, http://www.humana-military.com/library/pdf/chcbp-handbook.pdf.

15. Wm. John Camp, "Enrolling within 60 days," *Roll Call,* Newsletter of the Military Committee, ABA Family Law Section, Vol. 2008-1 Summer 2008, Appendix 2. http://meetings.abanet.org/webupload/commupload/FL115277/newsletterpubs/rc_sum08.pdf.

should be sent immediately after the divorce is finalized, and the former spouse should call two weeks later to confirm receipt and ask when to expect the CHCBP Identification Card (which is considered notification of approval). If the card is not received within that time, follow-up is needed as there may be missing paperwork causing a delay.

Paper ID cards come attached to an Enrollment Confirmation letter. A new letter, including a new ID card, is received each time quarterly premiums are paid and is good for three months.

> *Note:* All expired ID cards should be saved by the former spouse for claims processing and as proof of insurance coverage during each three month time frame. It's also a good idea to hand write any allergies, emergency contact numbers, etc. on the active paper card.

It can't be emphasized enough that the CHCBP program is run by HMHS, and it is *not* TRICARE. Even so, the former spouse will still list the service member as the sponsor and the service member's Social Security number will be used on all records and billing information.

This can be quite confusing for civilian medical offices. If they have dealt with the military health care system at all, they are used to seeing a dependent ID card, clearly listing the service member's Social Security number. The HMHS/CHCBP ID card does not list any Social Security number at all *(see* p. 35) and this often raises many questions.

The former spouse should advise the billing personnel ahead of time that when calling CHCBP, despite it not being TRICARE, they will be greeted with, "Welcome to TRICARE South" and they must continue to listen for options to locate the TRICARE administrator customer service area for CHCBP.

Ideally, billing offices should make a copy of the ID card and send it with the invoice claim. Should a former spouse receive a bill where coverage was denied, the first thing to check would be the Social Security number that the invoice was billed under when sent to CHCBP. Medical providers are often confused (and justifiably so) with former spouse patients who are no longer military dependents, yet they require billing under (use of) the service member's Social Security number.

Qualifying for Duration

Once eligibility and enrollment are completed (the first step), one can look at step two, qualifying for duration. The CHCBP handbook explains the 36 month coverage requirements as:

> "(1) For an unremarried former spouse of a member or former member, the coverage under the CHCBP is limited to 36 months after the later of:
>
> (a) The date on which the final decree of divorce, dissolution, or annulment occurs;
>
> (b) The date which is one year after the date of the divorce, dissolution, or annulment, if the former spouse is eligible for one-year transitional coverage under TRICARE; or
>
> (c) The date the member became ineligible for medical and dental care under a military health care plan as an active duty member or the date the member first ceases to be eligible for care under TAMP, whichever is later, if the former spouse first meets the requirements for being considered an unremarried former spouse during a period of continual coverage of the member for self and dependents."[16]

Note: The one-year transitional coverage mentioned in (b) refers to the 20/20/15 spouses who will receive four years of health coverage (one year under the 20/20/15 TRICARE program plus three more years (36 months) under CHCBP).

---

16. Humana Military Healthcare Services, "CHCBP Policy, Section E. Period of Coverage, Unremarried Former Spouse," *CHCBP Handbook*, p. 23, E. 1c (3), http://www.humana-military.com/library/pdf/chcbp-handbook.pdf.

Extending to Unlimited CHCBP Coverage

A former spouse enrolled in the 36 month CHCBP will receive an expiration letter *(see* p. 36-38) which includes a questionnaire and instructions on how to apply for extension to the unlimited coverage.

To qualify for the unlimited duration, the CHCBP Handbook, *Period of Coverage* states these criteria:

> "(2) The limitations for an unremarried former spouse do not apply and the length of coverage can be for an unlimited period of time, if the former spouse:
>
> (a) Has not remarried before the age of 55;
>
> (b) Was enrolled in the CHCBP or TRICARE as the *dependent* of an involuntary separated member during the 18 month period before the date of the divorce, dissolution, or annulment; and
>
> (c) Is receiving any portion of the retired or retainer pay of the member or former member, or an annuity based on the retired or retainer pay of the member; or
>
> (d) Has a court order for payment of any portion of the retired or retainer pay; or
>
> (e) Has a written agreement (whether voluntary or pursuant to a court order) which provides for an election by the member or former member to provide an annuity to the former spouse."[17]

> *Note:* The former spouse must meet both (a) and (b) but only meet either (c), (d), or (e).

---

17. Humana Military Healthcare Services, "CHCBP Policy, Section E. Period of Coverage, Unremarried Former Spouse," *CHCBP Handbook*, p. 23, E. 1c (2), http://www.humana-military.com/library/pdf/chcbp-handbook.pdf.

(a) Remarriage

To meet requirement (a), the former spouse makes a statement that he or she has not remarried before age 55.

(b) Prior CHCBP or TRICARE Enrollment

The handbook language of criteria 2(b) can cause confusion. Questions arise as to what is meant by "the dependent of an involuntary separated member" and the language further suggests the former spouse must be enrolled as a dependent for the entire 18 months prior to divorce (which would ultimately mean an 18 month marriage requirement).

The U.S. Code itself provides some clarification:

> "Who was enrolled in an approved health benefits plan under this chapter as a family member *at any time* during the 18-month period before the date of the divorce, dissolution, or annulment."[18]

The 36 month expiration letter from HMHS also refers to paragraph 2(b) using alternative language:

> "Was enrolled in, or covered by, an approved health benefits plan under Chapter 55, Title 10, U.S. Code, as the dependent of the retiree at *any time* during the 18 month period before the date of divorce, dissolution, or annulment. (Both TRICARE and CHCBP would qualify as such a plan.)"[19]

From the later references, the 18 month time reference appears to mean enrolled at *any time* during the prior 18 months of divorce.

The expiration letter and code language are better sources to provide an understanding of the qualifications required for transfer to the unlimited health care program.

---

18. U.S. Code Title 10 > Subtitle A > Part II > Chapter 55 > § 1078a. *Continued Health Benefits Coverage*, Jan. 5, 2009, http://www.law.cornell.edu/uscode/10/usc_sec_10_00001078---a000-.html.

19. *See* HMHS Expiration Notification Letter, sample at end of chapter

(c) Receives Retirement Pay or an Annuity

Requirement (c) applies to situations where the service member has already retired and the former spouse is receiving a portion of the retired pay and thus qualifies for unlimited coverage.

The reference to "annuity" refers to the Survivor Benefit Plan (SBP) payment. Upon the death of a retiree, retirement pay ceases, but a former spouse beneficiary of SBP will now receive an annuity payment instead of the retired pay award.

Since CHCBP unlimited health care relies on receipt of a portion of retired pay or an annuity, these two items (division of pay and participation in SBP) should most likely not be negotiated out of a divorce decree, nor waived or exchanged for receipt of some other negotiated asset.

(d) & (e) Will Receive Retirement Pay or Annuity

Requirements (d) and (e) apply when the service member has not retired, so the former spouse is not yet receiving any payments, but can still qualify for unlimited coverage using a court order awarding payment of any portion of the retired or retainer pay or an award of the annuity (an order to be the SBP beneficiary).

Application for Unlimited Health Care

HMHS sends a CHCBP expiration notification letter *(see* p. 36) to former spouses enrolled in the 36 month plan along with a questionnaire and instructions on how to extend to unlimited coverage. The former spouse will need to provide:

* A written statement of qualifications *(see* p. 39)
* Proof of meeting qualifications (a copy of the divorce decree and the *Certificate of Creditable Coverage*)
* The signed CHCBP renewal form along with payment for the next 3 months of premiums

Paperwork should be sent immediately. Two weeks later, the former spouse should follow-up by phone to confirm receipt and ask when to expect a new CHCBP Identification Card (considered notification of approval).

Remarriage

The CHCBP Handbook has a third paragraph under *Period of Coverage,* for an unremarried former spouse describing the only case where premium refunds are ever given:

> "(3) If an unremarried former spouse who is enrolled in the CHCBP subsequently remarries, enrollment in CHCBP will end as of the date of the marriage. Humana Military will refund any portion of the former spouse's previously paid premium for any days after CHCBP enrollment ends. Regardless of the period of coverage used by the former spouse, remarriage results in loss of all further eligibility for CHCBP coverage unless future eligibility can be subsequently established."[20]

Unmarried and unremarried are different terms:

> **Unmarried Former Spouse (UMFS):** A former spouse who has remarried but through death or divorce, is now unmarried again.
>
> **Unremarried Former Spouse (URFS):** A former spouse who has never remarried.

Questions have arisen concerning the paragraph (3) requirement not to remarry and the statement of prior paragraph (2)(a) "the limitations for an unremarried former spouse do not apply" and "the former spouse must not marry before age 55." The implication is a former spouse could remarry after this age when enrolled in the unlimited program. Thus, the two paragraphs seem to be in direct contradiction.

One could note that coverage terminates for remarriage under the 20/20/20 rules, 20/20/15 rules, and 36 month plan, so one might reason that paragraph (3) must overrule paragraph (2)(a). Wouldn't it be unfair for a former spouse, with no duration of marriage requirement, to be permitted remarriage when a spouse with 20 years of military exposure cannot?

---

20. Humana Military Healthcare Services, "CHCBP Policy, Section E. Period of Coverage, Unremarried Former Spouse," *CHCBP Handbook,* p. 23, E. 1c (3), http://www.humana-military.com/library/pdf/chcbp-handbook.pdf.

On the contrary, one can reason there must be some logic behind the age 55 statement (which also shows up in both the U.S. Code and the C.F.R. concerning CHCBP). Attorney Wm. John Camp found some logic as to how Congress derived this language:

> "This confusion in the statute may have come from an attempt by Congress to make the "unlimited CHCBP coverage" mirror the Spouse Equity Coverage for former spouses of federal employees offered through the Office of Personnel Management."[21]

Even the HMHS questionnaire only asks for a signed statement that one has not remarried prior to age 55, so if one were to remarry after age 55, the statement could not be considered fraud as the terms for unlimited care would be met and honestly stated.

How legal arguments would hold up, remains to be seen. Prior to remarrying, the CHCBP Grievance Coordinator might be the best person to contact for further information concerning this unresolved legal issue. The contact address is:

Regional Grievance Coordinator
8123 Data Point Dr, Ste. 400
San Antonio, TX 78229

Health Care for the Spouse of the Reservist

Reservist service member's years of service accrue on a point based system which can be converted to equivalent years toward retirement. Retirement for Reservists begins at age 60.

In the case of the 20/20/20 rules, a qualifying former spouse may need to obtain interim health care to fill some gap years (if for example, the divorce occurs at age 50 but military health care will not begin until the service member reaches age 60).

A former spouse of a reservist may also qualify for CHCBP. A reservist is a "member of the uniformed services," thus meeting the 3(a) eligibility requirement for former spouse health care.

---

21. Wm. John Camp, "The Continuation of Health Care Benefits Program (CHCBP) as a Long-Term Health Care Option for Former Military Spouses," *Roll Call*, Newsletter of the Military Committee, ABA Family Law Section, Vol. 2008-1 Summer 2008, Appendix 2. http://meetings.abanet.org/webupload/commupload/FL115277/newsletterpubs/rc_sum08.pdf.

Health Care Letters and Forms

Request for Certificate of Creditable Coverage (CoCC)

(date)

DEERS Support Office
Attn: CoCC
400 Gigling Road
Seaside, CA 93955-6771

Please send me a DEERS letter of credibility showing that I, (former spouse name) was enrolled in TRICARE up until (date).

My sponsor is (Service member's name and Social Security number).

Please mail a hard copy of the letter to my address below and also send a faxed copy to fax: (area code) _ _ _ - _ _ _ _.

I need this as soon as possible to qualify for Humana Military Healthcare coverage.

If you have any questions, please call and leave a message at (area code) _ _ _ - _ _ _ _.

Thank you,

(Former spouse's signature)

Name of former spouse
Address of former spouse
Email of former spouse

Certificate of Creditable Coverage (blank)

TRICARE - Military Managed Health Care Program
(formerly CHAMPUS)

Certificate of Creditable Coverage

IMPORTANT This certificate provides evidence of your prior health care coverage under one of the TRICARE administered programs. You may need to furnish this certificate if you become eligible under a group health plan that excludes coverage for certain medical conditions that you have before you enroll (also known as pre-existing conditions). This certificate may need to be provided if medical advice, diagnosis, care, or treatment was recommended or received for the condition within a certain time period (often six months to one year) prior to your enrollment in the new plan. If you become covered under another group health plan, check with the plan administrator to see if you need to provide this certificate. You may also need this certificate to buy, for yourself or your family, an insurance policy that does not exclude coverage for medical conditions that are present before you enroll.

1. Date of this certificate: _____

2. Participant (Sponsor) name: _____

3. Participant (Sponsor) Identification Number: _____

4. Names of individual(s) to whom this certificate applies:

   _____

5. All questions concerning this certificate should be directed to:
   Defense Manpower Data Center (DMDC) Support Office
   Attn: CoCC
   400 Gigling Road
   Seaside, CA 93955-6771

   For further information, call: 1-800-538-9552
   TTY/TDD: 1-866-363-2883

6. If the individual(s) identified in Line 4 above has/have at least 18 months of creditable coverage, check here ___ and skip Line 7. (Does not include any periods of coverage that occurred prior to a break in coverage of more than 63 days.)

7. Date coverage began: _____

8. Date coverage ended: _____ (or check if coverage continuing as of date of this certificate):

NOTE: *Separate certificates will be furnished if information is not identical for the participant and each dependent.*

DD Form 2837, CHCBP Enrollment Application

CONTINUED HEALTH CARE BENEFIT PROGRAM (CHCBP) APPLICATION

OMB No. 0704-0364
OMB Approval Expires Nov 30, 2008

The public reporting burden for this collection of information is estimated to average 15 minutes per response, including the time for reviewing instructions, searching existing data sources, gathering and maintaining the data needed, and completing and reviewing the collection of information. Send comments regarding this burden estimate or any other aspect of this collection of information, including suggestions for reducing the burden, to the Department of Defense, Executive Services Directorate (0704-0364). Respondents should be aware that notwithstanding any other provision of law, no person shall be subject to any penalty for failing to comply with a collection of information if it does not display a currently valid OMB control number.

PLEASE DO NOT RETURN YOUR APPLICATION TO THE ABOVE ORGANIZATION. RETURN COMPLETED APPLICATION WITH PREMIUM PAYMENT TO: Humana Military Healthcare Services, Inc., Attn: CHCBP, P.O. Box 740072, Louisville, KY 40201.

PRIVACY ACT STATEMENT

AUTHORITY: 10 U.S.C. 1086 and E.O. 9397.
PRINCIPAL PURPOSE(S): This form is used by certain former military health care beneficiaries to apply for coverage under the Continued Health Care Benefit Program (CHCBP). Please see 32 C.F.R. 199.20(d) for a list of the eligible beneficiaries.
ROUTINE USE(S): Disclosure may be made to Federal, state, local, foreign government agencies, private business entities and individual providers of care on matters relating to entitlement, fraud, program abuse, program integrity, or civil and criminal litigation related to the operation of the Continued Health Care Benefit Program.
DISCLOSURE: Voluntary; however, failure to furnish all requested information will result in the applicant not being enrolled in the Continued Health Care Benefit Program.

1. **APPLICANT NAME** *(Last, First, Middle Initial)*
2. **TELEPHONE NO.** *(Include Area Code)*
   a. HOME   b. WORK
3. **RESIDENCE ADDRESS** *(Street, Apartment No., City, State, ZIP Code)*
4. **MAILING ADDRESS** *(If different from Residence Address)*
5. **SERVICE MEMBER SPONSOR THROUGH WHOM YOU QUALIFY** *(If different from Applicant)*
   a. **NAME** *(Last, First, Middle Initial)*
   b. **SPONSOR'S SOCIAL SECURITY NUMBER**
6. **PERSON(S) TO BE ENROLLED IN CHCBP** *(Including Applicant)*

	a. NAME (Last, First, Middle Initial)	b. SSN OF INDIVIDUAL	c. DATE OF BIRTH (YYYYMMDD)	d. SEX (M/F)
(1) SPONSOR *(Submit copy of DD214 - Member 4 Copy)*				
(2) DEPENDENTS *(Submit copy of DD214 - Member 4 Copy)* *(Sponsor must enroll for dependents to be enrolled. List all family members. Use a separate sheet of paper if more space is needed.)*				
(3) UNREMARRIED FORMER SPOUSE *(Submit copy of final divorce decree.)*				
(4) CHILD LOSING MILITARY BENEFITS DUE TO AGE* *(Submit copy of Military ID Card)*				
(5) CHILD LOSING MILITARY BENEFITS FOR ANY OTHER REASON* *(Submit copy of proof of event that resulted in loss of benefits.)*				

*Children age 21 (23 if a full-time student) losing military coverage must apply separately for their own individual policy. If more than three children, use separate sheet of paper.

7. **TOTAL THREE-MONTH PREMIUM ENCLOSED:** *(Individual three-month premium is $933.00. Family three-month premium is $1,996.00.)*
   $ _____   PREMIUM PAID IS FOR: [ ] INDIVIDUAL COVERAGE [ ] FAMILY COVERAGE
   PAID BY: [ ] CHECK [ ] MONEY ORDER *(Check/money order payable to the United States Treasury)*

8. **APPLICANT'S SIGNATURE AND DATE**
   By signing this form, the applicant is certifying that the information provided on this form is true, accurate and complete. Federal funds are involved in this program and any false claims, statements, comments or concealment of a material fact may be subject to fine and imprisonment under applicable Federal law.

   a. SIGNATURE
   b. DATE SIGNED *(YYYYMMDD)*

DD Form 2837, CHCBP Application Instructions

CONTINUED HEALTH CARE BENEFIT PROGRAM (CHCBP) SUMMARY

WHAT IS THE CHCBP?

The Continued Health Care Benefit Program (CHCBP) is a program of temporary health benefit coverage for certain eligible individuals who lose military health benefits. The CHCBP is premium based, with the medical benefits under this program mirroring the benefits offered in the TRICARE Standard Program and functioning under most of the rules and procedures of TRICARE Standard.

ARE THERE SPECIFIC ENROLLMENT REQUIREMENTS?

Yes. Beneficiaries must elect coverage in the CHCBP within 60 days following: (1) loss of entitlement to the Military Health System; or (2) being notified of the CHCBP. Beneficiaries may not select the effective date of their CHCBP policy; the period of coverage must begin on the day after loss of military entitlement.

WHO IS ELIGIBLE?

(1) The sponsor; (2) certain unremarried former spouses; (3) a child who loses military benefits due to his or her age; and (4) a child placed in the legal custody of the sponsor.

WHAT ARE THE ENROLLMENT CATEGORIES?

CHCBP provides two types of coverage plans: individual and family. Individual coverage is available to the sponsor, an unremarried former spouse, and a child losing military benefits due to age. Family coverage is only available to the separating service member and his or her family members. Once the election is made, the sponsor's enrollment category can be changed from individual to family coverage under the following conditions: (1) birth of a child; (2) marriage of the sponsor; (3) legal adoption of a child by the sponsor; or (4) placement by a court of a child as a legal ward in the home of the sponsor. If one of the above events has occurred, the former member can change his or her enrollment from individual to family coverage, effective as of the date of the qualifying event. The sponsor must send a written request to Humana Military Healthcare Services, Inc., Attn: CHCBP, P.O. Box 740072, Louisville, KY 40201, no later than 60 days from the qualifying event and must include sufficient documentation to support the change in enrollment categories.

HOW DOES ONE ENROLL IN THE CHCBP?

In order to enroll in the CHCBP, an eligible individual must submit a completed enrollment application form, proof of eligibility, and payment in full for the first 90 days of coverage (check or money order made payable to the United States Treasury). The enrollment form may be requested from Humana Military Healthcare Services, Inc., by writing or calling them. The enrollment form can also be found on the Web at www.tricare.osd.mil or www.humana-military.com.

PROOF OF ELIGIBILITY:

Proof of eligibility must be submitted with the completed enrollment application and payment. The documentation that is required is shown in Sections 6(1) through 6(5) of the enrollment application, depending on the category of the individual applying. Additional information and documentation may be requested to confirm the applicant's eligibility.

HOW LONG IS COVERAGE OFFERED?

CHCBP coverage ranges from a period of 18 to 36 months, depending on the category of the beneficiary. Former active duty members and their family members are entitled to purchase up to 18 months of coverage. All other eligible beneficiaries are entitled to 36 months of coverage. Certain former spouses may be eligible for coverage beyond 36 months. All former spouses should review the criteria for extended coverage before enrolling in CHCBP to determine their eligibility for continued coverage beyond 36 months. CHCBP coverage is offered in increments of 90 days, renewable up to the total number of months referenced above.

WHAT DOES CHCBP COVERAGE COST?

The cost of CHCBP coverage depends on the category of enrollment, either individual or family. The premium for individual coverage is $933.00 per quarter and the premium for family coverage is $1,996.00 per quarter.

HOW IS COVERAGE RENEWED?

At least thirty days prior to the expiration of the current coverage period, a renewal notice will be sent to the enrollee. The enrollee must return the renewal notice and payment in full, by check, money order or major credit card, no later than 30 days after the end of the current coverage period. Failure to renew within the required time will result in the permanent loss of entitlement to purchase any additional CHCBP coverage.

DD Form 2837, CHCBP Application Instructions

CONTINUED HEALTH CARE BENEFIT PROGRAM (CHCBP)
SUMMARY *(Continued)*

ARE PREMIUMS REFUNDABLE?

Refunds of premiums paid for CHCBP coverage are not refundable other than in extraordinary circumstances, e.g., if the enrollee is no longer eligible for CHCBP coverage.

WHAT BENEFITS ARE OFFERED?

Health care coverage under the CHCBP mirrors the coverage of the TRICARE Standard benefit, which covers a majority of medical conditions. However, for some types of treatment, coverage can be limited. Prior to enrolling in the CHCBP, interested beneficiaries are encouraged to contact a TRICARE Service Center to ask specific questions regarding TRICARE Standard coverage.

WHAT ADDITIONAL COSTS ARE THERE?

When medical care is received, the beneficiary will be responsible for payment of certain deductible and cost-sharing amounts in connection with otherwise covered services and supplies. For detailed information concerning the amounts of cost-shares and deductibles, beneficiaries are encouraged to contact a TRICARE Service Center nearest their home.

HOW TO FILE A CLAIM:

Enrollees may request the provider to file medical claims on their behalf. If the provider does not file the claim, the enrollee will have to do so. It is helpful to attach a copy of the CHCBP enrollment card to the claim. Information regarding where to submit a claim can be found at the TRICARE Web Site www.tricare.osd.mil or by contacting either Humana Military Healthcare Services, Inc., or a TRICARE Service Center nearest the enrollee's residence.

If there are any problems with the processing of a CHCBP claim, the enrollee should contact the claims processor. If that is not successful, the enrollee may then write to the TRICARE Management Activity at the following address:

Beneficiary and Provider Services
TRICARE Management Activity
16401 East Centretech Parkway
Aurora, CO 80011-9066

HOW CAN PROVIDERS VERIFY CHCBP ELIGIBILITY?

Providers may call 1-800-444-5445 to verify the eligibility of the beneficiary or to obtain basic CHCBP information.

WHAT STEPS SHOULD ACTIVE DUTY MEMBERS TAKE WHEN SEPARATING FROM THE MILITARY?

Current active duty members anticipating separation from the military should ensure they participate in pre-separation counseling, which will provide information regarding various benefits available to members after leaving the military. Former members must also ensure that their correct status is recorded in DEERS upon separation.

HOW TO OBTAIN INFORMATION ABOUT CHCBP:

Humana Military Healthcare Services, Inc., provides administrative and educational support for the CHCBP. As part of this effort, they operate a toll-free line 24 hours a day. Beneficiary Service Representatives are available Monday through Friday 8:00 a.m. to 7:00 p.m. Eastern Time (except holidays).

ADDITIONAL INFORMATION:

Write or call:

Humana Military Healthcare Services, Inc.
Attn: CHCBP
P.O. Box 740072
Louisville, KY 40201

1-800-444-5445

or visit their Web Site at:
www.humana-military.com

Health Care ◄ 33

Quarterly Humana Military Healthcare Premiums Bill

```
                                                    Humana Military
                                                    Healthcare Services
                                                    Attn: CHCBP
                                                    500 West Main Street
                                                    P.O. Box 740072
                                                    Louisville, KY 40201-7472

                                                    HUMANA MILITARY
                                                    HEALTHCARE SERVICES
                                                    ★ ★ ★ ★ ★
(Date)

(Former Spouses Name
     and
     Address)
                                Quarterly Enrollment Fee:   $933.00
                                Initial Payment:            $933.00
RE: Quarterly Billing Statement  Amount Due:                $933.00
    Policyholder ID: _____  Due Date:
                                Billing Statement Period:
Dear _____
```

Thank you for choosing the Continued Health Care Benefit Program (CHCBP). We hope you are enjoying the benefits of your CHCBP membership.

Your CHCBP quarterly payment is now due. To prevent interruption of your CHCBP benefit and allow adequate time for the posting of your payment, it is important that you mail your payment before _____.

Please understand that if your payment is not received on time, we are required to disenroll you from the Continued Health Care Benefit Program. Also note, if you are disenrolled for non-payment of fees, you will not be able to re-enroll in this plan. If this notice has crossed in the mail with your payment, please disregard and accept our thanks in advance.

We look forward to serving you. If you have any questions, please contact one of our Beneficiary Services Representatives at 1-800-444-5445. We will be glad to assist you.

DETACH THIS PORTION AND KEEP FOR YOUR RECORDS

```
                                              Make checks payable to:
Policyholder ID: _____              The United States Treasury

Policyholder Name: _____                    Mail to:
Amount Due:      $933.00              Humana Military Healthcare Services
Due Date: _____             Continued Health Care Benefit Program
                                              P.O. Box 740072
                                           Louisville, KY 40201-7472

                                      ( ) I do not wish to renew coverage
Amount Enclosed or to be Charged $ _____

Payment Method:
_____ Check / Money Order / Cashier's Check (Please do not send cash)

Credit Card Payment (Please check one)
_____ Visa   _____ Master Card   _____ American Express   _____ Discover

Credit Card Number _____    Exp Date _____
                                                       (Month/Year)
Security Code _____ (Last 3 digits on back of card)


Signature of Cardholder _____
Required for credit card payment (Authorizes charge to your account)
```

CHCBP-010

Humana Military Healthcare Services Acceptance

```
                                          Humana Military
                                          Healthcare Services
                                          Attn: CHCBP
                                          500 West Main Street
                                          PO Box 740072
                                          Louisville, KY 40201-7472
```

(date)

HUMANA MILITARY
HEALTHCARE SERVICES
★ ★ ★ ★ ★

RE: Enrollment Confirmation
    Policyholder ID:

Dear

Welcome to the Continued Health Care Benefit Program.

We have recently completed your enrollment into the Continued Health Care Benefit Program (CHCBP). Your enrollment effective date of coverage is from _____ through _____. Your CHCBP identification card is attached below. Please present this card to your health care provider when receiving medical services. You may also recommend that the health care provider make a copy of the card. Whether you or your health care provider submit the claim, it is important to attach a copy of your card to the claim form. This will help to properly identify the claim.

In the future, you will be receiving premium notices on a quarterly basis. To ensure continued coverage, these premiums must be paid on time. As you pay each quarterly premium, you will be issued a new identification card. The identification card will show the start and end dates of each specific CHCBP enrollment period.

Information regarding CHCBP coverage of benefits, cost shares, and other important details can be found in the TRICARE Standard Handbook, at your local TRICARE Service Center, on our website at www.humana-military.com, or by contacting one of our Beneficiary Service Representatives at 1-800-444-5445.

Again, thank you for choosing the Continued Health Care Benefit Program.

Sincerely,

HMHS Director - Billing & Enrollment

CHCBP- 001

Humana Military Healthcare Services ID Card

Front of Membership Card (Blank)

> **Continued Health Care Benefit Program**
> A Department of Defense program administered by
> **HUMANA MILITARY**
> HEALTHCARE SERVICES
> ★ ★ ★ ★ ★
>
> Name:
>
> Birthdate: Effective Date:
>
>   End Date:

Back of Membership Card

> **HUMANA MILITARY**
> HEALTHCARE SERVICES
> ★ ★ ★ ★ ★
>
> Submit CHCBP claims to:
> TRICARE CHCBP Claims
> PO Box 7031
> Camden, SC 29020-7031
>
> – Information regarding CHCBP coverage of benefits, cost shares, and other important details can be found in the CHCBP Handbook, the TRICARE Prime Handbook, at your local TSC, by calling 1-800-444-5445, or by visiting our website at www.humana-military.com.
>
> – Some services require pre-authorization.
> – Cost shares and deductibles apply to this program.

Note: The former spouse follows TRICARE *Standard* rules, not *Prime* as indicated on the CHCBP ID card.

Humana Military Healthcare Expiration Letter

Humana Military
Healthcare Services
Attn: CHCBP
500 West Main Street
P.O. Box 740072
Louisville, KY 40201-7472

HUMANA MILITARY
HEALTHCARE SERVICES
★ ★ ★ ★ ★

(Date)

(Former Spouses Name
and
Address)

RE: Termination of Benefits Notification - Unremarried Former Spouse
 Policyholder ID:_____

Dear

This letter is to inform you that your eligibility to participate in the Continued health Care benefit Program will expire. Participation in CHCBP is limited to thirty-six (36) months for an unremarried former spouse, and our records indicate that your eligibility will expire as of _____.

The regulations governing CHCBP do however allow for extended coverage beyond 36 months in certain cases. Specifically, in the case of an unremarried former spouse of a member or former member whose divorce occurred prior to the end of transitional health care coverage, the period of eligibility for participation in CHCBP is unlimited if the former spouse meets the following criteria:

(A) Has not remarried before the age of 55,

 and

(B) Was enrolled in, or covered by, an approved health benefits plan under Chapter 55, Title 10, United States Code as the dependent of a retiree at any time during the 18-month period before the date of the divorce, dissolution, or annulment. (Both TRICARE and CHCBP would qualify as such a plan.)

A former spouse must *also* meet at least *one* of the following criteria in addition to both of the above criteria:

(C) Is receiving a portion of the retired or retainer pay of a member, or former member, or an annuity based on the retainer pay of the member; **or**

(D) Has a court order for payment of any portion of the retired or retainer pay; **or**

(E) Has a written agreement (whether voluntary or pursuant to a court order), which provides for an election by the member or former member to provide an annuity to the former spouse.

Humana Military Healthcare Expiration Letter

Should you meet the above criteria and wish to continue CHCBP coverage beyond 36 months, you must submit the following to our office:

1. Your signed statement of assurance that you have not remarried before the age of 55;

2. Proof that you meet criteria (B) above;

3. A copy of you final divorce decree or other authoritative evidence that you meet at least one of the requirements stated in (C) or (D) or (E) above; and

4. Your executed Renewal Notice, last page of this letter, together with a premium payment in the form of a check or money order for $933.00 made payable to the **United States Treasury**.

Upon receipt and acceptance of your documentation and premium, we will issue you an ID card and a written notice confirming your continued coverage. Please note that your premiums must continue to be received in our office by the due date specified on the renewal notice to maintain your CHCBP coverage.

If you do not qualify for the extended CHCBP coverage beyond 36 months based on the regulatory criteria outlined in this letter, your CHCBP coverage will be terminated on the date specified in the first paragraph of this letter.

If you have any questions, or need assistance, please contact one of our Beneficiary Service Representatives at 1-800-444-5445. We will be glad to assist you.

Again, thank you for choosing the Continued Health Care Benefit Program.

Sincerely,

Billing & Enrollment Manager

HMHS Renewal Notice (Attached to Expiration Letter)

RENEWAL NOTICE
CONTINUED HEALTH CARE BENEFIT PROGRAM

Return this page with your payment to:

**Humana Military Healthcare Services
Continued Health Care Benefit Program
P.O. Box 740071
Louisville, KY 40201-7472**

Sponsor Name: Policyholder ID:

Mark appropriate box and sign prior to mailing

( ) Check for $ _____ enclosed   ( ) I do not wish to renew coverage
Check or money order made
Payable to :
United States Treasury

By signing this form, the applicant is certifying that he/she meets the criteria for continued CHCBP coverage. Federal funds are involved in this program and any false claims, statements, or comments or concealment of a material fact may be subject to fine and imprisonment under applicable Federal Law.

Signature: _____ Date: _____

Former Spouse Statement for Unlimited Care

To: (Date)
Humana Military Healthcare Services
CHCBP
PO Box 740071
Louisville, KY 40201-7472

Subject: Extending to CHCBP Unlimited Coverage

I have not remarried before the age of 55.

I am currently enrolled in CHCBP meeting the qualifications of being covered in an approved health benefits plan under Chapter 55 Title 10.

I am enclosing copies of the relevant pages of my decree showing that I have a court order for payment of retired pay.

I am enclosing the signed renewal notice and a check for $933.00 for three months of premiums.

If you have any questions, my phone is (area code) _ _ _-_ _ _ _ and fax is (area code) _ _ _-_ _ _ _.

Sincerely,

(Former spouse's signature)

Name of former spouse   Att.
Address of former spouse   1) Decree / Court Order
Email of former spouse   2) Renewal notice
                                3) Premium Check
                                4) Certificate of Creditable
                                   Coverage

Copies of Court Orders

Certified copies of the decree are quite expensive. A low price is about $40 and how high prices can run depends upon the venue and number of pages.

Assuming it's affordable, sometimes it is easier to obtain certified copies at the time of divorce rather than later.

Consider the following list when deciding on the number of copies needed:

1. Two copies for personal records
2. One for the former spouse retired pay application
3. One for the Survivor Benefit Plan beneficiary election
4. One for the deemed SBP election
5. One for TRICARE for dependent children's records
6. One for the CHCBP health care application
7. An extra for unforeseen circumstances

If possible, lawyers should provide a copy of the divorce decree and all other court orders on a computer disc. When uncertified copies are needed, clients can print copies from this disc and replace the final page with a photocopy of the actual decree's signature page, thus making a complete copy and saving the certified cost.

Legal Fees

When asking for the opposing side to pay for all or part of the legal fees in a divorce, be sure to include the cost of certified copies of court orders. Since these costs are incurred after the divorce, they are often forgotten in negotiations. Attorneys might ask that they be paid in full by the initiator of the divorce or that they should at least be shared between the parties.

Military Benefits

Which State to Divorce In?

It is very important to be aware that there may be a choice of states to file in for divorce (also see Jurisdiction p. 42, Military Spouses Residency Relief Act p. 44, and Vested Retirement Pay p. 64).

While listing the pros and cons of each state's property division laws is not the purpose here, they must be considered before filing or responding to a filing for divorce.

State Comparison Checklist

Consider the following when comparing state laws:

1. Each state's equitable property division laws, including rules on pension division *(see* Vested Retirement Pay p.64)

2. The date of division used by each state when dividing marital assets, whether it is *date of divorce*, date of filing, date served, date the spouse moved out of the house, date of separation, or some other date

3. Each state's statute concerning calculations for the amount and duration of both alimony and child support

4. The cost involved in consulting a lawyer and/or a military divorce expert in each state

5. Litigation and travel expenses spanning two states when some issues will be decided in one state and the rest in another

6. Whether it is possible to file in the state where one intends to permanently reside (in order to avoid future interstate litigations) especially when both parties intend to relocate from the current state

Jurisdiction

An entire book could be devoted to addressing jurisdiction, especially when one considers service members located overseas or those entering marriages with foreign nationals. A brief overview is below and further reading can be found online through links at: http://www.militarydivorcetips.com/jurisdiction.html.

For a designated agent to process a retired pay court order, the order must clearly show the state has jurisdiction over the service member by *specifically stating* one of the following reasons:

> "1. The member resided in the territorial jurisdiction of the court at the time of the legal proceeding due to other than military assignment;
>
> 2. The member's domicile was in the territorial jurisdiction of the court at the time of the legal proceeding; or
>
> 3. The member consented to the jurisdiction of the court. The member indicates his or her consent to the jurisdiction of the court by participating in some way in the legal proceeding."[22]

The first refers to the court having jurisdiction if the service member lives in a state but is not under military assignment orders. For example, a service member assigned in New York, but living in New Jersey, is under New Jersey's jurisdiction.

The second refers to domicile which is established by indicators such as the state listed on the service member's driver's license, voter registration, car registration, bank accounts, and state income taxes. If the lawsuit occurs in the service member's domicile, that court has legal jurisdiction over the service member. The term *Home of Record* doe not necessarily translate to one's domicile.

The third issue of consent is defined by each state's law. Usually, if the service member files for divorce, the service member has automatically given consent to that court for jurisdiction. When the former spouse files for divorce, and the service member responds by filing an answer, the service member has acknowl-

---

22. DoD FMR Vol 7B Chapter 29, "Court Orders," *Former Spouse Payments from Retired Pay*, Feb. 2009, 290604, http://comptroller.defense.gov/fmr/07b/07b_29.pdf.

edged that state to have jurisdiction. Service members should research state options prior to filing or *answering* a suit. If another state is preferred for settlement, a possible strategy for the service member might be to file an objection (as opposed to an answer) concerning the state's legal jurisdiction.

Court orders cannot merely state that they "have Uniformed Services Former Spouse Protection Act (USFSPA) jurisdiction" but must state the *specific reason* for this jurisdiction:

> "If the court states that it has USFSPA jurisdiction, then it must state the basis for the finding, i.e., member's residence, member's domicile or member's consent."[23]

Saving/Losing the Retired Pay Division

The retired pay division can in some cases, be saved (from the viewpoint of the service member) or lost (from the viewpoint of the former spouse).

The following example summarizes exactly how critical a role jurisdiction can play in the division of retired pay. (Additional specific details can be found using the footnote reference.)

> **Example:** A former spouse sues for divorce in State A. The service member does not give consent or respond, and the court awards a default judgment issuing a former spouse award. The designated agent rejects this order due to lack of jurisdiction. Next, the former spouse sues for division in State B, the member's domicile. The service member's attorney, however, claims exclusive jurisdiction remains with State A, and since there is already an award in place, State B has no authority to make a new or further division. The end result is the former spouse is unable to obtain a valid court order and has lost the retirement pay award.[24]

---

23. DoD FMR Vol 7B Chapter 29, "State Law Jurisdiction," *Former Spouse Payments from Retired Pay,* Feb. 2009, 290605, http://comptroller.defense.gov/fmr/07b/07b_29.pdf.

24. Mark E. Sullivan, "Military Pension Division: The Servicemember's Strategy, Danger of a Default Judgment" Silent Partner, http://www.abanet.org/family/military/silent/mpd_servicemember.pdf

Servicemembers Civil Relief Act (SCRA)

In the case of active duty or deployed service members, the court order must also state compliance with the Servicemembers Civil Relief Act (SCRA) passed in 2003 as an amendment to the Soldiers' and Sailors' Civil Relief Act of 1940 (SSCRA).[25]

This act allows a service member to request a stay of proceedings due to military commitment, as well as avoid penalties for failure to appear. It protects the service member when duty calls and the service member is unable to respond or appear in court. It may also be used strategically to obtain a different state for jurisdiction. (This act also applies to other legal matters besides divorce, such as rent and mortgages, evictions, and life insurance).

Military Spouses Residency Relief Act (MSRRA)

The Military Spouses Residency Relief Act (MSRRA) of November 2009 was an amendment to SCRA. The aim was to eliminate spouses having to change voter registrations, driver's licenses, and tax filing states every time a military family relocates.

> "It just means spouses, like military members, now have the option to choose which state's income tax they wish to pay, provided they are domiciled in that state. Neither the SCRA nor the new MSRRA provision in the SCRA changed the rules about domicile. Domicile is where a person intends to permanently reside."[26]

Military experts in each applicable state should be consulted to determine if this act might provide alternative options for the former spouse when deciding where to file. The act might also help avoid expensive interstate litigations.

Domicile is a strategy subject best addressed by lawyers. Links to more information on the SCRA and MSRRA can be found online at http://www.militarydivorcetips.com/jurisdiction.html.

---

25. The U.S. Department of Justice, *Servicemembers Civil Relief Act*, http://www.justice.gov/crt/military/scratext.htm.

26. Holloman AFB, Legal Office Commentary, "Military Spouses Residency Relief Act Explained" http://www.holloman.af.mil/news/story.asp?id=123184574.

Moving Expenses - Travel and Transportation

During a Permanent Change of Station (PCS), the military provides several types of entitlements to assist with family relocation. In a military divorce, if the former spouse wishes to relocate from the service member's current duty station, there are no entitlements granted since usually there is no military order for relocation. Upon divorce, a former spouse, will lose the relocation privileges (travel and household goods) afforded a dependent under the travel and transportation entitlements of the service member.[27] Overseas spouses should consider the Early Return of Dependents (EROD) option prior to losing dependency status.[28]

A brief summary of possible relocation entitlements follows:

- *Temporary Lodging Expense (TLE) and Temporary Lodging Allowance (TLA):* allowances for the lodging and meal expenses incurred during temporary lodging (such as while household goods are being packed up) when relocating
- *Dislocation Allowance (DLA):* A dislocation allowance for expenses that are not reimbursed
- *Per Diem:* an allowance to assist with the cost of lodging and meals while relocating (during the traveling days)
- *Privately Owned Conveyance (POC):* a mileage allowance when service members elect to forgo the cost of air travel
- *Dependent Travel within Conus by Other than POC:* Dependents may be permitted reimbursement for travel up to the amount the military would have paid[29]

Considering the entitlements value, lawyers representing the former spouse might ask for compensation for this loss. If the service member caused this loss through the action of initiating the divorce, it could be argued for the member to share in any relocation costs. If a PCS move is pending, a delay of divorce should also be considered, to take advantage of relocating under orders.

---

27. U.S. Code Title 37 > Chapter 7 > § 404, *Travel and Transportation Allowances: General*, Jan. 5, 2009, http://www.law.cornell.edu/uscode/37/usc_sup_01_37_10_7.html

28. Soldier and Family Assistance Center, "Early Return of Dependents," http://www.imcom-europe.army.mil/sfac/admin/erd.htm

29. Rod Powers, "Military Travel (PCS) Move Entitlements," *About.com:U.S. Military*, http://usmilitary.about.com/od/travelpay/a/pcsentitlements.htm

Accrued Leave

Service members can accrue up to 60 days leave each year. When leaving the service, this leave can be *sold back*, meaning converted into separation pay; therefore, the current leave balance should be converted to a monetary figure and considered a divisible asset.

$$\text{Value of Accrued Leave} = \text{Number of days accrued Leave} \times \frac{\text{Base Pay}}{30 \text{ days}}$$

Thrift Savings Plan (TSP)

The Thrift Savings Plan (TSP) is a retirement savings and investment plan for Federal employees[30] where contributions grow tax-free until retirement. TSP should be treated as a divisible tax-deferred asset.

Commissary and Exchange Benefits

Commissary and Exchange benefits follow the 20/20/20 rules previously described under health care. Privileges are offered to a former spouse who:

1. Was married 20 years or more to a service member who

2. Served at least 20 years in the armed forces and

3. There is at least a 20 year overlap (there are at least 20 years of marriage while the service member served) and

4. Does not remarry[31]

In the case of remarriage, privileges are suspended but may be reinstated if the marriage ends due to death or divorce. This is different from the 20/20/20 rule for healthcare, which is never reinstated after remarriage. Former spouses, who do not meet the 20 year criteria but have children, should remember dependent children can continue to shop at both the commissary and the exchange even if their parent cannot make the purchase.

---

30. "Thrift Savings Plan," http://www.tsp.gov/.

31. U.S. Code Title 10 > Subtitle A > Part II > Chapter 54 > § 1062, *Commissary and Exchange Benefits*, Jan. 5, 2009, http://www.law.cornell.edu/uscode/10/usc_sup_01_10_10_A_20_II_30_54.html.

Last Will and Testament

Wills should be updated prior to divorce. Military legal assistance is readily available for the service member. Free assistance is also offered to dependents. Former spouses should consider taking advantage of this free assistance to revise or establish a will prior to divorce (prior to loss of dependency status). Wills should also be provided on a computer disc for easy future revision.

Military Spouse Preference Program

Dependent spouses may qualify for the Military Spouse Preference Program which provides them with preferential treatment when seeking certain Department of Defense (DoD) positions. Obtaining such employment prior to divorce might be in the interest of the former spouse. The base personnel office should be contacted for more information.

"The Military Spouse Preference Program:

* Applies to eligible spouses of active duty military members of the U.S. Armed Forces, including the U.S. Coast Guard and full-time National Guard, who are applying and referred for certain positions at DoD activities in the U.S., its territories and possessions, and in overseas areas;

* Applies only within the commuting area of the permanent duty station of the sponsor;

* Applies only if the spouse entered into the marriage with the military sponsor prior to the reporting date to the new duty assignment.

* Does not apply when the sponsor is separating or retiring."[32]

---

32. CPOL, "Military Spouse Preference Program," *Civilian Personnel Online*, http://cpol.army.mil/library/permiss/6314.html

Preserving USAA Membership

The United Services Automobile Association (USAA) offers insurance, banking, and investment opportunities to anyone who has honorably served in the U.S. military. In many cases this membership can be extended to children, widows, widowers, former spouses, and heirs.

USAA membership is another military-related benefit that can be an issue in pending divorces. Former spouses may wish to establish or preserve a USAA membership. USAA describes membership for eligible former spouses as:

> "Un-Remarried former spouses of USAA members who have or had a USAA auto or property insurance product while married."[33]

This does not say former spouses must remain unmarried to keep their insurance. When one becomes a USAA member, one remains a member for life. What it does say is before remarriage, the former spouse must have held a policy in his or her own right, under his or her own USAA membership number, while married. Former spouses, not meeting this rule, will move into the category of *other individuals* with limited access to USAA products.

When a divorce is pending, the parties involved should determine under whose USAA number the current auto or property insurance is actually listed. If the existing policies fall under the service member's number and the former spouse desires membership, one policy should be transferred to fall under the former spouse's USAA number.

---

33. United Services Automobile Association, "Widowers, Widows, and Former Spouses of USAA Members," *Why Choose USAA/Become a Member*, https://www.usaa.com/inet/ent_utils/McStaticPages?key=why_choose_usaa_eligibility_main&wa_ref=wcu_main_is_usaa_for_you.

The following scenario will illustrate this issue.

> **Example:** Captain Frank McGrath is married to Erika McGrath. Both have USAA membership numbers but the house and the car are listed solely under Frank's USAA number. Upon divorce, if no changes are made, Erika will lose her USAA membership ability concerning auto and property insurance, because she never held a policy under her own USAA number. The simple solution is to move one of the policies to fall under Erika's membership number prior to divorce. This not only assists Erika in her current situation, but if she remarries and has future children, she can now pass the membership on to them.

USAA membership can be shared with one's children, who in turn, can pass it down to their children. Purchase of a USAA insurance policy is a requirement for eligibility. Once a USAA member has purchased either auto, home, or renters insurance, his or her children are eligible to become USAA members.[34] When these children purchase a USAA insurance policy under their own membership number (at age 18 or older), then their children will be eligible for membership, and so on.

Whether to establish USAA membership or not is a matter of personal preference. The only intention here is to highlight the potential loss of eligibility for the former spouse and future generations. USAA continues to rank in the top two positions on Business Week's "Customer Service Champs" list. The company has a history of good business practices since 1922, free financial planning, no membership fees, and advisors that are not paid on commission. USAA divorce specialists can be contacted for more information and guidance at 1-800-531-8722, extension 75007.

---

34. United Services Automobile Association, "Securing USAA P&C Group Membership for Your Children," *Advice Center/Parent Resources*, https://www.usaa.com/inet/ent_utils/McStaticPages?key=advice_pass_membership_forward&SearchRanking=1&SearchLinkPhrase=securing%20USAA%20P[amp]C%20group%20membership.

Garnishments

Setting up garnishments to pay child support and alimony places a legal responsibility on the designated agent as opposed to relying on the good will of the service member. Garnishments ensure timely payments and also provide security. If something were to happen to the service member, such as being unreachable or in a medical incapacity, the payments will continue for the required duration. Garnishments also reduce communications which may be a desire of both parties, and garnishments are not stopped by bankruptcy filing.[35]

Alimony

Alimony,* also referred to as spousal maintenance or spousal support, is set by individual state laws. Lawyers will explain the rules concerning duration, amount, and remarriage applicable to their state. Alimony laws should be considered when deciding which state to proceed in for litigation (see Jurisdiction p.42).

On a tax return, alimony is deductible by the person paying it and declared as income by the person receiving it. While receiving alimony is a taxable transaction, alimony also qualifies for contributions to an Individual Retirement Account (IRA), so if possible, it should be invested. To avoid owing taxes at the end of the year, the person receiving alimony may wish to increase their withholding on their Form W-4, *Employees Withholding Allowance Certificate*. The person paying alimony might do the opposite.

Because alimony is tax deductible, strategic lawyers representing the service member might propose for the former spouse to waive receipt of retired pay and receive an equivalent amount in alimony, arguing that for the former spouse, the amount received will be taxable either way, as alimony or a retired pay award.

---

35. TheLaw.com, "Garnishment: Facts and Information," http://www.thelaw.com/guide/garnishment-facts-and-information/.

As with most military topics, however, one cannot look solely at one aspect of an issue. Retired pay's advantage is it increases with inflation and might continue as an annuity after the service member's death. Also, if the former spouse waives receipt of the retired pay award, there may be other connected losses, such as health care (*see* Extending to Unlimited CHCBP Coverage p. 23).

Child Support

Because the child support* figure depends on the individual state laws, lawyers certified in each state should be consulted to help predict the expected outcome of a child support award. Child support is another issue to consider when deciding which state to file in for divorce.

Unless a child support figure is willingly agreed upon, usually each side will try to reduce their income considered in the state's calculations. The end goal is to show either the need to receive more support or the inability to pay more support, depending upon the side represented.

The income of the former spouse is usually assigned from the Form W-2, *Wage and Tax Statement*, or tax returns. Questions arise when attributing income to the service member:

1. If a service member is living on base, living allowances such as *Basic Allowance for Housing* (BAH) or *Basic Allowance for Subsistence* (BAS) are not received. Will the state assign income to the service member equivalent to these costs?

2. If a service member is receiving any incentives or special pays such as overseas extension pay, flight pay, hostile fire pay, etc., will these be treated as income or are they considered temporary pay and excluded from calculations?

Attorneys will explain their state's position concerning military pay issues and child support. The child support obligation is usually secured by life insurance, discussed next. This requirement to maintain life insurance can actually be required of both parties.

---

*Alimony and child support as applicable to all families in general are covered in depth in the companion book, *Family Divorce Tips*. Here the focus is on unique issues solely surrounding a military divorce.

Life Insurance

When a divorce is pending, both parties should consider revising or establishing a life insurance policy.

Military members have Servicemembers' Group Life Insurance (SGLI) run by the Department of Veterans Affairs. Upon either separation or retirement, this can be converted to Veterans' Group Life Insurance (VGLI). After divorce, the service members must complete a new election certificate to remove the former spouse as their beneficiary. This does not happen automatically.

Two possible life insurance alternatives often used by military personnel and their dependents are the Armed Forces Benefit Association (AFBA) and the United Services Automobile Association (USAA). Former spouses may obtain their own life insurance through these or another civilian insurance.

Life insurance is often connected to child support. Often a noncustodial parent must maintain life insurance to ensure the support obligation will be paid even in the event of death. If the service member is the noncustodial parent, SGLI could be used for this coverage, assuming the beneficiary amount is sufficient. In such a case, the decree should order proof of the policy and beneficiary be provided to the former spouse on a reoccurring basis.

Often divorce decrees only require the noncustodial parent to maintain life insurance. In reality child support is a joint obligation, so it could be argued that both parents must maintain life insurance payable to the opposite party in the case of one's death. The amount of the insurance should be proportional to the percentages assigned each parent in state support calculations.

> **Example:** Jim and custodial parent, Amy have a combined child support amount of $1,000 divided 75/25. It might be ordered for Jim to obtain life insurance for 75 percent of the total obligation, and Amy to maintain life insurance for the remaining 25 percent, with each opposing party listed as the beneficiary. This ensures, should Amy pass away, Jim would not be 25 percent short, and vise versa.

Post 9/11 GI Bill for Education

The Post 9/11 GI Bill allows eligible service members to transfer unused educational benefits to their spouses and children on or after 1 August 2009.[36]

This benefit may be transferred to a spouse, a child (age 18 to 26), or shared between a spouse and children. The terms for spouse transfer are:

- "Must be enrolled in the Defense Enrollment Eligibility Reporting System (DEERS) and be eligible for benefits *at the time of transfer* to receive transferred educational benefits.
- May start to use the benefit immediately
- May use the benefit while the service member remains in the Armed Forces or after separation from active duty.
- Can use the benefit for up to 15 years after the service member's last separation from active duty.
- Is not eligible for the monthly stipend or books and supplies stipend while the member is serving on active duty."[37]

Concerning the division of marital property:

"A subsequent divorce will not affect the transferee's eligibility to receive educational benefits; however, after an individual has designated a spouse as a transferee under this section, the eligible individual retains the right to revoke or modify the transfer at any time."[38]

---

36. U.S. Department of Veterans Affairs, "Post 9/11 GI Bill Benefits," http://www.gibill.va.gov/.
37. Ibid. http://www.gibill.va.gov/gi_bill_info/ch33/transfer.htm
38. U.S. Department of Veterans Affairs, "Post 9/11 GI Bill Benefits," http://www.gibill.va.gov/documents/Post-911_Transferability.pdf.

> "The military member always retains the authority to change or revoke the transfer of benefits after benefits have been transferred. Transferred educational benefits may not be treated as marital property or as the asset of a marital estate subject to division in a divorce or other civil proceeding by law."[39]

The GI Bill, therefore, cannot be divided by the courts and the right to revoke cannot be taken away. Perhaps it should not be included in decrees at all, but at "an average start value estimated at $75,000 to $90,000,"[40] if the service member is not interested in using it, the benefit should not be overlooked. The service member can willingly choose to make the transfer and perhaps the former spouse would add some motivation toward this transfer by giving up something comparable. In such cases, the decree should also include some sort of stipulation as to compensation, should the service member later decide to revoke this decision.

> **Example:** A service member chooses to transfer the GI Bill to the former spouse, and knowing this, the former spouse willingly allows the decree to award the service member possession of an asset, their house. If the service member later revokes the benefit, the former spouse has no recourse action. If challenged, most likely the ruling would be the former spouse should have never participated in an exchange concerning the GI Bill benefit, as the benefit itself is not considered property or an asset, and perhaps should never have been "traded."

If in the same case, a condition had been included in the decree stipulating that if and when the service member should revoke this benefit, the former spouse would then receive some like in kind compensation, the conditions would be more equitable.

---

39. Military Officers Association of America, "The Post 9–11 GI Bill — All Aboard! Part 2," *Financial Frontlines, Jul. 20, 2009,* http://moaablogs.org/financial/2009/07/the-post-9-11-gi-bill%E2%80%94all-aboard-part-2/.

40. Tom Philpott, "DoD Defines New GI Bill Transfer Rules," *Today in the Military,* Apr. 30, 2009, http://www.military.com/features/0,15240,190065,00.html.

Similar issues could result in promises concerning children's college expenses.

> **Example:** A service member and former spouse agree to share college costs. The service member agrees to transfer the GI Bill benefits to the children and the former spouse agrees to receive and hold the marital EE Bonds for the children's college costs. At a later date, the service member can legally revoke the GI Bill benefit decision, whereas the former spouse would have to go back to court for any modification to the court ordered EE bond obligation.

Once again, it is within the service member's right to revoke the GI Bill benefit. A court cannot rule otherwise. Any *trade* proposals should be carefully considered with both legal and VA advice.

If the service member does wishes to make a transfer of benefits, it must be done before the former spouse or children are removed from DEERS. Processing takes time which could delay finalization of the divorce. (In Nov. 2009, GI Bill benefit processing was taking up to seven weeks.)[41]

A service member, who previously transferred the benefit to the spouse, may wish to revoke it upon divorce, perhaps to preserve the benefit for a future spouse. In a revocation case where the former spouse is currently using the GI Bill benefit, the former spouse should contact the Department of Veterans Affairs at (888) 442-4551 for advice concerning current and future education classes and required payments.

---

41. Patrick Campbell, "Average GI Bill Processing Time Now Nearly 7 Weeks Per Claim," *NewGIBill.org*, Nov. 6, 2009, http://www.newgibill.org/blog/average_gi_bill_processing_time_now_nearly_7_weeks_claim.

VA Home Loan

Negotiations involving VA Loans surround not only who will be awarded the home, but also the award of the continued use of the applicable VA Loan Certificate of Eligibility. The phone number for assistance with VA benefits is (800) 827-1000 and the home loan website page is: http://www.homeloans.va.gov.

Divorcing service members who have used their VA Certificate of Eligibility toward purchase of their home should contact the Department of Veterans Affairs for advice. The issue at hand concerns maintaining the eligibility and/or using this eligibility toward a future home purchase.

When a VA Loan has been used, to reestablish use of the VA Loan certificate for a future home purchase:

1. The loan must be paid in full and the house must no longer be owned by the person authorized to use the certificate, or

2. On a *one-time only* basis, eligibility may be restored if the prior VA loan has been paid in full but the property is still owned."[42]

If the service member plans to keep the home, the VA loan will proceed under the terms understood at the original signing and if needed, steps will be taken to remove the former spouse's name.

If the former spouse will be awarded the home along with the current VA Loan, the service member's name will be removed from the current loan, and the VA eligibility will be "tied up" so to speak. The eligibility will be unusable by the service member since the loan has not been paid off.

---

42. U.S. Department of Veterans Affairs, "Eligibility Frequently Asked Questions," http://www.homeloans.va.gov/faqelig.htm.

Sometimes, a portion of the eligibility may be available as described in this frequently asked question:

"Q: Only a portion of my eligibility is available at this time because my prior loan has not been paid in full even though I don't own the property anymore. Can I still obtain a VA guaranteed home loan?

A: Yes, depending on the circumstances. If a veteran has already used a portion of his or her eligibility and the used portion cannot yet be restored, any partial remaining eligibility would be available for use. The veteran would have to discuss with a lender whether the remaining balance would be sufficient for the loan amount sought and whether any down payment would be required."[43]

To restore full VA loan eligibility for future use, the house must be refinanced under a new loan in the name of the former spouse. In such a case, the original loan would be paid in full, and the service member would no longer own the house, thus meeting the criteria needed to fully restore eligibility.

Suppose a decision is made to sell the home. If the buyer wishes to assume the VA Loan, concerns arise not only with eligibility retention but also with possible consequences resulting from a potential default or foreclosure by the new owner. See the next frequently asked questions:

"Q: I sold the property I obtained with my prior VA loan on an assumption. Can I get my eligibility restored to use for a new loan?

A: In this case the veteran's eligibility can be restored only if the qualified assumer is also an eligible veteran who is willing to substitute his or her available eligibility for that of the original veteran. Otherwise, the original veteran cannot have eligibility restored until the assumer has paid off the VA loan.

---

43. U.S. Department of Veterans Affairs, "Eligibility Frequently Asked Questions," http://www.homeloans.va.gov/faqelig.htm.

Q: My prior VA loan was assumed, the assumer defaulted on the loan, and VA paid a claim to the lender. VA said it wasn't my fault and waived the debt. Now I need a new VA loan but I am told that my used eligibility cannot be restored. Why?

Or,

Q: My prior loan was foreclosed on, or I gave a deed in lieu of foreclosure, or the VA paid a compromise (partial) claim. Although I was released from liability on the loan and/or the debt was waived, I am told that I cannot have my used eligibility restored. Why?

A: In either case, although the veteran's debt was waived by VA, the Government still suffered a loss on the loan. The law does not permit the used portion of the veteran's eligibility to be restored until the loss has been repaid in full."[44]

All of the above would of course also apply to a former spouse who might default on an assumed VA loan. In the case of a default, the service member must either pay the debt or never have the VA loan eligibility reinstated.

A service member should be cautious when allowing others to assume the rights afforded by the VA certificate.

Veteran Spouse

Another option would be if the former spouse happens to also be a Veteran. A Veteran former spouse could substitute his or her certificate in place of the service member's, thus freeing up the service member's loan eligibility for future use (as explained in the second question on p. 57).

---

44. U.S. Department of Veterans Affairs, "Eligibility Frequently Asked Questions," http://www.homeloans.va.gov/faqelig.htm.

Designated Agents

The following offices are responsible for a service member's retired pay. They will be referred to as the *designated agent* hereafter:

    A. Army, Navy, Air Force, Marine Corps.
       DFAS-Cleveland Site
       DFAS-HGA/CL
       P.O. Box 998002
       Cleveland, OH 44199-8002
       Fax: 877-622-5930 or 216-522-6960

    B. United States Coast Guard
       Commanding Officer (L)
       Pay and Personnel Center
       444 Quincy Street
       Topeka, KS 66683-3591

    C. Public Health Service
       Office of General Counsel
       Department of Health and Human Service,
       Room 5362
       330 Independence Avenue, SW
       Washington, D.C. 20201

    D. National Oceanic and Atmospheric Administration
       Submit to Coast Guard address.[45]

---

45. DoD FMR Vol 7B Chapter 29, "Where to Send Applications for USFSPA Payments," *Former Spouse Payments from Retired Pay,* Feb. 2009, 290403, http://comptroller.defense.gov/fmr/07b/07b_29.pdf.

Preparation Checklist for Assistance

When contacting the designated agent, the following information should be readily available:

* Service member's Social Security number
* Former spouse's Social Security number
* Divorce date
* Rank at divorce
* Retirement date
* Rank at retirement
* Pay Entry Date (the date the service member first entered active duty)
* Years in service at divorce (exact number, including months)
* Years in service at retirement (exact number, including months)
* List of questions

Document the conversation. Keep a written sheet of paper that contains the:

* Date of the consultation phone call or visit
* Name, title and phone of the person contacted
* Topic discussed
* Questions discussed and answers given, including copies of documentation, such as references to U.S. Codes or Regulations
* Actions that were to be taken next
* Follow-up date to call back to check on the status of the issue discussed

Waiver of Privacy Act

Military divorce decrees should have a statement concerning waiver of the service member's rights to privacy when information is required to enforce the agreements declared in the decree. Such language might read:

> It is further ordered and decreed that service member does hereby waive any privacy or other rights as may be required for former spouse to obtain information relating to service member's date and time of retirement; last unit assignment; final rank, grade, and pay; present or past retired pay; or other information as may be required to enforce this award or required to revise this Order so as to make it enforceable.

Despite this language appearing in the decree, the former spouse should not interpret it as receiving the right to discuss the service member's records with the designated agent or any other office. In fact, when the former spouse calls the designated agent for assistance, most of the time a response within the first five minutes will be something to the effect of, "Due to the privacy act, I cannot discuss this matter with you."

Should the former spouse ask the designated agent's customer service representative to review the decree on file which shows the service member's waiver of the privacy act rights, the former spouse will then be told something to the effect of, "Due to the decree being under state law and the designated agent falling under federal law, this privacy waiver will not be enforced by the designated agent." In other words, the designated agent is under no obligation to follow something ordered by a particular state. The office is only obligated to follow Federal Law which says to comply with the privacy act.

Despite the limitations of the language waiving the right to privacy, the language should still be included in the decree to place the service member under a court ordered obligation to assist with providing accurate information to the former spouse. The language will still apply to the service member, even if there is no state authority over the designated agent.

In cases where the designated agent denies the former spouse information due to the Privacy Act, the former spouse has the following options:

1. The former spouse can try to rephrase the issue or question so it applies to all service members in general or present a hypothetical situation. Phrases such as "If a member..." or "How would this apply to a former spouse who..." can be used instead of using references to the specific situation. This type of language will usually result in receipt of the desired information. Despite their best intentions, the experience and knowledge of customer service personnel varies, so the only way to ensure one is receiving accurate information is to request the references, as in, "In what regulation would I find this so I'm able to read more?" or, "Could you provide an online reference to share with my lawyer?"

2. The former spouse can communicate with the service member, requesting the required information. If the service member is still in service, the former spouse might also consider placing the request through the service member's supervisor or commanding officer.

3. If the former spouse is unable to communicate with the service member, or the service member refuses to cooperate, the former spouse would have to use an attorney, and possibly the state court system, to make a request and/or file a motion that the service member has not complied with the decree. Sometimes a letter from an attorney, without actually filing an expensive motion within the court, is enough to receive a response.

Retirement Pay Overview

In 1982 Congress passed the Uniformed Services Former Spouses' Protection Act (USFSPA) allowing state courts to treat military disposable retired pay as divisible property in a divorce.

> "Subject to the limitations of this section, a court may treat disposable retired pay payable to a member for pay periods beginning after [retroactive to] June 25, 1981, either as property solely of the member or as property of the member and his [or her] spouse in accordance with the law of the jurisdiction of such court."[46]

The act itself gives the states the right to divide disposable retired pay as marital property. It does not discuss, however, how to divide retirement pay, or give the right or entitlement to a division of retirement pay to the former spouse (the divorce decree must do this). It also does not provide rules on the percentage to award a former spouse in a divorce decree (the state laws will do this). Lastly, the act does not specify how long a marriage must last to divide retired pay, only how long it must last for a federal designated agent to pay the retirement pay portion.

Given all these unknowns, it is in both the service member's and former spouse's interest to learn as much as possible concerning division prior to negotiations. This is true even if the marriage is viewed as *short term (see* 10/10 Rule for the Agent p. 68).

Ever since the passing of the USFSPA, this controversial topic continues to raise emotions in numerous point papers, articles, and discussions. The focus here is the application of the law (not the logic behind it). Understanding the intricacies of retirement pay is not a simple process and might require several reads.

---

46. U.S. Code Title 10 > Subtitle A > Part II > Chapter 71 > § 1408, "Payment of retired or retainer pay in compliance with court orders," Jan. 5, 2009, (c) (1), http://www4.law.cornell.edu/uscode/10/usc_sec_10_00001408----000-.html.

Vested Retirement Pay

While the USFSPA gives the states the right to divide disposable pay, it cannot be emphasized enough that the states are not instructed on how to accomplish this division.

Vested retirement pay, means the retirement pay is payable when the employee ceases to work. In the case of a military service member, retirement pay will not be received unless the member has served twenty years. A service member, who resigns prior to twenty years, receives no retirement pay. Consequently, military retirement pay is not considered *vested* until twenty years of service.

States have various laws in place addressing the issue of military retirement pay. Some examples of division laws are:

- Indiana and Arkansas require retirement pay to be vested.
- Alabama requires a marriage to have lasted ten years.
- Puerto Rico will not divide a noncontributory pension plan.[47]

Some states are creating orders to begin payment of retirement pay upon eligibility, even if the service member is not yet retired:

- New Mexico, Arizona, and California all have cases that took a stance requiring the service member to begin payments to the former spouse or else suffer the accrual of interest on the unpaid pension rights.[48]

This small state by state sampling shows how individual state laws play a significant role in a military divorce and to compare divorce decrees across states would be interesting but relatively meaningless. While this is often clear to the lawyers involved, for the service member and former spouse it can often be frustrating to discover a case favoring one's position, only to be told, "We can't use that because it's an out of state case."

---

47. Mark E. Sullivan, "Military Pension Division: The Servicemember's Strategy," Silent Partner, http://www.abanet.org/family/military/silent/mpd_servicemember.pdf

48. Mark E. Sullivan, "Military Pension Division: Scouting the Terrain," Silent Partner, http://www.abanet.org/family/military/silent/mpd_scoutingterrain.pdf

Disposable Retired Pay

The Uniformed Services Former Spouses' Protection Act (USFSPA), authorizes the designated agent to make payments from a service member's *Disposable Retired Pay*. Disposable retired pay is usually less than the gross retired pay. Disposable retired pay includes the gross monthly retired pay after the following are deducted out:

- Debts owed to the United States
- Court martial forfeitures of retired pay
- Pay waived to receive disability pay
- Survivor Benefit Plan (SBP) premiums.[49]

> **Example:** If a service member's gross pay is $3,000, with 25 percent ($750) waived for disability and the SBP premiums are $195, then the disposable retired pay is $2,055 ($3,000 - $750 - $195).

Retroactive or "Back Pay"

If alimony or the former spouse retirement pay is overdue, the designated agent will *not* make any retroactive payments to recover the obligation. "A former spouse can collect current retired pay award payments, but not retired pay award arrears." The designated agent will, however, pay up to two years "back pay" for child support.[50]

Since it takes the designated agent time to set up retiree accounts, often the service member will have to make the initial payments to the former spouse by check. If payments were ever to be put on hold awaiting litigation, when a final judgment is made, any back alimony or retirement pay, would again have to be paid directly by the service member to the former spouse.

---

49. U.S. Code Title 10 > Subtitle A > Part II > Chapter 71 > § 1408, "Payment of retired or retainer pay in compliance with court orders," Jan. 5, 2009, (a)(4) http://www4.law.cornell.edu/uscode/10/usc_sec_10_00001408----000-.html

50. DoD FMR Vol 7B Chapter 29, "Retired Pay Award," *Former Spouse Payments from Retired Pay*, Feb. 2009, 290304 and 290401, http://comptroller.defense.gov/fmr/07b/07b_29.pdf.

Retirement Pension and Death Beneficiaries

The service member's retirement pay is not a retirement pension. This is a very common misconception.

In fact, retirement pay is often looked at as reduced pay for reduced service. In the traditional sense, retirement separates an employee from the organization. A retired service member, however, is not viewed as separated from service since the member still receives pay (reduced pay for reduced services) and can actually be called back to duty.

With a pension plan, if the owner passes away, there is property to pass on to a beneficiary because money was *set aside* by the owner in the creation of the pension itself. In a pension plan the owner can withdraw the entire sum or "empty the account" so to speak. With the service member, however, there is no money that has been *set aside* for a potential withdrawal. Instead, retirement payments are dispersed from the annual federal budget.

Should the service member die before retirement, the former spouse will receive no retirement pay award. Should the service member die after retirement, the Survivor Benefit Plan (discussed later) can be used to preserve an award to the former spouse.

In the case of the former spouse's death, the former spouse's portion of the retirement pay will stop and the pay reverts back to the service member. There is no venue to pass the former spouse retirement pay award on to an heir.

Remarriage

Remarriage by the service member has no effect on the division of retired pay. Remarriage by the former spouse also has no effect on retired pay (unless receiving an award under the rules of an abused spouse, see p. 70).

> "*Unless the court order specifies otherwise*, retired pay award payments will not stop upon the designated agent's receipt of notice of the former spouse's remarriage."[51]

---

51. DoD FMR Vol 7B Chapter 29, "Termination and Suspension of Retired Pay Award Payments," *Former Spouse Payments from Retired Pay*, Feb. 2009, 291102, http://comptroller.defense.gov/fmr/07b/07b_29.pdf.

Uniformed Services Former Spouses' Protection Act

The Uniformed Services Former Spouses' Protection Act (USFSPA) is a controversial law passed in 1982 allowing states to divide a service member's retirement pay when dividing marital property. It also allows a former spouse to apply for alimony and child support payments from a service member's retired pay.

It does *not* award or guarantee a specific share (or percentage of retirement pay) to the former spouse.

The details of the USFSPA can be found in:

1. The Department of Defense (DoD) Financial Management Regulation (FMR), Vol. 7B, Chapter 29, *Former Spouse Payments from Retired Pay.* (Feb. 2009)[52]

2. U.S. Code Title 10, Subtitle A, Part II, Chapter 71, §1408 *Payment of Retired or Retainer Pay in Compliance with Court Orders.* (Jan. 2009)[53]

3. *Attorney Instruction Dividing Military Retired Pay,* by Garnishment Operations DFAS: DFAS-DGG/CL, DFAS Cleveland, Ohio (Revised Jan. 4, 2010).[54]

---

52. DoD FMR Vol. 7B, Ch. 29, *Former Spouse Payments from Retired Pay,* Feb. 2009, http://www.defenselink.mil/comptroller/fmr/07b/07b_29.pdf.

53. U.S. Code Title 10 > Subtitle A > Part II > Chapter 71 > § 1408, *Payment of retired or retainer pay in compliance with court orders,* Jan. 5, 2009, http://www.law.cornell.edu/uscode/10/usc_sec_10_00001408----000-.html.

54. DFAS Publication, *Attorney Instruction Dividing Military Retired Pay,* http://www.dfas.mil/garnishment/military/AttorneyInstruction-01-04-10.pdf.

10/10 Rule for the Agent (not Division)

For a former spouse to receive a portion of a service member's retired pay as a garnishment paid by the designated agent, the former spouse must have been married to the service member for 10 years during which time the member performed 10 years of creditable service.[55] This is commonly called the 10/10 Rule.

This does not mean a marriage must have lasted 10 years for states to divide retirement pay. What the 10/10 Rule means is for any marriage lasting under ten years, where a state divides retired pay, the service member will have to pay the former spouse directly. The designated agent will make payments when marriages last at least 10 years during the service members career.

Two advantages of the designated agent making the payment to the former spouse are:

- The designated agent will report the payments as taxable on a Form 1099-R issued to the former spouse (as opposed to listing all the pay on the service member's Form 1099-R) and
- Contact is reduced with the former spouse.[56]

In the case of *short term* marriages, even the smallest figures of retirement pay will add up. Suppose the former spouse's award resulted in receiving "only" $100 a month. This is $1,200 a year and assuming the former spouse lives 30 years past the retirement date, results in a total value of $36,000. The same scenario at $200 a month is a $72,000 value.

Annual cost of living adjustments would make the figure even greater, not to mention the investment potential and possible compounding growth.

Former spouses should stay away from any suggested waivers concerning retirement pay, regardless of how small the award, unless extremely confident that an equal trade has been offered.

---

55. DoD FMR Vol 7B Chapter 29, "Requirements that apply to a Retired Pay Award," *Former Spouse Payments from Retired Pay*, Feb. 2009, 290604, http://comptroller.defense.gov/fmr/07b/07b_29.pdf.

56. DFAS Publication, *Attorney Instruction Dividing Military Retired Pay*, http://www.dfas.mil/garnishment/military/AttorneyInstruction-01-04-10.pdf.

50 Percent Limit Rule for the Agent

Under the USFSPA rules, the designated agent will not make a former spouse payment that exceeds 50 percent of the member's disposable retired pay.[57]

> **Example:** If a retiree's disposable retired pay is $2,000, the most the designated agent will pay the former spouse is $1,000 (50% × $2,000).

While it is clear that the designated agent's limit is 50 percent, two stances have been taken on whether USFSPA actually sets a 50 percent cap on the total percentage a former spouse can be awarded by the states:

1. One view (similar to the reasoning discussed in the 10/10 Rule) interprets the "provision as only a limitation on payments made directly by the Secretaries of the Armed Services and not a limitation on the total percentage that the former spouse can receive."[58]

2. Some (for example, Missouri) think it is illogical to ignore the limit:

> "Why the government would care if it dispenses fifty percent or ninety percent escapes us, unless the fifty percent is the limit a nonmilitary spouse can receive through any means of disbursement".[59]

Lawyers will explain how their particular state addresses this issue.

If a state does award more than 50 percent, the service member will have to pay the additional amount (the amount exceeding 50 percent) directly to the former spouse.

---

57. DoD FMR Vol 7B Chapter 29, "Payment Amount Limitations," *Former Spouse Payments from Retired Pay*, Feb. 2009, 290901A, http://comptroller.defense.gov/fmr/07b/07b_29.pdf.

58. National Legal Research Group, Inc., "Military Service Benefits Update," *DivorceSource.com*, Part III. Retirement Benefits Other Issues, Federal Cap on Award, 1998, http://www.divorcesource.com/research/sample3.html

59. Ibid., http://www.divorcesource.com/research/sample3.html

65 Percent Limit Rule for the Agent

Under USFSPA, when the service member's pay is garnished for a former spouse award, alimony, and child support, the maximum amount the designated agent will pay combining all obligations is 65 percent of the member's disposable earnings.[60]

> **Example:** If a retiree's disposable pay is $2,000, then the most the designated agent is permitted to garnish is $1,300 (65 percent of $2,000). Of this $1,300, up to $1,000 (50 percent of $2,000) is permitted to be paid by the designated agent toward a former spouse retirement pay award (in accordance with the 50 percent limit rule previously discussed).

If the former spouse award, child support, and alimony sum to greater than 65 percent, the service member will have to make up the difference and the rule of *Order of Priority of Payments* comes into play.

Abused Spouses

If the member has been denied retired pay due to misconduct, the USFSPA provides for payments to abused spouses. Since these payments would be made by the designated agent, unless the member has another source of funds, the marriage must have lasted 10 years in accordance with the 10/10 Rule.

Payments are suspended upon remarriage of an abused former spouse receiving pay under these conditions but can later resume in the case of divorce, annulment, or death of the new spouse.

Details and qualifications for an abused former spouse receiving a portion of retirement pay (when the service member is ineligible) are found in the U.S. Code.[61]

---

60. DoD FMR Vol 7B Chapter 29, "Payment Amount Limitations," *Former Spouse Payments from Retired Pay*, Feb. 2009, 290901B, http://comptroller.defense.gov/fmr/07b/07b_29.pdf.

61. U.S. Code Title 10 > Subtitle A > Part II > Chapter 71 > § 1408, "Benefits for Dependents Who Are Victims of Abuse by Members Losing Right to Retired Pay," *Payment of retired or retainer pay in compliance with court orders*, (h), Jan. 5, 2009, http://www.law.cornell.edu/uscode/10/usc_sec_10_00001408----000-.html.

Order of Priority of Payments

The percentage rules play an even more significant role in the case of multiple garnishments.

When a former spouse is awarded a portion of retired pay, alimony, and child support, the former spouse may choose the priority for payments, and if no specification is made, payments are disbursed in this order:

1. Former spouse portion of retired pay
2. Child support
3. Alimony[62]

> **Example:** If a retiree's disposable pay is $2,000 and the former spouse (custodial parent) was awarded $750 in retirement pay and $600 in child support, then the designated agent would pay $750 to the former spouse and $550 would be garnished toward child support.
>
> The total garnished from the service member's pay is $1,300 ($750 + $550), in accordance with the 65 Percent Limit Rule. The retiree must send the former spouse an additional payment for the remaining $50 due in child support.

When the former spouse submits the DD Form 2293, *Application for Former Spouse Payments from Retired Pay*, (discussed later p. 133), the priority of payments should be indicated.

When choosing the order of payments, the former spouse should consider listing the child support payment last since child support offices are often able to assist in legal matters at no cost to the parents. On the contrary, if the former spouse has to recover unpaid alimony or retirement pay, hiring a lawyer might be necessary.

---

62. DoD FMR Vol 7B Chapter 29, "Priority of Payments, Multiple Awards," *Former Spouse Payments from Retired Pay*, Feb. 2009, 291001, http://comptroller.defense.gov/fmr/07b/07b_29.pdf.

Timely Account Set Up & Payments

It takes 30 to 60 days to establish the former spouse's account to begin payments and thus, the first payment could be at 90 days.

> "If the former spouse's application is approved, then payments will start no later than 90 days after the date the designated agent received the former spouse's complete application, or no later than 90 days after the date the member becomes eligible to receive military retired pay, whichever is later."[63]

The designated agent will not make retroactive payments so the service member must be ordered in the decree to make the initial payment(s) of retired pay to the former spouse *(see* Retroactive or "Back Pay" p. 65). It also takes 30 to 60 days for garnishments to begin, so if applicable, the service member must also be ordered and be prepared to make direct timely payments of alimony and child support.

Indemnification Statement - Civil Service Employment

Service members still on active duty have the option of leaving the service for federal employment (during which process they receive credit for service years), and thus, never officially retire from the military. An indemnification a clause is needed to ensure the former spouse still receives the award intended by the decree.

> "If [service member] fails to retire from military service and elects to "roll over" time in service into other federal government service in order to get credit for the same, then the [former spouse] shall be entitled to the [former spouse] share of any federal retirement pay or annuity received based on the parties' period of marriage during [service member's] period of military service. Service member shall notify... [*see* footnote link]."[64]

---

63. DoD FMR Vol 7B Chapter 29, "Starting Payments," *Former Spouse Payments from Retired Pay,* Feb. 2009, 290801, http://comptroller.defense.gov/fmr/07b/07b_29.pdf.

64. Mark E. Sullivan, "Getting Military Pension Division Orders Honored by DFAS," Silent Partner, http://www.abanet.org/family/military/silent/pension_division.pdf.

Computing the Division of Pay

While the USFSPA gives authority to the states to divide retired pay, it does not explain *how* to divide retired pay. The states apply their own laws when deciding what percentage to award a former spouse and what language to use in the decree. This book, the regulations, and the DFAS publication all have suggestions of acceptable computations and language to use.

The DoD Financial Management Regulation revised in 2009 offers some examples of computation and acceptable language. They fall into three categories:

1. Fixed amount or fixed percentage
2. A formula percentage
3. A hypothetical formula

Computation will be discussed first and discussion of language will follow. In its most basic form, there is one formula used to compute the former spouse award of retired pay:

		(a)		(b)		(c)
Former Spouse Award	=	Percent Awarded to the Former Spouse by the State	×	Marital Share	×	Retirement Pay Earned (at divorce or retirement)

At first glance, the issue for negotiation would appear to be the retirement pay figure (c), whether to use the amount earned at divorce time or the later figure in place at retirement. In reality, debatable issues arise in all three areas, (a), (b) and (c) discussed in the next sections.

Before delving into the three components of the formula, one should have an understanding of Cost of Living Adjustments (COLAs) and disability payments.

Cost of Living Adjustments (COLAs)

All percentage awards ensure the former spouse receives a proportionate share of every Cost of Living Adjustment (COLA) awarded from divorce date forward. (This is different from a Cost of Living Allowance, also referred to as COLA, but given as a pay adjustment to compensate for living in high-cost locations.)[65]

The government may award a Cost of Living Adjustment (hereafter referred to as COLA) to service members' pay to adjust for inflation.

This is not the same as the annual military pay raise increase. For a given year, Congress can award both a COLA increase and a pay raise increase and these percentages do not have to match.

Unless states otherwise, all formula awards allow each party to receive their respective share of all future COLAs:

> "Please note that all awards expressed as a percentage of disposable retired pay, including hypothetical awards, will automatically include a proportionate share of the member's Cost of Living Adjustments (COLAs) *unless the order states otherwise*. Also, hypothetical retired pay amounts will be adjusted for all retired pay COLAs from the hypothetical retirement date to the member's actual retirement date, unless stated otherwise."[66]

Designated agents can help provide explanations for personal computations. The purpose here is to understand the general concept and to have enough knowledge at retirement time to request an explanation of calculations to ensure the former spouse is neither over nor underpaid.

When a service member has not yet retired and the divorce decree award used the retirement pay *earned as of the date of divorce*, the effect of COLA increases can be complicated to understand. Service members may wonder why the former spouse's amount increases despite the fact the retirement award was limited.

---

65. Military.com, "2010 Cost-of-Living Allowance," *Military Pay Benefits*, http://www.military.com/benefits/military-pay/cost-of-living-allowance

66. DoD FMR Vol 7B Chapter 29, "Military Retired Pay Division Order," *Former Spouse Payments from Retired Pay*, Feb. 2009, Appendix A, p. 29-19, http://comptroller.defense.gov/fmr/07b/07b_29.pdf.

One way to explain increasing proportional COLAs is to imagine the retirement pay as a portion of land. At the time of divorce, the service member has earned "so much land" which the court divides between the former spouse and the service member:

Former Spouse	Service Member
Portion awarded to former spouse of retirement pay earned up to divorce date	Portion awarded to service member of retirement pay earned up to divorce date

Since division was as of the *date of divorce*, as the service member qualifies for more retirement pay, more "land" is added (white box) with no effect on the former spouse portion (award):

Former Spouse	Service Member	
Portion awarded to former spouse of retirement pay earned up to divorce date	Portion awarded to service member of retirement pay earned up to divorce date	Portion of retirement pay earned after divorce (belongs 100% to the service member)

In percentage awards, all COLAs granted after divorce, will apply (increase the value) to all sections (darker boxes). The former spouse portion increases, and the service member's portions awarded at and earned after divorce, likewise increase.

Former Spouse	Service Member	
Portion awarded to former spouse of retirement pay earned up to divorce date	Portion awarded to service member of retirement pay earned up to divorce date	Portion of retirement pay earned after divorce (belongs 100% to the service member)
+ all COLA awards after divorce date	+ all COLA awards after divorce date	+ all COLA awards after divorce date

COLA rates apply to other federal programs as well (such as Social Security). Increases are based on the previous year's Consumer Price Index (CPI) and it is possible to have no increase. The adjustments reflect the difference between the average CPI from the third quarter of one year to the next. Since the third quarter CPI for 2009 fell from the third quarter CPI of 2008, there was no COLA increase for 2010 (a first after 35 years of increases). No increase is expected for 2011 as well.[67]

The COLA applied to a retiree's pay may be further adjusted depending on:

1. The date the service member entered the service and the date the service member retired from the service, and

2. Whether the service member chose a Career Status Bonus at 15 years.

Example: In December 2005, a COLA increase of 4.1 percent went into effect for 2006. This meant that most retiree paychecks received a 4.1 percent increase beginning with the 1 January paycheck, but there were exceptions, as explained next.

COLA rates are reduced for those retiring in the year prior to the increase. Thus, members who actually retired in 2005 had their COLA rates for 2006 reduced. For 2006, retirees who entered service on September 8, 1980 or later received these rates:

* 4.1 percent (full amount) if retired before 1 January 2005

* 3.4 percent, if retired in the 1st quarter of 2005

* 2.8 percent, if retired in the 2nd quarter of 2005

* 1.4 percent, if retired in the 3rd quarter of 2005

* 0.0 percent, if retired in the 4th quarter of 2005[68]

---

67. Stan Hinden, "What Happened to my COLA?" *American Association of Retired Persons (AARP) Financial*, Nov. 2009, http://www.aarpfinancial.com/content/Learning/retPerspectives_hinden_1109.cfm.

68. DoD FMR Vol 7B Chapter 8, "Basic Pay Rates, Legislative and Cost of Living Adjustments to Retired Pay, "*Provisions of Pay Changes, Exceptions, and Special Computations,*" Sep. 2009, 0804, http://comptroller.defense.gov/fmr/07b/07b_08.pdf.

The other possible COLA reduction occurs for service members choosing the CSB/REDUX retirement system, where the service member receives a Career Status Bonus (CSB) at 15 years.

Example: "Under REDUX, the COLA is equal to CPI minus 1%...At age 62, the REDUX and High-3 retirement salaries are equal. But, REDUX COLAs for later years will again be set at CPI minus 1%."[69]

The designated agent always uses the High-3 retirement system (discussed later) for former spouse calculations, but makes former spouse adjustments to comply with the intentions of a decree if a service member falls under the CSB/REDUX retirement system.

Unadjusted COLA increases for the last several years are:[70]

In Dec. of Year	COLA Increased	For Year
1999	2.4%	2000
2000	3.5%	2001
2001	2.6%	2002
2002	1.4%	2003
2003	2.1%	2004
2004	2.7%	2005
2005	4.1%	2006
2006	3.3%	2007
2007	2.3%	2008
2008	5.8%	2009
2009	0.0%	2010

---

69. Office of the Secretary of Defense, "*CSB/REDUX Retirement System Details,*" Military Compensation, http://militarypay.defense.gov/retirement/ad/04_redux.html

70. Military Officers Association of America, "MOAA Cost of Living Adjustment (COLA) History," http://www.moaa.org/lac/lac_issues/lac_issues_major/lac_issues_major_retired/lac_cola.htm. (*See also,* footnote 67.)

Disability Pay

At retirement, a service member may waive a portion of retired pay and instead choose to receive an equivalent amount as Veterans Affairs disability pay. The advantages are VA disability pay is not taxable income (for state or federal taxes) and it is not divisible under USFSPA *(see* Disposable Retired Pay p. 65).

> **Example:** A service member with $2,000 gross monthly retired pay and a 10 percent disability could elect to waive $200 in pay to instead receive $200 in disability pay, thus reducing the monthly taxable pay to $1,800. (This is also the amount of the disposable retired pay, assuming there are no other pay factors to consider.)

When disability occurs after divorce, concerns begin to arise when looking at the division of retired pay.

> **Example A, Disability Pay Indemnification:** A service member retires receiving $2,000 in gross monthly retired pay. The division is 25 percent to the former spouse and 75 percent to the service member. Assuming there is never any disability pay, the former spouse receives $500 (25% × $2,000) and the service member receives $1,500 (75% × $2,000) monthly.
>
> When a 10 percent disability occurs after divorce, the designated agent removes the disability pay first, "off the top," reducing the disposable retired pay to $1,800 ($2,000 less $200 in disability). This causes the former spouse to now receive a reduction to $450 a month (25 percent of $1,800) and the service member to receive a monthly increase to $1,550 (75 percent of $1,800 plus $200 in disability pay).

The problem is the court awarded former spouse portion of the retirement pay should not be reduced for disability occurring after divorce. To protect the former spouse award, lawyers will add an indemnification reimbursement clause to the divorce decree.

Indemnification Language - Disability Waiver

An indemnification statement will require reimbursement for any actions taken by the service member that would reduce the former spouse's court awarded portion of retirement pay. A general indemnification statement might be best to cover all possible situations causing a reduction in pay, but it can also be very specific.

Examples of such clauses are:

> **General:** It is further ordered and decreed that service member be and is hereby specifically directed, on penalty of contempt, to pay former spouse's interest in the disposable retired pay as ordered in this decree. Service member is specifically directed that he/she is not relieved of that obligation except to the extent that he/she is specifically notified that one hundred percent (100%) of former spouse's interest in the retirement benefit has been directly paid by the designated agent. It is further ordered and decreed that any election of benefits which may hereafter be made by service member shall not reduce the amount equal to the percentage of disposable retired pay the Court has herein awarded to former spouse.

> Or

> **Specific:** "If husband receives VA disability pay and this event causes a reduction of husband's disposable retired pay, thus reducing his former wife's share thereof, husband will pay directly to his former wife each month any amount that is withheld from husband by the designated agent for the above reason."[71]

The argument in favor of indemnification clauses is the former spouse's interest must be protected and the service member

---

71. JustAnswer.com "What is the law in regards XX pay being awarded to an ex spouse as alimony?" Military Law, Aug. 2009, http://www.justanswer.com/questions/2dvag-what-is-the-law-in-regards-to-disability-pay-being-awarded.

should not have the ability to take actions to reduce the court award. Virginia courts have ruled on this in the appeal case of *Owen v Owen*:

> "Conceivably, husband's disability payments could eliminate completely the wife's benefits. Such a result is irrational and does not comport with the clear intent expressed by the language of the PSA [property settlement agreement]."[72]

While states may consider rulings in other states, some courts wish to hear only about rulings that occurred within their state, and may choose to apply only local law to make a final decision.

Indemnification clauses can also include an order for the service member to take action should the former spouse award not be paid in full. This language acts as a "catch all" protecting the former spouse for any unforeseen future events:

> **General "catch all:"** It is further ordered and decreed that service member shall not pursue any course of action which would defeat, reduce or limit former spouse's right to receive former spouse's full separate property share of service member's retired pay as awarded herein. It is further ordered and decreed if the designated agent is not allowed to pay former spouse the full amount of former spouse's entitlement pursuant to this decree for *whatever reason*, then the service member is hereby ordered, within seven (7) days of being notified by former spouse that former spouse is not receiving the full amount of former spouse's interest in the retired pay, to execute and deliver to the *designated agent* such forms or documents which may then be necessary to effect an *allotment* payable to former spouse in the amount of the difference between the amount being paid directly to the former spouse by the designated agent and the full amount of the former spouse's interest in the retired pay.

---

72. Owen v. Owen, 14 Va. Appeal Record No. 0479-96-4, Oct. 1, 1996, http://www.courts.state.va.us/opinions/opncavtx/0479964.txt

The required allotment through the designated agent documents proper payment for audit trail purposes. It ensures the former spouse is paid timely, on the first of the month, and eliminates the need for contact between the service member and former spouse. It also secures payment for the former spouse should anything happen to the service member (such as a medical incapacity) or some other unforeseen situation where the service member's bank account could potentially run out of funds (causing the former spouse not to be paid).

Indemnification clauses can also require interest to be paid on unpaid obligations. It is also possible to choose language that holds both parties accountable for any future damages (such as legal fees incurred for having to go back to court due to the other's actions).

While an indemnification statement is preferable, all is not necessarily lost if a divorce decree has been finalized without one. There are cases where state courts have ruled concerning the *intention of the parties involved* and in such cases, these rulings concluded that the intention at the time of divorce was for neither party to take any action to reduce the amounts awarded in the divorce decree.

> "Even if there is no expressed indemnity clause in the property settlement agreement, the court may find that indemnification was implicit. In other words, there was no intent for one of the parties to reduce the other's benefit by electing disability benefits."[73]

The key point here is in cases with no indemnification clause, both the service member and former spouse might once again end up in court, so it is in everyone's best interest both financially and emotionally to understand and resolve this topic prior to signing the divorce decree.

---

73. Pension Analysis Consultants, Inc., "The Disability Issue in the Distribution of Military Retirement Benefits," *MilitaryDivorceOnline.com* Indemnity, Mar. 22, 2005, http://www.militarydivorceonline.com/worddocashtm/the_disability_issue_in_the_distribution_of_military_retirement_renefits.htm.

Disability Indemnification Logic - Protecting the Former Spouse

The logic behind this position (of including indemnification so the former spouse award will not be reduced due to disability claimed at a later date) can be better understood by looking at an example.

The basic idea is that while it is the service member's legal right to waive a portion of retired pay, the waived amount should come from the portion the service member was awarded.

Imagine the retirement pay as a portion of land. At the time of divorce, the active service member has earned "so much land" which the court divides between the former spouse and the service member. There was no disability pay at the time, so the portion split was in accordance with federal law:

Former Spouse	Service Member
Portion awarded to former spouse	Portion awarded to service member

Recall Example A, Disability Pay (p.78) where a service member has $2,000 monthly gross retired pay, a 10 percent disability, and a 25 percent former spouse award. The monthly intention of the divorce decree was to pay $500 to the former spouse and $1,500 to the service member.

Decree Intention	
Former Spouse	**Service Member**
$500	$1,500

Ideally, when a 10 percent disability occurs after divorce, the disability would be waived from the service member's portion of "land" with no effect on the former spouse award as illustrated:

Ideally	
Former Spouse	**Service Member**
$500	$1,350 taxable pay ($1,500 - $150 waived) + $150 disability pay (10% × $1,500) $1,500 total pay

In reality, the designated agent removes the disability pay "off the top" prior to dividing the pay (in accordance with the USFSPA definition of disposable retired pay). As a result, the designated agent divides only $1,800 ($2,000 - $200 (the 10 percent disability pay)). The service member receives $1,550 ($200 in disability pay + $1,350 (75% of $1,800)) and the former spouse receives a reduced amount of $450 (25% of $1,800).

In reality	
Former Spouse	**Service Member**
$450	$1,350 taxable pay (75% × $1,800) + $200 disability pay (10% × $2,000) $1,550 total pay

The indemnification clause now comes into play. The indemnification clause is needed in the decree to require the service member to send an additional payment of $50 to the former spouse. This will bring the totals back to a $500/$1,500 split as originally intended. (These figures are shown mathematically on the next page with an additional explanation of the tax benefits).

Note: If the former spouse award was restricted to the retirement pay *earned as of the date of divorce,* the concept is the same. The "land" is divided as of divorce (gray boxes), more "land" (white box) is added after the divorce, and the disability pay occurring after divorce would *ideally* be waived from the service member's portion as shown below:

Ideally		
Former Spouse	**Service Member**	
Portion awarded to former spouse of retirement pay earned up to divorce date	Portion awarded to service member of retirement pay earned up to divorce date	Portion of retirement pay earned after divorce (belongs 100% to the service member)
	Disability pay should be waived from any of the above portion belonging to the service member – with no impact on a former spouse	

Since the designated agent will not create the *ideal* division, the indemnification statement and reimbursement are again required.

Example A: Disability Pay Indemnification and Tax Benefits

The service member and the former spouse both receive a proportional tax benefit when the service member chooses disability pay and there is an indemnification clause requiring reimbursement (also see Taxes Incident to Divorce and IRS Form 1099-R p. 169).

> **Example A,** (disability from p. 78): A 10 percent disabled member receives $2,000 monthly, has a 25 percent former spouse award, and has an indemnification statement.

Before disability is waived (divorce decree intention):

$2,000 Retirement Pay	$2,000 Retirement Pay
× 75% for Service Member	× 25% for Former Spouse
$1,500 to the Service Member	$500 to the Former Spouse

Taxable pay received:
  $1,500 for the Service member
  $500 for the Former Spouse

After disability is applied:

$2,000 Retirement Pay
-$ 200 Disability Pay (calculated from 10% × $2,000)
$1,800 Disposable Pay (after disability is taken "off the top")

$1,800 Disposable Pay	$1,800 Disposable Pay
× 75% for Service Member	× 25% for Former Spouse
$1,350 to the Service Member	$ 450 to the Former Spouse

Taxable pay received (decree awards reduced by 10 percent):
  $1,350 for the Service Member ($1,500 was reduced by $150)
  $ 450 for the Former Spouse ($500 was reduced by $50)

Non-Taxable pay:
  $200 for the Service Member
  $ 50 for the Former Spouse (sent from the Service Member)

Take-home pay (matches the divorce decree intentions):
  $1,500 for the Service Member ($1,350.00 + $200 - $50)
  $ 500 for the Former Spouse ($450 + $50)

When the Disability Percent Exceeds the Service Member Award

Up to this point, the scenario discussed a disability percentage (10 percent) that was less than the service member's percentage awarded in the decree (75 percent). Controversial arguments begin to enter the picture when the disability percentage exceeds the service member's percentage of the retirement award.

Instead of a 10 percent disability, consider instead the service member declared 80 percent disabled. Then, there is not enough of the court awarded portion (75 percent) to cover the disability pay. What is intended by the law in this case? Should the former spouse lose some of the awarded portion of retirement pay since disability pay cannot be divided or should the service member still reimburse the spouse?

In the scenario, the divorce decree was expected to award $500 to the former spouse and $1,500 to the service member. If an 80 percent disability occurred after divorce, the designated agent would pay the service member $1,600 (80% × $2,000) in disability pay and divide the retirement pay into $300 (75% × $400) for the service member and $100 (25% × $400) for the former spouse.

```
 $2,000 Retirement Pay
-$1,600 Disability Pay (calculated from 80% × $2,000)
 $  400 Disposable Pay
```

$ 400 Disposable Pay	$ 400 Disposable Pay
× 75% for Service Member	× 25% for Former Spouse
$ 300 for the Service Member	$ 100 for the Former Spouse

The indemnification clause would require the service member to reimburse the former spouse $400 to comply with the intention of the divorce decree and bring the totals back to the appropriate $500/$1,500 split. The total *take-home* pay for the service member would then be reduced to $1,500 ($1,600 disability + $300 taxable - $400 sent to the former spouse) which appears correct according to the intentions of the divorce decree. The taxable awards (declared in the decree) to both parties have been reduced by 80 percent:

Taxable pay received (decree awards reduced by 80 percent):
$300 for the Service Member ($1,500 less $1,200 disability pay)
$100 for the Former Spouse ($500 less $400 disability pay)

The question arises, however, whether this indemnification repayment of $400 is in accordance with federal law.

Disability pay is not to be divided. Only $300 was received in non-taxable pay, so how does the service member send $400 to the former spouse without using pay from the disability portion received? It appears the service member is now using a portion of the disability pay to send $400 to the former spouse.

The answer is reimbursement must come from another source of funds. The state award for division at divorce time was correct as there was no disability in place at the time of divorce. The former spouse should not be penalized for something that occurred after the fact and disability pay should not be a potential tool used by service members to reduce payment to former spouses.

In theory, as long as there is another funding source, even if a service member became 100 percent disabled after divorce, the former spouse would still receive the awarded amount of pay:

> *From Florida:*
> Indemnification protects the former spouse's interest in retirement pay (as stated in the divorce decree) by providing for an alternative source of payment (from non-disability sources) by the service member in the case where a voluntary act reduces the amount awarded to the former spouse.[74]

An Iowa court also upheld this position saying the issue was not dividing disability pay but instead, whether service members can be ordered to indemnify former spouses for the reduction in their share of the retirement pay:

> "The court held, however, that the order is only valid if the military spouse is able to satisfy the indemnification from a source of funds other than disability benefits."[75]

---

74. District Court of Appeal, First District, State of Florida, "Blann V Blann, Appeal from the circuit court for Clay County. Opinion, CASE NO. 1D07-0100," Nov 2007, http://opinions.1dca.org/written/opinions2007/11-20-07/07-0100.pdf.

75. FindArticles.com, "In property division, ex-spouse entitled to indemnification for disability benefit deductions from military spouse's pension," *Law Reporter*, Dec. 2004, http://findarticles.com/p/articles/mi_qa3898/is_200412/ai_n9471024/.

The National Legal Research Group also reported:

> "[A] husband's agreement to pay specified percentage of gross retirement benefits to wife was enforceable even though he had waived part of those benefits to receive disability pay."[76]

Application of the USFSPA concerning disability pay indemnification continues to be an emotionally debatable topic in all states. However, some relief has come for a disability rating of 50 percent or greater (discussed next).

Concurrent Retirement Disability Pay (CRDP)

In January 2004, a nine year phase-in began restoring retired payments that had been waived for VA Disability Pay, in the form of a new payment, Concurrent Retirement Disability Pay (CRDP). By 2014, all members with a disability rating of 50 percent or more, will no longer be waiving disability pay, but instead receive it concurrently with their retired pay.[77]

This means no reimbursements will be necessary from a 50 percent or greater disabled service member to the former spouse, since in such cases, the former spouse receives the full award.

Former spouses still need indemnification clauses in their decree to protect against future unknown pay changes, especially in cases where the service member has not yet retired and the disability rating (if any) is unknown.

In addition, some eligible service members can choose to receive Combat Related Special Compensation (CRSC) which wipes out the receipt of CRDP, and has detrimental effects (similar to that of disability pay) on the former spouse award. The proper way to protect a former spouse award is to have a clause requiring reimbursement for *any actions* taken by the service member that result in a reduction of the award provided for in the final decree.

---

76. National Legal Research Group, Inc., "Military Service Benefits Update," *DivorceSource.com*, Part II. Retirement Benefits Conversion to Disability Benefits or Other Compensation, 1998, http://www.divorcesource.com/research/sample3.html.

77. Military.com, "Concurrent Retirement and Disability Pay (CRDP) Overview," http://www.military.com/benefits/military-pay/retired-pay/retired-concurrent-receipt-overview

Retirement Pay and Social Security

Since 1957, Military personnel have not contributed a percentage of their salary toward retirement benefits. They pay taxes into the Social Security trust fund and collect full Social Security benefits in addition to their military retired pay. Military retired pay and Social Security are not offset against each other.[78]

A divorced spouse may be eligible and elect to claim social security benefits based on the ex-spouse's income if certain criteria are met and in some cases the ex-spouse does not have to actually be retired. Details can be found on the Social Security website.[79]

---

78. Congressional Research Service (CRS), "Military Retired Pay and Social Security," *CRS Issue Brief for Congress: Military Retirement Major Legislative Issues,* Mar 14, 2006, http://www.fas.org/sgp/crs/natsec/IB85159.pdf.

79. Social Security Administration, Benefits for a Divorced Spouse, http://www.socialsecurity.gov/pubs/10035.html.

State Percentage to the Former Spouse (a)

In its most basic form, there is one formula used to compute the former spouse award of retired pay:

	(a)		(b)		(c)
Former Spouse Award =	Percent Awarded to the Former Spouse by the State	×	Marital Share	×	Retirement Pay Earned (at divorce or retirement)

The first component, (a), the *Percent Awarded to the Former Spouse by the State*, is decided by individual state guidelines on equitable division of marital property.

In general, the term *separate property* refers to property that can be traced directly to one party. Perhaps it was owned prior to marriage or a direct gift.

On the contrary, the term *community property* refers to property that is jointly owned. Community property states generally consider all property acquired after marriage to be community property, to be divided equally in a divorce, a 50/50 split.

The community property states are Arizona, California, Idaho, Louisiana, Nevada, New Mexico, Texas, Washington, and Wisconsin and will usually use a 50 percent division for the first figure (a) in the formula. Colorado (not a community property state) also awards 50 percent of retirement pay to the former spouse.[80]

A state can ultimately declare any figure either ordered or mutually agreed upon, even if over 50 percent *(see* 50 Percent Limit Rule for the Agent p. 69). For example, a state might declare an uneven (60/40) division if the former spouse has been out of the workforce for several years. Attorneys should be able to predict the percentage figure to be used by their particular state when computing a former spouse award. Both sides should be cautious not to voluntarily waive their percentage rights provided by the state.

---

80. Carl O. Graham, "Colorado Formula for Military Retirement Division," Military Divorce Guide, http://www.military-divorce-guide.com/military-retirement-colorado-division.htm.

Marital Share (b)

The Marital Share (or Marital Fraction) is the second figure (b) in the core formula. It represents the overlap time of marriage and total military service.

Former Spouse Award	=	(a) Percent Awarded to the Former Spouse by the State	×	(b) Marital Share	×	(c) Retirement Pay Earned (at divorce or retirement)

The Marital Share (b) cannot be greater than 1 and is carried out to six decimal places. The formula for the Marital Share is:

$$\text{(b) Marital Share} = \frac{\text{Months of Marriage Overlap Time}}{\text{Total Months of Service}}$$

Months of Marriage Overlap Time: is the number of months the service member was both married and in service.

Total Months of Service: refers to the total number of months the service member spent (or will spend) in service before retiring. It is the total number of months for the service member's entire career.

The designated agent does not consider days or partial months, so negotiations should decide how to round partial months.

Example 1: The entire service career was during the marriage.

A marriage existed 25 years during which 20 were also service years. The Marital Share equals 1.

Months of Marriage Overlap = 20 years × 12 months = 240
Months of Service = 20 years × 12 months = 240

$$\text{Marital Share} = \frac{240 \text{ Months of Marriage Overlap Time}}{240 \text{ Total Months of Service}}$$

Marital Share = 1.000000 (carry decimals to six places)

Example 2: The retiree married after service began.

> A retired service member has 21 years creditable service. The marriage existed for 15 years (10 years in service plus 5 years after retirement). The Marital Share is .476190.
>
> Months of Marriage Overlap = 10 years × 12 months = 120
> Months of Service = 21 years × 12 months = 252
>
> $$\frac{\text{Marital}}{\text{Share}} = \frac{120 \text{ Months of Marriage Overlap Time}}{252 \text{ Total Months of Service}}$$
>
> Marital Share = 0.476190

Example 3: The member is not retired (denominator is unknown).

> A marriage existed for the past 15 years and the service member currently has 16 years in service up to the divorce. The Marital Share is unknown.
>
> Months of Marriage Overlap = 15 years × 12 months = 180
> Months of Service = unknown × 12 months = unknown
>
> $$\frac{\text{Marital}}{\text{Share}} = \frac{180 \text{ Months of Marriage Overlap Time}}{\text{Unknown Total Months of Service}}$$
>
> Marital Share = Unknown

Date of Divorce Variation: Some states divide retirement pay as of the *date of divorce*. The following variation of the Marital Share results in an actual figure for the unretired member in Example 3:

(b) Marital Share	=	*Marital Share Variation* Months of Marriage Overlap Time Total Months of Service *up to divorce*

> Months of Marriage Overlap = 15 years × 12 months = 180
> Months of Service *up to Divorce* = 16 years × 12 months = 192
>
> $$\frac{\text{Marital}}{\text{Share}} = \frac{180 \text{ Months of Marriage Overlap Time}}{192 \text{ Months of Service } up\ to\ Divorce}$$
>
> Marital Share = 0.937500

This variation of the Marital Share definition is favorable to the former spouse, because it "locks" the denominator, preventing it from increasing and thus, avoiding any reduction to this component (b). (This variation is used again in Example C, p. 97.)

Marital Share for Reservists

When computing the Marital Share for a reservist, there are two basic choices. Both choices should be calculated and compared to decide which favors the service member and which favors the former spouse. The choices are to use months or to use points:

1. Compute the Marital Share as a fraction of months, as just described (or the variation thereof, using the *date of divorce* months as the denominator).

$$\frac{\text{Marital Share}}{\text{for Reserve}} = \frac{\text{Months of Marriage Overlap Time}}{\text{Total Months of Service}}$$

2. Compute the Marital Share as a fraction of points (or a variation thereof, using the *date of divorce* points as the denominator).

$$\frac{\text{Marital Share}}{\text{for Reserve}} = \frac{\text{Points Earned During Marriage}}{\text{Total Reserve Retirement Points}}$$

An example illustrating this choice is summarized below:

Example: A service member served 5 years unmarried on active duty and served 15 years married as a reserve. Upon retirement, the member has 2,725 points, 900 of which were earned during marriage (overlap points).[81]

Choice 1, Marital Share based on total months:

$$\frac{\text{Marital Share}}{\text{for Reserve}} = \frac{\text{Months of Marriage Overlap Time}}{\text{Total Months of Service}}$$

Marital Share for Reserve = 180 Months (Computed from 15 yrs. × 12 months) / 240 Total Months (Computed from 20 yrs. × 12 mos.)

Marital Share for Reserve = .750000 or 75%

---

81. Mark E. Sullivan, "Military Pension Division: The Spouse's Strategy," Silent Partner, www.abanet.org/family/military/silent/mpd_spouse.pdf.

Choice 2, Marital Share based on total points:

$$\text{Marital Share for Reserve} = \frac{\text{Points Earned During Marriage}}{\text{Total Reserve Retirement Points}}$$

$$\text{Marital Share for Reserve} = \frac{900 \text{ Points Earned During Marriage}}{2{,}725 \text{ Total Reserve Retirement Points}}$$

$$\text{Marital Share for Reserve} = .330275 \text{ or } 33.0275\%$$

In the example, the service member might argue for the lower percentage stating that only 900 points were earned during the marriage time frame. On the contrary, the argument in favor of the former spouse could point out that for 15 years, the former spouse participated in military life, regardless of the number of active days each year, and thus deserves the higher percentage. The final decision must be worked out through negotiations.

The calculations concerning actually achieving reserve points are beyond the scope of this book. More information concerning reservists can be found online at http://www.militarydivorce-tips.com/reservist.html.

The purpose of the example is to illustrate how the Marital Share computation can be interpreted and thus, altered strategically when making the final computation for the former spouse award.

Former Spouse Percentage

Once the Marital Share is computed, the former spouse percentage, the percent used in the language of a decree, can be figured.

Recall, the core formula which refers to the actual (or sometimes hypothetical) amount or award the former spouse will receive:

| Former Spouse Award | = | (a) Percent Awarded to the Former Spouse by the State | × | (b) Marital Share | × | (c) Retirement Pay Earned (at divorce or retirement) |

Multiply the first two components (a) and (b) of this formula to calculate the former spouse percentage that might be used in a divorce decree:

| Former Spouse Percentage | = | (a) Percent Awarded to the Former Spouse by the State | × | (b) Marital Share |

Often, the former spouse percentage is the percent used in the language of the decree. After computing this figure, one can compare the different language options and negotiate as to whether the Retirement Pay Earned (c) should be that in place at *date of divorce*, or that in place *at retirement*, or a negotiated figure.

Three more examples are provided illustrating multiplying the Percent Awarded to the Former Spouse by the State (a), times the Marital Share (b), to arrive at the former spouse percentage.

All three assume the Percent Awarded to the Former Spouse by the State is 50 percent. This could be different as previously explained *(see* State Percentage to Former Spouse p. 89).

Entering the 50 percent awarded by the state results in:

| Former Spouse Percentage | = | (a) 50% | × | (b) Marital Share |

Example B: *Divorce after Retirement*

A couple married on 1 June 1990 and divorced on 1 June 2009. The service member entered service on 1 June 1985 and retired after 20 years on 1 June 2005. The marriage overlap was 15 years, from 1 June 1990 to 1 June 2005.

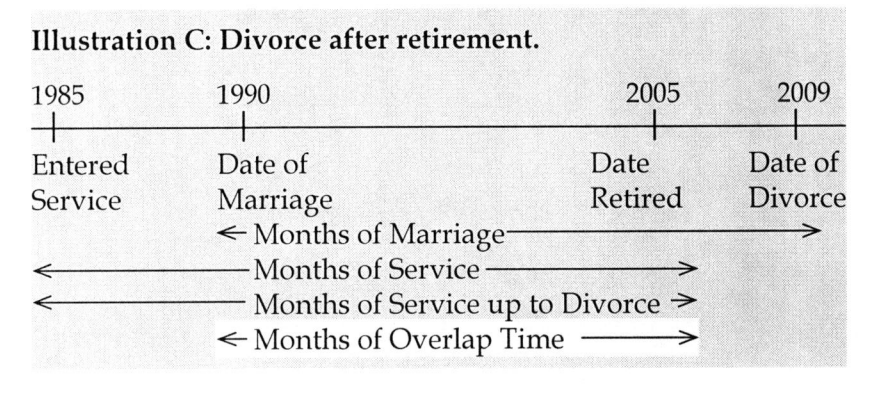

Illustration C: Divorce after retirement.

```
1985              1990                          2005         2009
+—————————————————+————————————————————————————+————————————+
Entered           Date of                      Date         Date of
Service           Marriage                     Retired      Divorce
                  ←— Months of Marriage ———————————————————→
←———————————————— Months of Service ————————————→
←———————————————— Months of Service up to Divorce →
                  ←— Months of Overlap Time ——→
```

| Former Spouse Award | = | (a) Percent Awarded to the Former Spouse by the State | × | (b) Marital Share | × | (c) Retirement Pay Earned (at divorce or retirement) |

a. The state awarded 50 percent to the former spouse.
b. The marital share equals 0.750000.

$$\text{(b) Marital Share} = \frac{\text{Months of Marriage Overlap Time}}{\text{Total Months of Service}}$$

$$\text{Marital Share} = \frac{180 \text{ Months of Marriage Overlap Time}}{240 \text{ Total Months of Service}}$$

Marital Share = .750000

Former Spouse Award = (a) × (b) × (c)
Former Spouse Award = 50% × .75 × Retirement Pay
Former Spouse Award = .375000 × Retirement Pay
The Former Spouse Percentage is 37.5000 percent.

Example C: *Service Member Not Yet Retired*

A couple married on 1 December 1994 and divorced on 1 June 2009. The service member entered service on 1 June 2000 and has not yet retired. The marriage overlap is 9 years from 2000 to 2009.

Illustration B: Service date began after the marriage date.

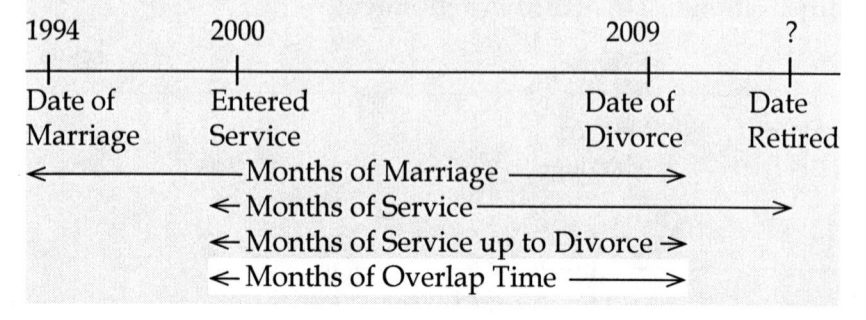

```
1994              2000                         2009            ?
 +-----------------+----------------------------+---------------+
Date of           Entered                      Date of         Date
Marriage          Service                      Divorce         Retired
    <————————————— Months of Marriage —————————>
           <— Months of Service ——————————————————————————————>
           <— Months of Service up to Divorce —>
           <— Months of Overlap Time ————————>
```

Former Spouse Award	=	(a) Percent Awarded to the Former Spouse by the State	×	(b) Marital Share	×	(c) Retirement Pay Earned (at divorce or retirement)

a. The state awarded 50 percent to the former spouse.
b. The marital share equals unknown.

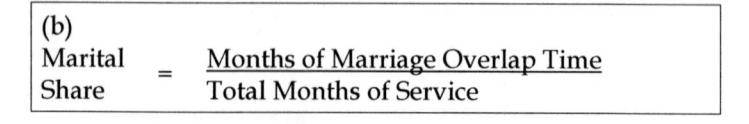

$$\text{(b) Marital Share} = \frac{\text{Months of Marriage Overlap Time}}{\text{Total Months of Service}}$$

$$\text{Marital Share} = \frac{108 \text{ Months of Marriage Overlap Time}}{\text{unknown Total Months of Service}}$$

Marital Share = unknown

The marital share is unknown. Because of this, an exact final spouse percentage would not be used in the language of the decree. Instead, the decree will describe a formula, stating the denominator to use is equal to "total months of service."

Example D: *Marital Share as of Date of Divorce*

A couple married on 1 December 1990 and divorced (after 14 years 6 months) on 1 June 2005. The service member entered service on 1 June 1989, currentlyhas 16 years service, and has not yet retired.

Illustration C: Service date began before the marriage date.

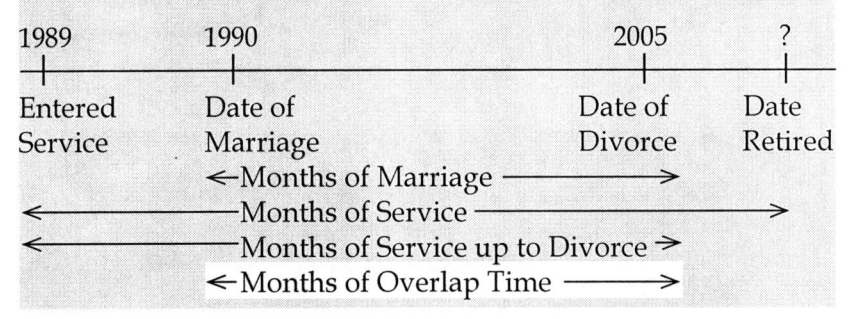

```
1989            1990                        2005            ?
 +---------------+---------------------------+---------------+
Entered        Date of                     Date of         Date
Service        Marriage                    Divorce         Retired
               <-- Months of Marriage -->
 <------------------- Months of Service ------------------->
 <--------- Months of Service up to Divorce -->
 <-- Months of Overlap Time -->
```

	(a)		(b)		(c)
Former Spouse Award =	Percent Awarded to the Former Spouse by the State	×	Marital Share	×	Retirement Pay Earned (at divorce or retirement)

a. The state awarded 50 percent to the former spouse.
b. The marital share equals 0.906250.

(b) Marital Share	=	Months of Marriage Overlap Time / Months of Service *up to Divorce*

$$\text{Marital Share} = \frac{174 \text{ Months of Marriage Overlap Time}}{192 \text{ Months of Service up to Divorce}}$$

Marital Share = .906250

Former Spouse Award = (a) × (b) × (c)
Former Spouse Award = 50% × .906250 × Retirement Pay
Former Spouse Award = .453125 × Retirement Pay
The Former Spouse Percentage is 45.3125 percent.

Retirement Pay Figure (c)

The retirement pay figure (c) is the third figure in the core formula used to compute retired pay:

Former Spouse Award	=	(a) Percent Awarded to the Former Spouse by the State	×	(b) Marital Share	×	(c) Retirement Pay Earned (at divorce or retirement)

USFSPA does not specify how to divide retirement pay:

> "The amount of a former spouse's award is entirely a matter of state law...and the court order must provide [the designated agent] with all the information necessary to compute the award."[82]

While it would be impossible to explain each state's marital property laws, this section provides an overview of the various options for component (c) in the core formula and of the numerous viewpoints surrounding the choices.

Usually only unresolved items are brought before a judge. When considering bringing issues before a local judge, past state rulings should assist lawyers and clients in trying to predict the likely outcomes. Several arguments have arisen concerning the retirement pay figure.

Favoring the Former Spouse

Those favoring the former spouse might argue for a retirement pay figure based on the rank at retirement. The general line of reasoning behind this position gives consideration to the supporting role a former spouse plays in a service member's career. This role does not necessarily have to be as public as in hosting spousal parties, but can be as simple as being present for household goods shipments to allow the service member to report for duty.

---

82. DFAS Publication, *Attorney Instruction Dividing Military Retired Pay*, IV, http://www.dfas.mil/garnishment/military/AttorneyInstruction-01-04-10.pdf.

Another argument concerns the difficulty of former spouses to pursue their own careers and establish retirement accounts due to constraints such as frequent moves, staying with children when the service member deploys or works odd hours, etc.

Lastly, some will argue that former spouse contributions in the years prior to divorce affect promotions in later years. After all, without the prior promotions, the service member would not have reached the retirement rank.

Favoring the Service Member

Arguments for the service member will usually question how supportive or significant the role of the former spouse could possibly have been since the marriage itself has fallen apart. Perhaps the role of the former spouse has even been detrimental to the career.

Further arguments focus on the fact that the former spouse will not be present in the upcoming years toward retirement, so why give credit to pay earned during this period?

Length of marriage might also come into play. For example, if a marriage lasted only two years, the former spouse could have a difficult time arguing for a retirement pay figure based on the pay in place at retirement. On the contrary, if promotion occurs next month, strong arguments could be made for the former spouse to receive an award based on that rank.

Four Variations for Retirement Pay Language

Compelling arguments for both sides result in four variations for the retirement pay figure, component (c):

1. *Pay at the Rank on Date of Divorce:*
2. *Pay at Retirement but Based on the Rank at Divorce*
3. *Pay at Retirement based on Rank at Retirement*
4. *Negotiated Amount*

Pay at the Rank on Date of Divorce

The first choice for the retirement pay figure is the pay earned as of the date of divorce. Sometimes state laws use a variation of this using the date of separation, date of filing, or some other date. This language favors the service member by ensuring the former spouse does not benefit from any pay increases or promotions that might occur after divorce date.

> **Retired Service Member:** For calculations, a retired service member (choosing this option) uses the current retirement pay being received. This is the amount earned as of the date of divorce.
>
> **Not Yet Retired Service Member:** A service member not yet retired must calculate a hypothetical retirement figure. The hypothetical retired pay amount is computed as if the service member had retired on the *date of divorce* (*see* Hypothetical Formula Language p. 111).

Pay Scale at Retirement but Based on Rank at Divorce

The second choice is to use the pay scale in place at retirement time but based on the rank at divorce. Suppose a major with fifteen years in service divorces in 2005 and retires after 20 years, as a colonel in 2010. This option would limit the former spouse award to the retirement pay of a major, but the retirement pay using the pay chart of a major in 2010, not 2005.

The supporting argument here is the former spouse contributed to the achievement of the rank of major and thus should be entitled to that portion of final retirement pay. This option allows the former spouse to benefit from all pay raises awarded from date of divorce through retirement, applicable to the rank of major.

The language of the decree could either limit this award to the current years in service (favoring the service member) or use the years in service as of retirement, which would result in an even greater amount for the former spouse and also compensate for service members who might stay in service past twenty years. In other words, while the award is based on the 2010 pay scale for a major, the decree must also specify whether the award will be based on a major with fifteen years service or a major with the longevity (in this case 20 years of service) in place at retirement.

Pay at Retirement Based on Rank at Retirement

The third choice is the pay amount in place at retirement based on the retirement rank. For a service member still in service, this is the least favorable language for the service member and the most favorable for the former spouse. The former spouse will benefit from any pay increases or promotions occurring after the divorce.

> **Example:** A major divorces in 2005 and later retires as a colonel in 2010. If the decree awards a retired pay figure as that *in place at retirement*, the former spouse will receive an award based on the pay of a colonel, including applicable longevity (all the service member's years in service).

Negotiated Amount

The fourth option is a court ordered negotiated amount.

There are cases where both parties wish to part ways amicably and for no other reason than wishing each other well, arrive at a negotiated figure.

Negotiated amounts might also occur when discussing benefits. If the major's marriage lasted 19 years (during service) the major might agree to delay divorce finalization until 20 years (which would allow the former spouse to receive health care, commissary and exchange (BX/PX) benefits under the 20/20/20 rule with the condition that the former spouse agree to use the retirement figure for the rank of a major with 19 years service. The divorce would be finalized after 20 years, but a *negotiated figure* of a major with 19 years service would be used in the decree language.

This does not mean the service member and former spouse must live together for the remaining year. One is just setting the date of the filing of the final order into the future. There are pros and cons to this suggestion (especially if one member wishes to remarry sooner) but that is not the issue here. The illustration is only an example of how a negotiated amount might be used.

Negotiated amounts might also occur concerning promotions, discussed next.

Promotions, Line Numbers, and Crossing Entry Dates

When a service member is selected or scheduled with a line number for promotion, negotiations should consider whether the retirement pay will be based on the new rank or the existing rank.

> **Example:** A divorcing major has a line number and is expecting to promote to lieutenant colonel in the next three months. The former spouse could argue for retirement pay based on the new promotion rank, lieutenant colonel. The position being that the former spouse participated in all of the marriage achieving the promotion and thus deserves to benefit from it.

Again, each state has the authority to make its own decisions. Texas is one state where this argument will most likely fail should it be brought before a judge. This is because of past rulings:

> "In *Grier v. Grier*, the Texas Supreme Court held that the wife of a major who was on the promotion list for lieutenant colonel at the time of divorce could only share in the retired pay of a major."[83]

A former spouse's lawyer might also try to delay the divorce until the promotion date to lock in the favorable outcome for the former spouse. Of course, lawyers representing the service member should watch carefully for such delay tactics.

In addition to promotions, pay increases are earned for longevity (for crossing service entry date anniversaries) such as after 2, 3, 4, 6, etc., years in service (*see* Military Pay Charts p. 123). These anniversary dates should also be considered when strategically trying to increase or decrease the award to the former spouse.

If an agreement is reached to use a figure from future promotion, the divorce itself does not have to be delayed. The language can specifically state that the retirement pay figure to be used in the computation should be that of the higher pay grade. The major can still get a timely divorce, but the decree will require computation to be calculated based on the rank of lieutenant colonel.

---

83. Mark E. Sullivan, "Military Pension Division: The Service Member's Strategy," Silent Partner, http://www.abanet.org/family/military/silent/mpd_servicemember.pdf.

Language for Division of Pay

The first step, when deciding which language to use in a military divorce decree, is to gain an understanding of the three main components (discussed previously) used in computing the former spouse award of retirement pay:

a. Percent Awarded to the Former Spouse by the State

b. Marital Share

c. Retirement Pay (at time of divorce or time of retirement)

	(a)		(b)		(c)
Former Spouse Award =	Percent Awarded to the Former Spouse by the State	×	Marital Share	×	Retirement Pay Earned (at divorce or retirement)

With so many variations of the components, there will be a wide range of language descriptions for pay division. Acceptable language falls into one of three categories:

1. Fixed amount or fixed percentage

2. A formula

3. A hypothetical formula

The best language for the service member is the fixed amount as it restricts the award to the former spouse by limiting the amount as well as avoiding any COLA increases.

The best language for the former spouse is a fixed percentage (assuming the percentage is as high as possible) based on final retirement pay.

Anything that differs from these two options will have pros and cons attached for either side.

An example will be used to illustrate language that might be used in a decree.

Example E: *Language for Division of Pay*

The following information is known prior to divorce:
- State award: a 50 percent division
- Service member entered service: 1 June 1989
- Marriage date: 1 December 1990
- Projected Divorced date: 1 June 2005
- Hypothetical Retirement Date: 1 June 2005 (divorce date)
- Length of Marriage: 14.5 years or 174 months
- Marriage Overlap Time: 14.5 years or 174 months
- Rank at divorce (and for 36 months prior): Major, O-4
- Length of service (creditable years) at divorce: 16 years

The following information is unknown at divorce, but it occurs at retirement and is used to illustrate Steps 6 through 9:
- Retirement date and rank: 1 October 2009, Lt. Colonel, O-5
- Rank for 36 months prior to retirement: Lt. Colonel, O-5

Retirement Award Steps Checklist (also see p. 122):

Prior to Divorce:
1. Calculate the percentage awarded to the former spouse.
2. Compute the (hypothetical) retired pay base.
3. Choose the language to be used in the divorce decree.
4. Compute the (hypothetical) retired pay multiplier.
5. Compute the (hypothetical) retired pay amount, including tentative division amounts.

At retirement:
6. If a hypothetical formula was used, adjust the hypothetical retired pay to *present value* by adding all COLAs.
7. Compute the actual retired pay multiplier.
8. Compute the service member's actual retired pay base and actual retired pay amount.
9. If a hypothetical formula was used, convert the former spouse hypothetical award to an actual percentage and final award amount.

Step 1 — Percentage Awarded to Former Spouse

Calculate the Former Spouse Percentage using the formula:

Former Spouse Award	=	(a) Percent Awarded to the Former Spouse by the State	×	(b) Marital Share	×	(c) Retirement Pay Earned (at divorce or retirement)

The first two components provide the Former Spouse Percentage:

Former Spouse Percentage	=	(a) Percent Awarded to the Former Spouse by the State	×	(b) Marital Share

and the Marital Share was defined as:

(b) Marital Share	=	Months of Marriage Overlap Time / Total Months of Service

Calculate the Former Spouse Percentage: (a) × (b) as shown:

Choice 1, Actual Retirement Date:
For Example E, the Former Spouse Percentage is unknown.

Former Spouse Percentage	=	(a) 50%	×	(b) 174 Months (Dec. 1990 to Jun. 2005) unknown

Choice 2, Date of Divorce Variation:
Using a denominator of months *up to divorce*, for Example E, the Former Spouse Percentage is 45.3125%.

Former Spouse Percentage	=	(a) 50%	×	(b) 174 months (Dec. 1990 to Jun. 2005) 192 months (Jun. 1989 to Jun. 2005)

Former Spouse Percentage	=	50%	×	0.906250	= 45.3125%

Step 2 — The Retired (or Hypothetical Retired) Pay Base

The Retired Pay Base (also called the Hypothetical Retired Pay Base if the service member is not yet retired) is the figure upon which the basic pay is calculated. (Service members with 20 years receive 50 percent of the retired pay base. Those who serve longer, receive a higher percentage.)

For service members with a service entry date prior to September 8, 1980, the retired pay base is the member's basic pay at retirement. Members entering service on or after this date, use the average highest 36 months of pay (the High-3 pay) on retirement (or hypothetical retirement) date for their retired (or hypothetical retired) pay base, which is *usually* the last 36 months of pay.[84]

To compute the amount, using the High-3 method, create a spreadsheet with columns for: the *Dates of Possible Pay Increases* for the 36 months prior to divorce, the *Number of Months* included in each date range, the *Rank*, and the *Years of Service*.

Possible pay increases can occur on 1 January (a possible annual pay raise), on promotion, and each time a service member crosses the service entry anniversary date. Create rows grouping months with a division each time there is a possible pay increase.

For Example E, with a 1 June service entry date, the result is:

Dates of Possible Pay Increases	# of Months	Rank	Cumulative Years of Service		
Jun.-Dec. 02	7	0-4	13		
Jan.-May 03	5	0-4	13		
Jun.-Dec. 03	7	0-4	14		
Jan.-May 04	5	0-4	14		
Jun.-Dec. 04	7	0-4	15		
Jan.-May 05	5	0-4	15		
Totals	36				

---

84. DFAS Publication, *Attorney Instruction Dividing Military Retired Pay*, IV. D Hypothetical Retired Pay Awards, (1), http://www.dfas.mil/garnishment/military/AttorneyInstruction-01-04-10.pdf.

Next, add a column for the *Monthly Pay Amounts Received* using pay charts at www.dfas.mil/militarypay/militarypaytables.html or at the end of this section. Locate the service member's rank in the far left column and locate the number of years in service along the top row (*see* marked pay chart examples p. 123-126). The intersection of the rank and years in service is the monthly pay figure received.

Add a final column for the *Total Pay* (the *Number of Months* (A) multiplied by the *Monthly Pay Received* (B)).

Dates of Possible Pay Increases	(A) # of Mos.	Rank	Cumulative Years of Service	(B) Monthly Pay Amounts Received	(A) × (B) Months x Monthly Pay = Total Pay
Jun.-Dec. 02	7	0-4	13	$ 4,930.20	$ 34,511.40
Jan.-May 03	5	0-4	13	$ 5,201.40	$ 26,007.00
Jun.-Dec. 03	7	0-4	14	$ 5,372.70	$ 37,608.90
Jan.-May 04	5	0-4	14	$ 5,571.60	$ 27,858.00
Jun.-Dec. 04	7	0-4	15	$ 5,571.60	$ 39,001.20
Jan.-May 05	5	0-4	15	$ 5,766.60	$ 28,833.00
Totals	36				$193,819.50

Take the average of the member's highest 36 months of pay, rounded down to the lowest dollar, to calculate the retired pay base (hypothetical in Example E, for a member not yet retired).

Hypothetical Retired Pay Base = $\dfrac{\text{36 Months Highest Pay Total (High-3 Pay)}}{\text{36 Months}}$

Hypothetical Retired Pay Base = $\dfrac{\$193{,}819.50}{\text{36 Months}}$

Hypothetical Retired Pay Base = $5,383 (always round cents down)

Step 3: Choosing the Language

Fixed Amount or Percentage Language

Steps 1 and 2 provide enough information for the first language option, a Fixed Amount or Percentage. The suggested wording is:

> [Active Duty and Reservist] "The former spouse is awarded ___ percent [or dollar amount per month] of the member's disposable military retired pay."[85]

Using Example E, a *fixed dollar amount* would read:

> "The former spouse is awarded **$5,383 per month** of the member's disposable military retired pay."

A *Fixed Dollar Amount* is the best choice for the service member and is not in the best interest of the former spouse. It prevents the former spouse from receiving all future Cost of Living Adjustments (COLAs).

Choosing a *Fixed Percentage* for Example E requires use of the *Date of Divorce* variation of the Marital Share (computed on p. 105), which provides a figure of 45.3125 percent (instead of an unknown) when the member is not retired:

> "The former spouse is awarded **45.3125 percent** of the member's disposable military retired pay."

The *Fixed Percentage* language will result in computation of the former spouse award based on *final* retirement pay (as opposed to retirement pay earned as of divorce date). For this reason, service members not yet retired will want to avoid using this language.

For retired service members (as in Example B on p. 95), future pay and promotions are not a concern, so the *Fixed Percentage* language works well. A *Fixed Percentage* language for Example B would read:

> "The former spouse is awarded **37.5000 percent** of the member's disposable military retired pay"

---

85. DFAS Publication, *Attorney Instruction Dividing Military Retired Pay*, IV. A, http://www.dfas.mil/garnishment/military/AttorneyInstruction-01-04-10.pdf.

Formula Percentage Language

Steps 1 and 2 also provide enough information for the Formula Percentage language. This wording ensures receipt of all Cost of Living Adjustments (COLAs). The suggested wording is:

> [Active duty formula] "The former spouse is awarded a percentage of the member's disposable military retired pay, to be computed by multiplying 50% times a fraction, the numerator of which is _____ **[this must state the exact number for the designated agent to accept the award]** months of marriage during the member's creditable military service, divided by the member's total number of months of creditable military service."[86]

Mathematically written this language says:

$$\text{Former Spouse Award} = 50\% \times \frac{\text{Months Marriage Overlap}}{\text{Total Months of Service}} \times \text{Retirement Pay Earned at retirement}$$

The first thing to note is this wording automatically awards 50 percent by the state.

Second, if the member is still in service, the denominator will favor the service member. The longer the service member chooses to stay in service, the greater the denominator will become which in effect, reduces the amount received by the former spouse. (This proposal uses the traditional definition of Marital Share.)

On the other hand one cannot claim the regulation's suggested language has forgotten the former spouse. As written, the third component (retirement pay) will be based on *final* retirement pay, which favors the former spouse. This may be a concern for the service member who may try to negotiate for an alternate ending or for use of the hypothetical formula language instead.

---

86. DoD FMR Vol 7B Chapter 29, "Military Retired Pay Division Order," *Former Spouse Payments from Retired Pay*, Feb. 2009, Appendix A, Figure 1, http://comptroller.defense.gov/fmr/07b/07b_29.pdf.

For Example E, a Formula Percentage Language would result in an unknown award until retirement time and would read:

> "The former spouse is awarded a percentage of the member's disposable military retired pay, to be computed by multiplying 50% times a fraction, the numerator of which is **174 months** of marriage during the member's creditable military service, divided by the member's total number of months of creditable military service."

Variations

The designated agent will accept language variations if all variables are provided for the award to be computed.

> **Example:** Using *date of divorce* helps the spouse: "The former spouse is awarded a percentage of the member's disposable military retired pay, to be computed by multiplying 50% times a fraction, the numerator of which is **174 months** of marriage during the member's creditable military service, divided by the denominator which is **192 months** total creditable military service, including both active and reserve years."

> **Example:** Perhaps use a negotiation of 20 years: "The former spouse is awarded a percentage of the member's disposable military retired pay, to be computed by multiplying 50% times a fraction, the numerator of which is **174 months** of marriage during the member's creditable military service, divided by the denominator which is **240 months** total creditable military service, including both active and reserve years."

The suggested reservist language also uses the final retirement pay figure and total points at retirement for the denominator:

> [Reservist formula] "The former spouse is awarded a percentage of the member's disposable military retired pay, to be computed by multiplying 50% times a fraction, the numerator of which is _____ Reserve retirement points earned during the period of the marriage, divided by the member's total number of Reserve retirement points earned."

Hypothetical Formula Language

The hypothetical formula is often chosen when the member has not yet retired. It automatically results in receipt of all COLA increases unless stated otherwise.[87] It prevents the former spouse from benefiting from any pay increases due to promotions.

Depending on the language chosen, it may or may not prevent pay scale increases applicable to longevity or the current rank at divorce. Days and partial months are not considered in the agent's calculations, so should not be used in the language. (Negotiations should decide whether to round partial months up or down.)

Both active and reserve members entering service prior to September 8, 1980 should check the regulation for some alternate language suggestions. All service members, regardless of service entry date may use the options explained next.

Hypothetical Active Duty

> Choice 1, *Actual Retirement Date*: [Active duty hypothetical calculated as of member's actual retirement date] "The former spouse is awarded ____% of the disposable military retired pay the member would have received had the member retired on his [or her] *actual* retirement date with the rank of _____ and with ____ years of creditable service."

Or

> Choice 2, *Date of Divorce*: [Active duty hypothetical calculated as of time of division, for all members regardless of service entry date] "The former spouse is awarded ____% of the disposable military retired pay the member would have received had the member retired with a retired pay base of _____ and with ____ years of creditable service on _____."[88]

---

87. DoD FMR Vol 7B Chapter 29, "Military Retired Pay Division Order," *Former Spouse Payments from Retired Pay*, Feb. 2009, Appendix A, Figure 1, http://comptroller.defense.gov/fmr/07b/07b_29.pdf.

88. Ibid., Appendix A, Figure 1, http://www.defenselink.mil/comptroller/fmr/07b/07b_29.pdf.

Completing Hypothetical Language Choice 1

Choice 1, in effect, avoids Step 2 by ordering the agent to calculate the hypothetical retired pay amount. This language results in a higher award for the former spouse because it uses the pay scale in place at retirement time. (Reasoning for this was discussed earlier p. 100.)

Despite using the rank at divorce, the pay used in calculations will be at the rate (pay scale) for the same rank, but at the year of retirement. Completing the language using Example E reads:

> "The former spouse is awarded **45.3125 percent** of the disposable military retired pay the member would have received had the member retired on his [or her] *actual* retirement date with the rank of **major** and with **16 years** of creditable service."

This means, the former spouse will receive 45.3125 percent of calculations using the 2009 pay of a major with 16 years toward retirement (as opposed to calculations using the 2005 pay of a major with 16 years toward retirement). Thus, the longer the member remains in service, the higher the former spouse award.

Some logic behind the Choice 1 language is a former spouse should be compensated when the member's actions (waiting to retire) delay the court award. Additionally, the former spouse was present for the rank earned as of divorce and thus should benefit from all pay scale increases awarded to that particular rank.

Completing Hypothetical Language Choice 2

Steps 1 and 2 for Example E provide enough information to complete the Hypothetical Language Choice 2. Using the *Date of Divorce* variation for Marital Share computation (although another percentage could be negotiated) results in:

> "The former spouse is awarded **45.3125 percent** of the disposable military retired pay the member would have received had the member retired with a retired pay base of **$5,383** and with **16 years** of creditable service on **1 June 2005**."

Hypothetical Reservist Language

For reservists, the basic ideas and concepts will be the same, but language can be adjusted to use the point based system.

> Choice 1: [Reservist hypothetical calculated as of the date the member becomes eligible to receive retired pay] "The former spouse is awarded ___% of the disposable military retired pay the member would have received had the member become eligible to receive retired pay on the date he [or she] *attained age 60*, with the rank of ___, with ___ Reserve retirement points, and with ___ years of service for basic pay purposes."

Or

> Choice 2: [Reservist hypothetical calculated as of time of division, for all members regardless of service entry date] "The former spouse is awarded ___% of the disposable military retired pay the member would have received had the member become eligible to receive military retired pay with a retired pay base of ___ and with ___ Reserve retirement points on ___."[89]

Remaining in Service - Avoiding the Award

The longer a member remains in service, the longer the delay of division. In fact if the member never retires, the former spouse will never receive the division award.

Some states are beginning to address this issue by creating orders to begin payment of retirement pay upon eligibility.[90] In such cases the service member must make payments directly to the former spouse. (This is a highly controversial issue and only mentioned to bring awareness to current developments. Further information is online at http://www.militarydivorcetips.com/states.html. *See also*, Vested Retirement Pay p. 64.)

---

89. DoD FMR Vol 7B Chapter 29, "Military Retired Pay Division Order," *Former Spouse Payments from Retired Pay*, Feb. 2009, Appendix A, Figure 1, http://comptroller.defense.gov/fmr/07b/07b_29.pdf.

90. Mathew B Tully, "Ins and Outs of Retirement Pay and Divorce," ArmyTimes.com, http://www.armytimes.com/community/ask_lawyer/military_askthelawyer_070716w/

Hypothetical Award Amount

If the retired pay multiplier (discussed next) and the retired pay base (from Step 2) are known, the monetary amount of the division can be computed. Turning all this information into a monetary figure (which may or may not be expressed in the decree) is where it begins to have real significance to both parties.

The core formula to compute the monetary amount of the *total* retired pay (the service member's retired pay before division) is:

Gross Retired Pay	=	Retired Pay Multiplier	×	Retired Pay Base (the High-3 average from Step 2)

For Example E, the Retired Pay Base was calculated in Step 2, so the next computation needed is the Retired Pay Multiplier.

Step 4 — The (Hypothetical) Retired Pay Multiplier

The *standard retired pay multiplier* is defined as the service member's creditable years of service multiplied by 2.5 percent. (For a Reservist, divide the reserve retirement points upon which the award is based by 360, for the years of creditable service.)[91]

Retired Pay Multiplier	=	2.5%	×	Years Creditable Service

The 2.5 percent is from the High-3 Year Average Retirement System where each year of service is worth 2.5 percent toward the final retirement pay; hence a 20 year career results in receipt of 50 percent (2.5% × 20) of the High-3 pay.

Under the CSB/REDUX retirement system, the service member receives a Career Status Bonus (CSB) at 15 years in service. A CSB/REDUX reduced retired pay multiplier is then used to compute the retired pay until age 62. For the former spouse, however, the *standard* retired pay multiplier (described above) is *always* used. The former spouse percentage is adjusted at age 62 to ensure the award is not effected by the service member's career choice.[92]

---

91. DFAS Publication, *Attorney Instruction Dividing Military Retired Pay*, IV. D, Hypothetical Retired Pay Awards, (1), http://www.dfas.mil/garnishment/military/AttorneyInstruction-01-04-10.pdf.

92. Ibid.

For Example E, the hypothetical retired pay multiplier uses the formula from the previous page, but with hypothetical figures:

Hypothetical Retired Pay Multiplier	=	2.5%	×	Hypothetical Years Creditable Service up to Divorce

Hypothetical Retired Pay Multiplier = 0.025 × 16

Hypothetical Retired Pay Multiplier = .400000 or 40.0000%

Recall that at 20 years, service members qualify for 50 percent of the retired pay base. In Example E, after 16 years of service, the service member had earned 40 percent of the retired pay base.

Step 5 — The (Hypothetical) Retired Pay Amount

The hypothetical retired pay amount is the *total* amount of retired pay the service member would receive had the service member hypothetically retired on the date of divorce. (The same formula from the previous page is used, but with hypothetical amounts.)

The hypothetical retired pay amount for Example E results in:

Hypothetical Gross Retired Pay	=	Hypothetical Retired Pay Multiplier	×	Hypothetical Retired Pay Base (the High-3 average)

Hypothetical Gross Retired Pay = 40.00% × $5,383 (from Step 2)

Hypothetical Gross Retired Pay = $2,153.00 (always round cents down)

Had the service member hypothetically retired on the divorce date, the service member's retired pay, before any division, would have been $2,153.

Dividing the Hypothetical Retired Pay

Using the total hypothetical retired pay and the percentage awarded to the former spouse, the service member and former spouse can estimate an expected minimum amount the former spouse will receive. This monetary amount may or may not be specifically expressed in the divorce decree.

For Example E, using the core formula with the *Date of Divorce Marital Share* (the variation) results in:

		(a)		(b)		(c)
Former Spouse Award	=	Percent Awarded to the Former Spouse by the State	×	Marital Share	×	Retirement Pay Earned (at divorce or retirement)

		(a)		(b)		(c)
Former Spouse Award	=	50%	×	$\frac{174}{192}$	×	Hypothetical Retirement Pay

		(a) × (b)		
Former Spouse Award	=	45.3125% (also computed in Step 1)	×	$2,153 (from Step 5)

Former Spouse Award	=	$975.58

For Example E, hypothetically, if the service member had retired on the divorce date, (assuming no deductions such as for disability, etc.) the gross retired pay of $2,153 is also equal to the disposable retired pay. The monetary award to the former spouse would equal $975.58 (45.3125 percent of the member's $2,153 disposable retired pay). The service member would receive $1,177.42 ($2,153 - $975.58).

The next steps explain how the designated agent calculates any adjustments at actual retirement time to the former spouse's percentage used in the hypothetical language of a decree. This should be understood prior to signing a divorce decree and re-checked at retirement. (It is possible for the COLA step to be forgotten.)

Calculations at Retirement Time

In Example E, hypothetical language Choice 2 awards the former spouse 45.3125 percent of the hypothetical retirement pay, earned as of *date of divorce*, including all COLAs thereafter. This is not 45.3125 percent of the *final* disposable retirement pay. In fact, as will be shown next, the former spouse award (actual percentage) will be 30.8444 percent. This is not a reduction but an adjustment.

Step 6 — *Hypothetical to Present Value (add COLAs)*

The designated agent will adjust the hypothetical retired pay to *present value* by adding all COLAs that occurred from divorce date up to the service member's actual retirement date. Care should be taken in the first computation as the COLA award is reduced for the year in which the member actually retires *(see* COLA p. 76).

In Example E, with divorce on 1 June 2005, and the actual retirement on 1 October 2009, the designated agent adds COLAs from 2006 through 2009. Using the Hypothetical Retired Pay of $2,153 computed in Step 5, the formula is repeated for each year and cents are rounded down. (A COLA rate table is on p. 77)

| Hypothetical Retired Pay | × | (1 + COLA Increase) | = | New Hypothetical Retired Pay |

For Example E, since COLA is reduced for the year in which the member retires, the full COLA increase of 4.1 percent is reduced to 2.8 percent for 2006. (DoD FMR Vol. 7B Ch.8 has reduction rates.)

$2,153 × 1.028 = $2,213

In Dec. 2006 the 3.3% increase awarded for 2007 results in:

$2,213 × 1.033 = $2,286

In Dec. 2007 the 2.3% increase awarded for 2008 results in:

$2,286 × 1.023 = $2,338

In Dec. 2008 the 5.8% increase awarded for 2009 results in:

$2,338 × 1.058 = $2,473

Thus, the hypothetical pay increased from $2,153 to $2,473. The former spouse receives 45.3125 percent of this, equal to $1,120.58.

Step 7—Compute the Actual Retired Pay Multiplier

Compute the actual retired pay multiplier using the concepts from Step 4, The Hypothetical Retired Pay Multiplier.

The years of creditable service will be 20 years plus the 4 months of June, July, August, and September expressed as a fraction (4 divided by 12 months in the year).

Retired Pay Multiplier = 2.5% × Years Creditable Service

Retired Pay Multiplier = 2.5% × (20 years + (4 months/12 months))

Retired Pay Multiplier = 0.025 × (20 + 0.3333)

Retired Pay Multiplier = 0.025 × 20.3333

Retired Pay Multiplier = .508333 or 50.8333%

The service member was in service over 20 years, so the retired pay multiplier has gone over 50 percent. ("A member who served 32 years would receive 80 percent of their base pay and a member who served 42 years would receive 105 percent of their base pay. In most cases, there is no longer a cap on the percentage multiplier to be utilized in the computation of retired pay.")[93]

---

93. Military.com, *Military Retired Pay Overview*, http://www.military.com/benefits/military-pay/retired-pay/military-retired-pay-overview.

Step 8 - Service Member's Actual Retired Pay Base

Compute the actual retired pay base using High-3 concepts from Step 2, The Retired Pay Base (p. 106-107), (also see marked pay chart examples p. 127-130):

Dates of Possible Pay Increases	# of Mos.	Rank	Years of Service Completed by Member	Monthly Pay	Months x Monthly Pay
Oct.-Dec. 06	3	O-5	17	$ 6,630.60	$ 19,891.80
Jan.-May 07	5	O-5	17	$ 6,776.40	$ 33,882.00
Jun.-Dec. 07	7	O-5	18	$ 6,968.10	$ 48,776.70
Jan.-May 08	5	O-5	18	$ 7,212.00	$ 36,060.00
Jun.-Dec. 08	7	O-5	19	$ 7,212.00	$ 50,484.00
Jan.-May 09	5	O-5	19	$ 7,493.40	$ 37,467.00
Jun.-Sep. 09	4	O-5	20	$ 7,697.40	$ 30,789.60
Totals	36				$257,351.10

Retired Pay Base = 36 Months Highest Pay Total (High-3 Pay) / 36 Months

Retired Pay Base = $257,351.10 / 36 Months

Retired Pay Base = $7,148 (always round cents down)

Part II: Compute the service member's gross retired pay using concepts explained previously in Step 5, Retired Pay Amount:

Gross Retired Pay = Retired Multiplier × Retired Pay Base

Gross Retired Pay = 50.8333% (from Step 7) × $7,148

Gross Retired Pay = $3,633 (always round cents down)

Step 9 – Convert the Former Spouse Hypothetical Retired Pay Percentage to an Actual Percentage

In Step 6, adjusting for COLA increases converted the hypothetical retirement pay of $2,153 at time of divorce to a present value of $2,473 at time of retirement. This figure can be used to compute the actual former spouse percentage.

Method A

The former spouse will receive 45.3125 percent of $2,153 (the hypothetical pay including COLAs) as shown below

| Adjusted Former Spouse Award | = | Decree Percentage Awarded to the Former Spouse | × | Adjusted Hypothetical Pay (Award + all COLAs) |

Adjusted Former Spouse Award = 45.3125% × $2,473

Adjusted Former Spouse Award = $1,120.58

To compute the actual percentage of retirement pay awarded to the former spouse, divide the former spouse pay amount by the retiree pay amount.

| Former Spouse Actual Percentage | = | Actual Former Spouse Pay / Retiree Gross Pay Amount |

Former Spouse Actual Percentage = $1,120.58 (from above) / $3,633 (Step 8 Part II, Gross Retired Pay)

Former Spouse Actual Percentage = .308444 or 30.8444%

The former spouse award (actual percentage) at retirement will be 30.8444 percent. The former spouse percentage was adjusted from the 45.3125 percent stated in the decree because the service member earned more pay after divorce, pay the former spouse was not entitled to due to the restriction by the hypothetical award.

Method B

Another method used to arrive at the actual percentage and actual amount for the former spouse uses a hypothetical percentage.

$$\text{Hypothetical Percentage} = \frac{\text{Service Member's Hypothetical Pay after COLAs}}{\text{Service Member's Actual Gross Retired Pay}}$$

$$\text{Hypothetical Percentage} = \frac{\$2{,}473 \text{ (from Step 6, Hypothetical to Present Value)}}{\$3{,}633 \text{ (from Step 8, Retired Pay Base)}}$$

$$\text{Hypothetical Percentage} = .680704 \text{ or } 68.0704\%$$

This shows that at the time of divorce, the service member had earned 68.0704 percent of the final amount to be received as retirement pay. The former spouse will receive 45.3125 percent (the percentage awarded in the divorce decree) of the above percentage (the retirement pay percentage earned as of divorce date).

$$\text{Former Spouse Actual Percentage} = \text{Percentage Awarded the Former Spouse in Decree} \times \text{Hypothetical Percentage}$$

$$\text{Former Spouse Actual Percentage} = 45.3125\% \times .680704$$

$$\text{Former Spouse Actual Percentage} = .308444 \text{ or } 30.8444\%$$

The former spouse's actual adjusted percentage at retirement is 30.8444 percent of the final retirement pay.

$$\text{Adjusted Former Spouse Award} = \text{Former Spouse Actual Percentage} \times \text{Final Retirement Pay}$$

$$\text{Adjusted Former Spouse Award} = 30.8444\% \times \$3{,}633$$

$$\text{Adjusted Former Spouse Award} = \$1{,}120.58$$

Both methods have the same results, but sometimes one method is more easily understood than the other.

Note: All adjustments are computed based on gross retired pay figures. The actual award paid by the agent may be less due to reductions for disability, SBP, etc. and in such cases, indemnification would be required.

Summary of Retirement Award Steps Checklist

Step 1: Compute the Former Spouse Percentage Award.

$$\text{Former Spouse Percentage} = \text{Percent Awarded to the Former Spouse by the State} \times \text{Marital Share}$$

Step 2: Compute the (Hypothetical) Retired Pay Base (High-3 rule).

$$\text{Retired Pay Base (High-3 average)} = \frac{\text{36 Months Highest Pay Total (High-3 Pay)}}{\text{36 Months}}$$

Step 3: Choose the language for the divorce decree.

Step 4: Compute the (Hypothetical) Retired Pay Multiplier.

$$\text{Retired Pay Multiplier} = 2.5\% \times \text{Years Creditable Service}$$

Step 5: Compute the (Hypothetical) Retired Pay Amount.

$$\text{Gross Retired Pay} = \text{Retired Pay Multiplier} \times \text{Retired Pay Base}$$

After Retirement - Check the Pay Received

Step 6: Hypothetical Awards: Adjust the Hypothetical Retired Pay for each year of COLAs to compute the *present value*.

$$\text{Hypothetical Retired Pay} \times (1+\text{COLA Increase}) = \text{New Hypothetical Retired Pay}$$

Step 7: Compute the Actual Retired Pay Multiplier *(see* Step 4).

Step 8: Compute the Actual Retired Pay Base using the rules for Step 2 and the Actual Retired Pay using the rules in Step 5.

Step 9: Convert the former spouse hypothetical retired pay percentage to an actual percentage and compute the final former spouse monetary award.

Military Pay Charts 2002-2010

Effective: January 1, 2002

Pay Grade	Under 2	Over 2	Over 3	Over 4	Over 6	Over 8	Over 10	Over 12	Over 14	Over 16	Over 18	Over 20	Over 22	Over 24
O-10 1/ & 2/												11,601.90	11,659.20	11,901.30
O-9 1/ & 2/												10,147.50	10,293.60	10,504.80
O-8 2/	7,180.20	7,415.40	7,571.10	7,614.90	7,809.30	8,135.10	8,210.70	8,519.70	8,608.50	8,874.30	9,259.50	9,614.70		
O-7 2/	5,966.40	6,371.70	6,418.20	6,657.90	6,840.30	7,051.20	7,271.80	7,472.70	8,135.10	8,694.90	8,694.90			
O-6 2/	4,422.00	4,857.90	5,176.80		5,196.60	5,418.90	5,448.50	5,073.30	5,628.60	6,305.70	6,627.00	6,948.30	7,131.00	7,316.10
O-5 2/	3,537.00	4,152.60	4,440.30	4,494.30	4,673.10	4,813.50	4,930.20	5,413.50	5,755.80	5,919.00	6,079.80	6,262.80		
O-4 2/	3,023.70	3,681.90	3,927.60	3,982.50	4,210.50	4,395.90	4,696.20	4,930.20	5,092.50	5,255.70	5,310.60			
O-3 2/	2,796.60	3,170.40	3,421.80	3,698.70	3,875.70	4,070.10	4,232.40	4,441.20	4,549.50					
O-2 2/	2,416.20	2,751.90	3,169.50	3,276.30	3,344.10									
O-1 2/	2,097.60	2,183.10	2,638.50											
O-3E 2/ & 3/				3,698.70	3,875.70	4,070.10	4,232.40	4,441.20	4,617.00	4,717.50	4,855.20			
O-2E 2/ & 3/				3,276.30	3,344.10	3,450.30	3,630.00	3,768.90	3,872.40					
O-1E 2/ & 3/				2,638.50	2,818.20	2,922.30	3,028.50	3,133.20	3,276.30					
W-5 2/												4,965.60	5,136.00	5,307.00
W-4 2/	2,889.60	3,108.60	3,198.00	3,285.90	3,437.10	3,586.50	3,737.70	3,885.30	4,038.00	4,184.40	4,334.40	4,480.80	4,632.60	4,782.00
W-3 2/	2,638.80	2,862.00		2,898.90	3,017.40	3,152.40	3,330.90	3,439.50	3,558.30	3,693.90	3,828.60	3,963.60	4,098.30	4,233.30
W-2 2/	2,321.40	2,454.00	2,569.80	2,654.10	2,726.40	2,875.20	2,984.40	3,093.90	3,200.40	3,318.00	3,438.90	3,559.80	3,680.10	3,801.30
W-1 2/	2,049.90	2,217.60	2,330.10	2,402.70	2,511.90	2,624.70	2,737.80	2,850.00	2,963.70	3,077.10	3,189.90	3,275.10		
E-9 2/ & 4/								3,423.90	3,501.30	3,599.40	3,830.40	3,944.10	4,098.30	4,251.30
E-8 2/						2,858.10	2,940.60	3,017.70	3,110.10	3,210.30	3,314.70	3,420.30	3,573.00	3,724.80
E-7 2/	1,986.90	2,169.00	2,251.50	2,332.50	2,417.40	2,562.90	2,645.10	2,726.40	2,808.00	2,892.60	2,975.10	3,057.30	3,200.40	3,292.80
E-6 2/	1,701.00	1,870.80	1,953.60	2,033.70	2,117.40	2,254.50	2,337.10	2,417.40	2,499.30	2,558.10	2,602.80			
E-5 2/	1,561.50	1,665.30	1,745.70	1,828.50	1,912.80	2,030.10	2,110.20	2,193.30						
E-4 2/	1,443.60	1,517.40	1,599.60	1,680.30	1,752.30									
E-3 2/	1,303.50	1,385.40	1,468.50											
E-2 2/	1,239.30													
E-1 (4mos +) 2/	1,105.50													
E-1 (<4 mos) 2/	1,022.70													

NOTES:
1. While serving as JCS/Vice JCS, CNO, CMC, Army/Air Force CS, basic pay is $13,598.10 (See note 2).
2. Basic pay for an O-7 to O-10 is limited by Level III of the Executive Schedule which is $11,516.70. Basic pa for O-6 and below is limited by Level V of the Executive Schedule which is $10,133.40.
3. Applicable to O-1 to O-3 with at least 4 years & 1 day of active duty as a warrant and/or enlisted member.

BASIC PAY—EFFECTIVE JANUARY 1, 2003[1/]

Cumulative Years of Service

Pay Grade	2 or less	Over 2	Over 3	Over 4	Over 6	Over 8	Over 10	Over 12	Over 14	Over 16	Over 18	Over 20	Over 22	Over 24	Over 26
O-10[2/]	0.00	0.00	0.00	0.00	0.00	0.00	0.00	0.00	0.00	0.00	0.00	12,077.70	12,137.10	12,389.40	12,829.20
O-9	0.00	0.00	0.00	0.00	0.00	0.00	0.00	0.00	0.00	0.00	0.00	10,563.60	10,715.70	10,935.60	11,319.60
O-8	7,474.50	7,719.30	7,881.60	7,927.20	8,129.40	8,468.70	8,547.30	8,868.90	8,961.30	9,238.20	9,639.00	10,008.90	10,255.80	10,255.80	10,255.80
O-7	6,210.90	6,499.20	6,633.00	6,739.20	6,930.90	7,120.80	7,339.40	7,552.40	7,779.00	8,468.70	9,051.30	9,051.30	9,051.30	9,051.30	9,096.90
O-6	4,603.20	5,057.10	5,388.90	5,388.90	5,409.60	5,641.20	5,672.10	5,672.10	5,994.60	6,564.30	6,898.80	7,233.30	7,423.50	7,616.10	7,989.90
O-5	3,837.60	4,323.00	4,622.40	4,678.50	4,864.80	4,977.00	5,222.70	5,403.00	5,635.50	5,991.90	6,161.70	6,329.10	6,519.60	6,519.60	6,519.60
O-4	3,311.10	3,832.80	4,088.70	4,145.70	4,383.00	4,637.70	4,954.50	5,201.40	5,372.70	5,471.10	5,528.40	5,528.40	5,528.40	5,528.40	5,528.40
O-3	2,911.20	3,300.30	3,562.20	3,883.50	4,069.50	4,273.50	4,405.80	4,623.30	4,736.10	4,736.10	4,736.10	4,736.10	4,736.10	4,736.10	4,736.10
O-2	2,515.20	2,864.70	3,299.40	3,410.70	3,481.20	3,481.20	3,481.20	3,481.20	3,481.20	3,481.20	3,481.20	3,481.20	3,481.20	3,481.20	3,481.20
O-1	2,183.70	2,272.50	2,746.80	2,746.80	2,746.80	2,746.80	2,746.80	2,746.80	2,746.80	2,746.80	2,746.80	2,746.80	2,746.80	2,746.80	2,746.80
O-3E[3/]	0.00	0.00	0.00	3,883.50	4,069.50	4,273.50	4,405.80	4,623.30	4,806.30	4,911.00	5,054.40				
O-2E[3/]	0.00	0.00	0.00	3,410.70	3,481.20	3,591.90	3,778.80	3,923.40	4,031.10	4,031.10	4,031.10				
O-1E[3/]	0.00	0.00	0.00	2,746.80	2,933.70	3,042.00	3,152.70	3,261.60	3,410.70	3,410.70	3,410.70				
W-5	0.00	0.00	0.00	0.00	0.00	0.00	0.00	0.00	0.00	0.00	0.00	5,169.30	5,346.60	5,524.50	5,703.30
W-4	3,008.10	3,236.10	3,329.10	3,420.60	3,578.10	3,733.50	3,891.00	4,044.60	4,203.60	4,356.00	4,512.00	4,664.40	4,822.50	4,978.20	5,137.50
W-3	2,747.10	2,862.00	2,979.30	3,017.70	3,141.00	3,281.70	3,467.40	3,580.50	3,771.90	3,915.60	4,058.40	4,201.50	4,266.30	4,407.00	4,548.00
W-2	2,416.50	2,554.50	2,675.10	2,763.00	2,838.30	2,993.10	3,148.50	3,264.00	3,376.50	3,453.90	3,579.90	3,705.90	3,831.00	3,957.30	3,957.30
W-1	2,133.90	2,308.50	2,425.50	2,501.10	2,662.50	2,782.20	2,888.40	3,006.90	3,085.20	3,203.40	3,320.70	3,409.50	3,409.50	3,409.50	3,409.50
E-9[4/]	0.00	0.00	0.00	0.00	0.00	0.00	3,564.30	3,645.00	3,747.00	3,867.00	3,987.30	4,180.80	4,344.30	4,506.30	4,757.40
E-8	0.00	0.00	0.00	0.00	0.00	2,975.40	3,061.20	3,141.30	3,237.60	3,342.00	3,530.10	3,625.50	3,787.50	3,877.50	4,099.20
E-7	2,068.50	2,257.80	2,343.90	2,428.20	2,516.40	2,667.90	2,753.40	2,838.30	2,990.40	3,066.30	3,138.60	3,182.70	3,331.50	3,427.80	3,671.40
E-6	1,770.60	1,947.60	2,033.70	2,117.10	2,204.10	2,400.90	2,477.40	2,562.30	2,636.70	2,663.10	2,709.60	2,709.60	2,709.60	2,709.60	2,709.60
E-5	1,625.40	1,733.70	1,817.40	1,903.50	2,037.00	2,151.90	2,236.80	2,283.30	2,283.30	2,283.30	2,283.30	2,283.30	2,283.30	2,283.30	2,283.30
E-4	1,502.70	1,579.80	1,665.30	1,749.30	1,824.00										
E-3	1,356.90	1,442.10	1,528.80	1,528.80	1,528.80	1,528.80	1,528.80	1,528.80	1,528.80	1,528.80	1,528.80	1,528.80	1,528.80	1,528.80	1,528.80
E-2	1,290.00	1,290.00	1,290.00	1,290.00	1,290.00	1,290.00	1,290.00	1,290.00	1,290.00	1,290.00	1,290.00	1,290.00	1,290.00	1,290.00	1,290.00
E-1 4 mos +	1,150.80	1,150.80	1,150.80	1,150.80	1,150.80	1,150.80	1,150.80	1,150.80	1,150.80	1,150.80	1,150.80	1,150.80	1,150.80	1,150.80	1,150.80

NOTES:

1. While serving as JCS/Vice JCS, CNO, CMC, Army/Air Force CS, basic pay is $14,155.50 (See note 2).
2. Basic pay for an O-7 to O-10 is limited by Level III of the Executive Schedule which is $11,874.90. Basic pay for O-6 and below is limited by Level V of the Executive Schedule which is $10,449.90.
3. Applicable to O-1 to O-3 with at least 4 years & 1 day of active duty as a warrant and/or enlisted member.

Figures in Step 2

BASIC PAY—EFFECTIVE JANUARY 1, 2004[1/]

Cumulative Years of Service

Pay Grade	2 or less	Over 2	Over 3	Over 4	Over 6	Over 8	Over 10	Over 12	Over 14	Over 16	Over 18	Over 20	Over 22	Over 24	Over 26
O-10[2/]	0.00	0.00	0.00	0.00	0.00	0.00	0.00	0.00	0.00	0.00	0.00	12524.70	12586.70	12847.80	13303.80
O-9	0.00	0.00	0.00	0.00	0.00	0.00	0.00	0.00	0.00	0.00	0.00	10954.50	11112.30	11340.30	11738.40
O-8	7751.10	8004.90	8173.20	8220.60	8430.30	8781.90	8863.50	9197.10	9292.80	9579.90	9995.70	10379.10	10635.30	10635.30	10635.30
O-7	6440.70	6739.80	6878.40	6988.50	7187.40	7384.20	7611.90	7839.00	8066.70	8781.90	9386.10	9386.10	9386.10	9386.10	9433.50
O-6	4773.60	5244.30	5588.40	5588.40	5609.70	5850.00	5882.10	5882.10	6216.30	6807.30	7154.10	7500.90	7698.30	7897.80	8285.40
O-5	3979.50	4482.90	4793.40	4851.60	5044.80	5161.20	5415.90	5602.80	5844.00	6213.60	6389.70	6563.40	6760.80	6760.80	6760.80
O-4	3433.50	3974.70	4239.90	4299.00	4545.30	4809.30	5137.80	5394.00	5571.60	5673.60	5733.00	5733.00	5733.00	5733.00	5733.00
O-3	3018.90	3422.40	3693.90	4027.20	4220.10	4431.60	4568.70	4794.30	4911.30	4911.30	4911.30	4911.30	4911.30	4911.30	4911.30
O-2	2608.20	2970.60	3421.50	3537.00	3609.90	3609.90	3609.90	3609.90	3609.90	3609.90	3609.90	3609.90	3609.90	3609.50	3609.50
O-1	2264.40	2356.50	2848.50	2848.50	2848.50	2848.50	2848.50	2848.50	2848.50	2848.50	2848.50	2848.50	2848.50	2848.50	2848.50
O-3E[3/]	0.00	0.00	0.00	4027.20	4220.10	4431.60	4568.70	4794.30	4984.20	5092.80	5241.30	5241.30	5241.30	5241.30	5241.30
O-2E[3/]	0.00	0.00	0.00	3537.00	3609.90	3724.80	3918.60	4068.60	4180.20	4180.20	4180.20	4180.20	4180.20	4180.20	4180.20
O-1E[3/]	0.00	0.00	0.00	2848.50	3042.30	3154.50	3269.40	3382.20	3537.00	3537.00	3537.00	3537.00	3537.00	3537.00	3537.00
W-5	0.00	0.00	0.00	0.00	0.00	0.00	0.00	0.00	0.00	0.00	0.00	5360.70	5544.30	5728.80	5914.20
W-4	3119.40	3355.80	3452.40	3547.20	3710.40	3871.50	4035.00	4194.30	4359.00	4617.30	4782.60	4944.30	5112.00	5277.00	5445.90
W-3	2848.80	2967.90	3089.40	3129.30	3257.10	3403.20	3595.80	3786.30	3988.80	4140.60	4291.80	4356.90	4424.10	4570.20	4716.30
W-2	2505.90	2649.00	2774.10	2865.30	2943.30	3157.80	3321.60	3443.40	3562.20	3643.80	3712.50	3843.00	3972.60	4103.70	4103.70
W-1	2212.80	2394.00	2515.20	2593.50	2802.30	2928.30	3039.90	3164.70	3247.20	3321.90	3443.70	3535.80	3535.80	3535.80	3535.80
E-9[4/]	0.00	0.00	0.00	0.00	0.00	0.00	3769.20	3854.70	3962.40	4089.30	4216.50	4421.10	4594.20	4776.60	5054.70
E-8	0.00	0.00	0.00	0.00	0.00	3085.50	3222.00	3306.30	3407.70	3517.50	3715.50	3815.70	3986.40	4081.20	4314.30
E-7	2145.00	2341.20	2430.60	2549.70	2642.10	2801.40	2891.10	2980.20	3139.80	3219.60	3295.50	3341.70	3498.00	3599.10	3855.00
E-6	1855.50	2041.20	2131.20	2218.80	2310.00	2516.10	2596.20	2685.30	2763.30	2790.90	2809.80	2809.80	2809.80	2809.80	2809.80
E-5	1700.10	1813.50	1901.10	1991.10	2130.60	2250.90	2339.70	2367.90	2367.90	2367.90	2367.90	2367.90	2367.90	2367.90	2367.90
E-4	1558.20	1638.30	1726.80	1814.10	1891.50										
E-3	1407.00	1495.50	1585.50	1585.50	1585.50										
E-2	1337.70	1337.70	1337.70	1337.70	1337.70										
E-1 4 mos +	1193.40	1193.40	1193.40	1193.40	1193.40										

NOTES:

1. While serving as JCS/Vice JCS, CNO, CMC, Army/Air Force CS, basic pay is $14,634.20 (See note 2).
2. Basic pay for an O-7 to O-10 is limited by Level III of the Executive Schedule which is $12,050.00. Basic pay for O-6 and below is limited by Level V of the Executive Schedule which is $10,608.30
3. Applicable to O-1 to O-3 with at least 4 years & 1 day of active duty or 1460 points as a warrant and/or enlisted member. See DoDFMR for more detailed explanation on who is eligible for this special basic pay rate.

PROPOSED BASIC PAY—EFFECTIVE JANUARY 1, 2005[1]

Pay Grade	2 or less	Over 2	Over 3	Over 4	Over 6	Over 8	Over 10	Cumulative Years of Service Over 12	Over 14	Over 16	Over 18	Over 20	Over 22	Over 24	Over 26
O-10[2]	0.00	0.00	0.00	0.00	0.00	0.00	0.00	0.00	0.00	0.00	0.00	12,963.00	13,026.60	13,297.50	13,769.40
O-9	0.00	0.00	0.00	0.00	0.00	0.00	0.00	0.00	0.00	0.00	0.00	11,337.90	11,501.10	11,737.20	12,149.10
O-8	8,022.30	8,285.10	8,459.40	8,508.30	8,725.50	9,089.40	9,173.70	9,519.00	9,618.00	9,915.30	10,345.50	10,742.40	11,007.60	11,007.60	11,007.60
O-7	6,666.00	6,975.60	7,119.00	7,233.00	7,439.10	7,642.50	7,878.30	8,113.50	8,349.00	9,089.40	9,714.60	9,714.60	9,714.60	9,714.60	9,763.80
O-6	4,940.70	5,427.90	5,784.00	5,784.00	5,805.90	6,054.90	6,087.90	6,087.90	6,433.80	7,045.50	7,404.60	7,763.40	7,967.70	8,174.10	8,575.50
O-5	4,118.70	4,639.80	4,961.10	5,021.40	5,221.50	5,341.80	5,605.50	5,799.00	6,048.60	6,431.10	6,613.20	6,793.20	6,997.50	6,997.50	6,997.50
O-4	3,553.80	4,113.90	4,388.40	4,449.60	4,704.30	4,977.60	5,317.50	5,582.70	5,766.60	5,872.20	5,933.70	5,933.70	5,933.70	5,933.70	5,933.70
O-3	3,124.50	3,542.10	3,823.20	4,168.20	4,367.70	4,586.70	4,728.60	4,962.00	5,083.20	5,083.20	5,083.20	5,083.20	5,083.20	5,083.20	5,083.20
O-2	2,699.40	3,074.70	3,541.50	3,660.90	3,736.20	3,736.20	3,736.20	3,736.20	3,736.20	3,736.20	3,736.20	3,736.20	3,736.20	3,736.20	3,736.20
O-1	2,343.60	2,439.00	2,948.10	2,948.10	2,948.10	2,948.10	2,948.10	2,948.10	2,948.10	2,948.10	2,948.10	2,948.10	2,948.10	2,948.10	2,948.10
O-3E[3]	0.00	0.00	0.00	0.00	0.00	4,168.20	4,367.70	4,586.70	4,728.60	5,158.50	4,962.00	5,424.60	5,271.00	5,424.60	5,424.60
O-2E[3]	0.00	0.00	0.00	0.00	0.00	3,660.90	3,855.30	3,736.20	4,055.70	4,211.10	4,326.60	4,326.60	4,326.60	4,326.60	4,326.60
O-1E[3]	0.00	0.00	0.00	0.00	0.00	2,948.10	3,264.90	3,148.80	3,383.70	3,500.70	3,660.90	3,660.90	3,660.90	3,660.90	3,660.90
W-5	0.00	0.00	0.00	0.00	0.00	0.00	0.00	0.00	0.00	0.00	0.00	5,548.20	5,738.40	5,929.20	6,121.20
W-4	3,228.60	3,473.40	3,573.30	3,671.40	3,840.30	4,007.10	4,176.30	4,341.00	4,511.70	4,779.40	4,950.00	5,117.40	5,290.80	5,461.80	5,636.40
W-3	2,948.40	3,071.70	3,197.40	3,238.80	3,371.10	3,522.30	3,721.80	3,918.90	4,128.30	4,285.50	4,442.10	4,509.30	4,578.90	4,730.10	4,881.30
W-2	2,593.50	2,741.70	2,871.30	2,965.50	3,046.20	3,268.20	3,438.00	3,564.00	3,687.00	3,771.30	3,842.40	3,977.40	4,111.50	4,247.40	4,247.40
W-1	2,290.20	2,477.70	2,603.10	2,684.40	2,900.40	3,030.90	3,146.40	3,275.40	3,360.90	3,438.30	3,564.30	3,659.70	3,659.70	3,659.70	3,659.70
E-9[4]	0.00	0.00	0.00	0.00	0.00	0.00	0.00	3,901.20	3,989.70	4,101.00	4,232.40	4,364.10	4,575.90	4,943.70	5,231.70
E-8	0.00	0.00	0.00	0.00	0.00	3,193.50	3,334.80	3,422.10	3,527.10	3,640.50	3,845.40	3,949.20	4,125.90	4,224.00	4,465.20
E-7	2,220.00	2,423.10	2,515.80	2,638.80	2,734.50	2,899.50	2,992.20	3,084.60	3,249.60	3,332.40	3,410.70	3,458.70	3,620.40	3,725.10	3,990.00
E-6	1,920.30	2,112.60	2,205.90	2,296.50	2,391.00	2,604.30	2,687.10	2,779.20	2,859.90	2,888.70	2,908.20	2,908.20	2,908.20	2,908.20	2,908.20
E-5	1,759.50	1,877.10	1,967.70	2,060.70	2,205.30	2,329.80	2,421.60	2,450.70	2,450.70	2,450.70	2,450.70	2,450.70	2,450.70	2,450.70	2,450.70
E-4	1,612.80	1,695.60	1,787.10	1,877.70	1,957.80										
E-3	1,456.20	1,547.70	1,641.00	1,641.00	1,641.00		NOTES:								
E-2	1,384.50	1,384.50	1,384.50	1,384.50	1,384.50										
E-1 4 mos +	1,235.10	1,235.10	1,235.10	1,235.10	1,235.10										

NOTES:
1. While serving as JCS/Vice JCS, CNO, CMC, Army/Air Force CS, commander of a unified or specified combatant command, basic pay is $15,146.40 (See note 2).
2. Basic pay for an O-7 to O-10 is limited by Level III of the Executive Schedule which is $12,433.20. Basic pay for O-6 and below is limited by Level V of the Executive Schedule which is $10,950.00.
3. Applicable to O-1 to O-3 with at least 4 years & 1 day of active duty or more than 1460 points as a warrant and/or enlisted member. See DoDFMR for more detailed explanation on who is eligible for this special basic pay rate.

BASIC PAY—EFFECTIVE JANUARY 1, 2006[1]

Pay Grade	2 or less	Over 2	Over 3	Over 4	Over 6	Over 8	Over 10	Over 12	Over 14	Over 16	Over 18	Over 20	Over 22	Over 24	Over 26
O-10[2]	0.00	0.00	0.00	0.00	0.00	0.00	0.00	0.00	0.00	0.00	0.00	13,365.00	13,430.40	13,709.70	14,196.30
O-9	0.00	0.00	0.00	0.00	0.00	0.00	0.00	0.00	0.00	0.00	0.00	11,689.50	11,857.50	12,101.10	12,525.60
O-8	8,271.00	8,541.90	8,721.60	8,772.00	8,996.10	9,371.10	9,458.10	9,814.20	9,916.20	10,222.80	10,666.20	11,075.40	11,348.70	11,348.70	11,348.70
O-7	6,872.70	7,191.90	7,339.80	7,457.10	7,669.80	7,879.50	8,122.50	8,364.90	8,607.90	9,371.10	10,015.80	10,015.80	10,015.80	10,015.80	10,066.50
O-6	5,094.00	5,596.20	5,963.40	5,985.90	6,242.70	6,276.60	6,276.60	6,276.60	6,633.30	7,263.90	7,634.10	8,004.00	8,214.60	8,427.60	8,841.30
O-5	4,246.50	4,783.50	5,115.00	5,177.10	5,383.50	5,507.40	5,779.20	5,978.70	6,236.10	6,630.60	6,818.10	7,003.80	7,214.40	7,214.40	7,214.40
O-4	3,663.90	4,241.40	4,524.30	4,587.60	4,850.10	5,131.80	5,482.20	5,755.80	5,945.40	6,054.30	6,117.60	6,117.60	6,117.60	6,117.60	6,117.60
O-3	3,221.40	3,651.90	3,941.70	4,297.50	4,503.00	4,728.90	4,875.30	5,115.90	5,240.70	5,240.70	5,240.70	5,240.70	5,240.70	5,240.70	5,240.70
O-2	2,783.10	3,170.10	3,651.00	3,774.30	3,852.00	3,852.00	3,852.00	3,852.00	3,852.00	3,852.00	3,852.00	3,852.00	3,852.00	3,852.00	3,852.00
O-1	2,416.20	2,514.60	3,039.60	3,039.60	3,039.60	3,039.60	3,039.60	3,039.60	3,039.60	3,039.60	3,039.60	3,039.60	3,039.60	3,039.60	3,039.60
O-3E[3]	0.00	0.00	0.00	4,297.50	4,503.00	4,728.90	4,875.30	5,115.90	5,318.40	5,434.50	5,592.90	5,592.90	5,592.90	5,592.90	5,592.90
O-2E[3]	0.00	0.00	0.00	3,774.30	3,852.00	3,974.70	4,181.40	4,341.60	4,460.70	4,460.70	4,460.70	4,460.70	4,460.70	4,460.70	4,460.70
O-1E[3]	0.00	0.00	0.00	3,039.60	3,246.30	3,366.00	3,488.70	3,609.30	3,774.30	3,774.30	3,774.30	3,774.30	3,774.30	3,774.30	3,774.30
W-5	0.00	0.00	0.00	0.00	0.00	0.00	0.00	0.00	0.00	0.00	0.00	5,720.10	5,916.30	6,113.10	6,311.10
W-4	3,328.80	3,581.10	3,684.00	3,785.10	3,959.40	4,131.30	4,305.90	4,475.70	4,651.50	4,927.20	5,103.60	5,276.10	5,454.90	5,631.00	5,811.00
W-3	3,039.90	3,166.80	3,296.40	3,339.30	3,475.50	3,631.50	3,837.30	4,040.40	4,256.40	4,418.40	4,579.80	4,649.10	4,720.80	4,876.80	5,032.50
W-2	2,673.90	2,826.60	2,960.40	3,057.30	3,140.70	3,369.60	3,544.50	3,674.40	3,801.30	3,888.30	3,961.50	4,100.70	4,239.00	4,379.10	4,379.10
W-1	2,361.30	2,554.50	2,683.80	2,767.50	2,990.40	3,124.80	3,243.90	3,376.80	3,465.00	3,544.80	3,674.70	3,773.10	3,773.10	3,773.10	3,773.10
E-9[4]	0.00	0.00	0.00	0.00	0.00	0.00	4,022.10	4,113.30	4,228.20	4,363.50	4,499.40	4,717.80	4,902.30	5,097.00	5,394.00
E-8	0.00	0.00	0.00	0.00	0.00	3,292.50	3,438.30	3,528.30	3,636.30	3,753.30	3,964.50	4,071.60	4,253.70	4,354.80	4,603.50
E-7	2,288.70	2,498.10	2,593.80	2,720.70	2,819.40	2,989.50	3,084.90	3,180.30	3,350.40	3,435.60	3,516.30	3,565.80	3,732.60	3,840.60	4,113.60
E-6	1,979.70	2,178.00	2,274.30	2,367.60	2,465.10	2,685.00	2,770.50	2,865.30	2,948.70	2,978.10	2,998.50	2,998.50	2,998.50	2,998.50	2,998.50
E-5	1,814.10	1,935.30	2,028.60	2,124.60	2,273.70	2,402.10	2,496.60	2,526.60	2,526.60	2,526.60	2,526.60	2,526.60	2,526.60	2,526.60	2,526.60
E-4	1,662.90	1,748.10	1,842.60	1,935.90	2,018.40										
E-3	1,501.20	1,595.70	1,692.00	1,692.00	1,692.00	1,692.00	1,692.00	1,692.00	1,692.00	1,692.00	1,692.00	1,692.00	1,692.00	1,692.00	1,692.00
E-2	1,427.40	1,427.40	1,427.40	1,427.40	1,427.40	1,427.40	1,427.40	1,427.40	1,427.40	1,427.40	1,427.40	1,427.40	1,427.40	1,427.40	1,427.40
E-1 4 mos +	1,273.50	1,273.50	1,273.50	1,273.50	1,273.50	1,273.50	1,273.50	1,273.50	1,273.50	1,273.50	1,273.50	1,273.50	1,273.50	1,273.50	1,273.50

Cumulative Years of Service

Figure in Step 8

NOTES:

1. While serving as JCS/Vice JCS, CNO, CMC, Army/Air Force Chief of Staff, commander of a unified or specified combatant command, basic pay is $15,615.90 (See note 2).
2. Basic pay for an O-7 to O-10 is limited by Level III of the Executive Schedule which is $12,666.60. Basic pay for O-6 and below is limited by Level V of the Executive Schedule which is $11,158.20.
3. Applicable to O-1 to O-3 with at least 4 years & 1 day of active duty or more than 1460 points as a warrant and/or enlisted member. See DoDFMR for more detailed explanation on who is eligible for this special basic pay rate.

BASIC PAY—EFFECTIVE JANUARY 1, 2007[1]

Cumulative Years of Service

Pay Grade	2 or less	Over 2	Over 3	Over 4	Over 6	Over 8	Over 10	Over 12	Over 14	Over 16	Over 18	Over 20	Over 22	Over 24
O-10[2]												13,659.00	13,725.90	14,011.20
O-9												11,946.60	12,118.50	12,367.20
O-8	8,453.10	8,729.70	8,913.60	8,964.90	9,194.10	9,577.20	9,666.30	10,030.20	10,134.30	10,517.80	10,900.80	11,319.00	11,598.30	11,598.30
O-7	7,023.90	7,350.00	7,501.20	7,621.20	7,838.40	8,052.90	8,301.30	8,548.80	8,797.20	9,577.20	10,236.00	10,236.00	10,236.00	10,236.00
O-6	5,206.20	5,719.20	6,094.50	6,094.50	6,117.60	6,380.10	6,414.60	6,414.60	6,779.10	7,423.80	7,802.10	8,180.10	8,395.20	8,613.00
O-5	4,339.80	4,888.80	5,227.50	5,291.10	5,502.00	5,628.60	5,906.40	6,110.10	6,373.20	6,776.40	6,968.10	7,158.00	7,373.10	7,373.10
O-4	3,744.60	4,334.70	4,623.90	4,688.40	4,956.90	5,244.60	5,602.80	5,882.40	6,076.20	6,187.50	6,252.30	6,252.30	6,252.30	6,252.30
O-3	3,292.20	3,732.30	4,028.40	4,392.00	4,602.00	4,833.00	4,982.70	5,228.40	5,355.90	5,355.90	5,355.90	5,355.90	5,355.90	5,355.90
O-2	2,844.30	3,239.70	3,731.40	3,857.40	3,936.60	3,936.60	3,936.60	3,936.60	3,936.60	3,936.60	3,936.60	3,936.60	3,936.60	3,936.60
O-1	2,469.30	2,569.80	3,106.50	3,106.50	3,106.50	3,106.50	3,106.50	3,106.50	3,106.50	3,106.50	3,106.50	3,106.50	3,106.50	3,106.50
O-3[3]				4,392.00	4,602.00	4,833.00	4,982.70	5,228.40	5,435.40	5,554.20	5,715.90			
O-2[3]				3,857.40	3,936.60	4,062.00	4,273.50	4,437.00	4,558.80	4,558.80	4,558.80			
O-1[3]				3,106.50	3,317.70	3,440.10	3,565.50	3,688.80	3,857.40	3,857.40	3,857.40			
W-5												5,845.80	6,046.50	6,247.50
W-4	3,402.00	3,660.00	3,765.00	3,868.50	4,046.40	4,222.20	4,400.70	4,574.10	4,753.80	5,035.50	5,215.80	5,392.20	5,574.90	5,754.90
W-3	3,106.80	3,236.40	3,369.00	3,412.80	3,552.00	3,711.30	3,921.60	4,129.20	4,350.00	4,515.60	4,680.60	4,751.40	4,824.60	4,984.20
W-2	2,732.70	2,888.70	3,025.50	3,124.50	3,209.70	3,443.70	3,622.50	3,755.10	3,885.00	3,973.80	4,048.80	4,191.00	4,332.30	4,475.40
W-1	2,413.20	2,610.60	2,742.90	2,828.40	3,056.10	3,193.50	3,315.30	3,451.20	3,541.20	3,622.80	3,755.40	3,856.20	3,856.20	3,856.20
E-9[4]							4,110.50	4,203.90	4,321.20	4,459.50	4,598.40	4,821.60	5,010.30	5,209.20
E-8						3,364.80	3,513.90	3,606.00	3,716.40	3,835.80	4,051.80	4,161.30	4,347.30	4,450.50
E-7	2,339.10	2,553.00	2,650.80	2,780.70	2,881.50	3,055.20	3,152.70	3,250.20	3,424.20	3,511.20	3,593.70	3,644.10	3,814.80	3,925.20
E-6	2,023.20	2,226.00	2,324.40	2,419.80	2,519.40	2,744.10	2,831.40	2,928.30	3,013.50	3,043.50	3,064.50	3,064.50	3,064.50	3,064.50
E-5	1,854.00	1,977.90	2,073.30	2,171.40	2,323.80	2,454.90	2,551.50	2,582.10	2,582.10	2,582.10	2,582.10	2,582.10	2,582.10	2,582.10
E-4	1,699.50	1,786.50	1,883.10	1,978.50	2,062.80	2,062.80	2,062.80	2,062.80	2,062.80	2,062.80	2,062.80	2,062.80	2,062.80	2,062.80
E-3	1,534.20	1,630.80	1,729.20	1,729.20	1,729.20	1,729.20	1,729.20	1,729.20	1,729.20	1,729.20	1,729.20	1,729.20	1,729.20	1,729.20
E-2	1,458.90	1,458.90	1,458.90	1,458.90	1,458.90	1,458.90	1,458.90	1,458.90	1,458.90	1,458.90	1,458.90	1,458.90	1,458.90	1,458.90
E-1[5]	1,301.40	1,301.40	1,301.40	1,301.40	1,301.40	1,301.40	1,301.40	1,301.40	1,301.40	1,301.40	1,301.40	1,301.40	1,301.40	1,301.40

Figures in Step 8

Military Pay Charts ◀ 129

BASIC PAY—EFFECTIVE JANUARY 1, 2008

Pay Grade	2 or less	Over 2	Over 3	Over 4	Over 6	Over 8	Over 10	Over 12	Over 14	Over 16	Over 18	Over 20	Over 22	Over 24	Over 26	Over 28	Over 30	Over 32
O-10[2]												14,137.20	14,206.20	14,501.70	15,016.50	15,016.50	15,767.10	15,767.10
O-9												12,364.80	12,542.70	12,800.10	13,249.20	13,249.20	13,911.90	13,911.90
O-8	8,748.90	9,035.10	9,225.60	9,278.70	9,516.00	9,912.30	10,004.70	10,381.20	10,488.90	10,913.50	11,282.40	11,715.30	12,004.20	12,004.20	12,004.20	12,004.20	12,304.50	12,304.50
O-7	7,269.60	7,607.40	7,763.70	7,887.90	8,112.60	8,334.90	8,591.70	8,847.90	9,105.00	9,912.00	10,594.20	10,594.20	10,594.20	10,594.20	10,647.90	10,647.90	10,860.90	10,860.90
O-6	5,388.30	5,919.30	6,307.80	6,307.80	6,331.80	6,603.30	6,639.00	6,639.00	7,016.40	7,683.60	8,075.10	8,466.30	8,688.90	8,914.50	9,351.90	9,351.90	9,538.80	9,538.80
O-5	4,491.60	5,059.80	5,410.50	5,476.20	5,694.60	5,825.70	6,113.10	6,324.00	6,596.40	7,013.70	7,212.00	7,408.50	7,631.10	7,631.10	7,631.10	7,631.10	7,631.10	7,631.10
O-4	3,875.70	4,486.50	4,785.60	4,852.50	5,130.30	5,428.20	5,799.00	6,088.20	6,288.90	6,404.10	6,471.00	6,471.00	6,471.00	6,471.00	6,471.00	6,471.00	6,471.00	6,471.00
O-3	3,407.40	3,862.80	4,169.40	4,545.60	4,763.10	5,002.20	5,157.00	5,411.40	5,543.40	5,543.40	5,543.40	5,543.40	5,543.40	5,543.40	5,543.40	5,543.40	5,543.40	5,543.40
O-2	2,943.90	3,353.10	3,861.90	3,992.40	4,074.30	4,074.30	4,074.30	4,074.30	4,074.30	4,074.30	4,074.30	4,074.30	4,074.30	4,074.30	4,074.30	4,074.30	4,074.30	4,074.30
O-1	2,555.70	2,659.80	3,215.10	3,215.10	3,215.10	3,215.10	3,215.10	3,215.10	3,215.10	3,215.10	3,215.10	3,215.10	3,215.10	3,215.10	3,215.10	3,215.10	3,215.10	3,215.10
O-3[3]				4,545.60	4,763.10	5,002.20	5,157.00	5,411.40	5,625.60	5,748.60	5,916.00	5,916.00	5,916.00	5,916.00	5,916.00	5,916.00	5,916.00	5,916.00
O-2[3]				3,992.40	4,074.30	4,204.20	4,423.20	4,592.40	4,718.40	4,718.40	4,718.40	4,718.40	4,718.40	4,718.40	4,718.40	4,718.40	4,718.40	4,718.40
O-1[3]				3,215.10	3,433.80	3,560.40	3,690.30	3,817.80	3,992.40	3,992.40	3,992.40	3,992.40	3,992.40	3,992.40	3,992.40	3,992.40	3,992.40	3,992.40
W-5												6,261.30	6,579.00	6,815.40	7,077.60	7,077.60	7,431.60	7,431.60
W-4	3,521.10	3,788.10	3,896.70	4,003.80	4,188.00	4,370.10	4,554.60	4,832.70	5,076.00	5,307.60	5,496.90	5,681.70	5,953.50	6,176.40	6,431.10	6,431.10	6,559.50	6,559.50
W-3	3,215.40	3,349.80	3,486.90	3,532.20	3,676.20	3,959.70	4,254.90	4,393.80	4,554.30	4,719.90	5,017.50	5,218.80	5,339.10	5,466.90	5,640.90	5,640.90	5,640.90	5,640.90
W-2	2,845.50	3,114.60	3,197.40	3,254.70	3,439.20	3,726.00	3,867.90	4,008.00	4,179.00	4,312.50	4,434.00	4,578.60	4,674.00	4,749.90	4,749.90	4,749.90	4,749.90	4,749.90
W-1	2,497.80	2,766.00	2,838.90	2,991.60	3,172.50	3,438.60	3,562.80	3,736.50	3,907.50	4,041.90	4,165.50	4,316.10	4,316.10	4,316.10	4,316.10	4,316.10	4,316.10	4,316.10
E-9[4]							4,254.60	4,350.90	4,472.40	4,615.50	4,759.20	4,990.50	5,185.80	5,391.60	5,705.70	5,705.70	5,991.00	5,991.00
E-8						3,482.70	3,636.90	3,732.30	3,846.60	3,970.20	4,193.70	4,306.80	4,499.40	4,606.20	4,869.60	4,869.60	4,967.10	4,967.10
E-7	2,421.00	2,642.40	2,743.50	2,877.90	2,982.30	3,162.00	3,263.10	3,443.10	3,592.50	3,694.50	3,803.10	3,845.40	3,986.70	4,062.60	4,351.20	4,351.20	4,351.20	4,351.20
E-6	2,094.00	2,304.00	2,405.70	2,504.40	2,607.60	2,840.10	2,930.40	3,105.00	3,158.70	3,197.70	3,243.30	3,243.30	3,243.30	3,243.30	3,243.30	3,243.30	3,243.30	3,243.30
E-5	1,918.80	2,047.20	2,145.90	2,247.30	2,405.10	2,570.70	2,705.40	2,722.20	2,722.20	2,722.20	2,722.20	2,722.20	2,722.20	2,722.20	2,722.20	2,722.20	2,722.20	2,722.20
E-4	1,758.90	1,848.90	1,949.10	2,047.80	2,135.10	2,135.10	2,135.10	2,135.10	2,135.10	2,135.10	2,135.10	2,135.10	2,135.10	2,135.10	2,135.10	2,135.10	2,135.10	2,135.10
E-3	1,587.90	1,687.80	1,789.80	1,789.80	1,789.80	1,789.80	1,789.80	1,789.80	1,789.80	1,789.80	1,789.80	1,789.80	1,789.80	1,789.80	1,789.80	1,789.80	1,789.80	1,789.80
E-2	1,509.90	1,509.90	1,509.90	1,509.90	1,509.90	1,509.90	1,509.90	1,509.90	1,509.90	1,509.90	1,509.90	1,509.90	1,509.90	1,509.90	1,509.90	1,509.90	1,509.90	1,509.90
E-1[6]	1,347.00	0.00																

Figure in Step 8

2008 chart for the 3.5% delayed pay raise, retroactive to 1 Jan 2008, http://www.dfas.mil/militarypay/militarypaytables/militarypaypriorrates/2008MilitaryPayCharts35.pdf

BASIC PAY—EFFECTIVE JANUARY 1, 2009

Pay Grade	2 or less	Over 2	Over 3	Over 4	Over 6	Over 8	Over 10	Over 12	Over 14	Over 16	Over 18	Over 20	Over 22	Over 24	Over 26	Over 28	Over 30	Over 32
O-10[2]												14,688.60	14,760.30	15,067.20	15,602.10	15,602.10	16,382.10	16,382.10
O-9												12,846.90	13,032.00	13,299.30	13,765.80	13,765.80	14,454.60	14,454.60
O-8	9,090.00	9,387.60	9,585.30	9,640.50	9,887.10	10,299.00	10,395.00	10,786.20	10,888.10	11,296.30	11,792.50	12,172.20	12,472.50	12,472.50	12,472.50	12,472.50	12,784.50	12,784.50
O-7	7,553.10	7,904.10	8,066.40	8,195.40	8,429.10	8,660.10	8,926.80	9,192.90	9,460.20	10,299.00	11,007.30	11,007.30	11,007.30	11,007.30	11,063.10	11,063.10	11,284.50	11,284.50
O-6	5,598.30	6,150.30	6,553.80	6,553.80	6,578.70	6,860.70	6,897.90	6,897.90	7,290.00	7,983.00	8,390.10	8,796.60	9,027.90	9,262.20	9,716.70	9,716.70	9,910.80	9,910.80
O-5	4,666.80	5,257.20	5,621.40	5,689.80	5,916.60	6,052.80	6,351.60	6,570.60	6,853.80	7,287.30	7,493.40	7,697.40	7,928.70	7,928.70	7,928.70	7,928.70	7,928.70	7,928.70
O-4	4,026.90	4,661.40	4,972.20	5,041.80	5,330.40	5,640.00	6,025.20	6,325.50	6,534.30	6,654.00	6,723.30	6,723.30	6,723.30	6,723.30	6,723.30	6,723.30	6,723.30	6,723.30
O-3	3,540.30	4,013.40	4,332.00	4,722.90	4,948.80	5,197.20	5,358.00	5,622.30	5,759.70	5,759.70	5,759.70	5,759.70	5,759.70	5,759.70	5,759.70	5,759.70	5,759.70	5,759.70
O-2	3,058.80	3,483.90	4,012.50	4,148.10	4,233.30	4,233.30	4,233.30	4,233.30	4,233.30	4,233.30	4,233.30	4,233.30	4,233.30	4,233.30	4,233.30	4,233.30	4,233.30	4,233.30
O-1	2,655.30	2,763.60	3,340.50	3,340.50	3,340.50	3,340.50	3,340.50	3,340.50	3,340.50	3,340.50	3,340.50	3,340.50	3,340.50	3,340.50	3,340.50	3,340.50	3,340.50	3,340.50
O-3[3]				4,722.90	4,948.80	5,197.20	5,358.00	5,622.30	5,844.90	5,972.70	6,146.70	6,146.70	6,146.70	6,146.70	6,146.70	6,146.70	6,146.70	6,146.70
O-2[3]				4,148.10	4,233.30	4,368.30	4,595.70	4,771.50	4,902.30	4,902.30	4,902.30	4,902.30	4,902.30	4,902.30	4,902.30	4,902.30	4,902.30	4,902.30
O-1[3]				3,340.50	3,567.60	3,699.30	3,834.30	3,966.60	4,148.10	4,148.10	4,148.10	4,148.10	4,148.10	4,148.10	4,148.10	4,148.10	4,148.10	4,148.10
W-5												6,505.50	6,835.50	7,081.20	7,353.60	7,353.60	7,721.40	7,721.40
W-4	3,658.50	3,935.70	4,048.80	4,159.80	4,351.20	4,540.50	4,732.20	5,021.10	5,274.00	5,514.60	5,711.40	5,903.40	6,185.70	6,417.30	6,681.90	6,681.90	6,815.40	6,815.40
W-3	3,340.80	3,480.30	3,622.80	3,669.90	3,819.60	4,114.20	4,420.80	4,565.10	4,731.90	4,904.10	5,213.10	5,422.20	5,547.30	5,680.20	5,860.80	5,860.80	5,860.80	5,860.80
W-2	2,956.50	3,236.10	3,322.20	3,381.60	3,573.30	3,871.20	4,018.80	4,164.30	4,341.90	4,480.80	4,606.80	4,757.10	4,856.40	4,935.00	4,935.00	4,935.00	4,935.00	4,935.00
W-1	2,595.30	2,874.60	2,949.60	3,108.30	3,296.10	3,572.70	3,701.70	3,882.30	4,059.90	4,199.40	4,328.10	4,484.40	4,484.40	4,484.40	4,484.40	4,484.40	4,484.40	4,484.40
E-9[4]							4,420.50	4,520.70	4,646.70	4,795.50	4,944.90	5,185.20	5,388.00	5,601.90	5,928.30	5,928.30	6,224.70	6,224.70
E-8						3,618.60	3,778.80	3,877.80	3,996.60	4,125.00	4,357.20	4,474.80	4,674.90	4,785.90	5,059.50	5,059.50	5,160.90	5,160.90
E-7	2,515.50	2,745.60	2,850.60	2,990.10	3,098.70	3,285.30	3,390.30	3,577.20	3,732.60	3,838.50	3,951.30	3,995.40	4,142.10	4,221.00	4,521.00	4,521.00	4,521.00	4,521.00
E-6	2,175.60	2,394.90	2,499.60	2,602.20	2,709.90	2,950.80	3,044.70	3,226.20	3,282.00	3,322.50	3,369.90	3,369.90	3,369.90	3,369.90	3,369.90	3,369.90	3,369.90	3,369.90
E-5	1,993.50	2,127.00	2,229.60	2,334.90	2,499.00	2,670.90	2,811.00	2,828.40	2,828.40	2,828.40	2,828.40	2,828.40	2,828.40	2,828.40	2,828.40	2,828.40	2,828.40	2,828.40
E-4	1,827.60	1,920.90	2,025.00	2,127.60	2,218.50	2,218.50	2,218.50	2,218.50	2,218.50	2,218.50	2,218.50	2,218.50	2,218.50	2,218.50	2,218.50	2,218.50	2,218.50	2,218.50
E-3	1,649.70	1,753.50	1,859.70	1,859.70	1,859.70	1,859.70	1,859.70	1,859.70	1,859.70	1,859.70	1,859.70	1,859.70	1,859.70	1,859.70	1,859.70	1,859.70	1,859.70	1,859.70
E-2	1,568.70	1,568.70	1,568.70	1,568.70	1,568.70	1,568.70	1,568.70	1,568.70	1,568.70	1,568.70	1,568.70	1,568.70	1,568.70	1,568.70	1,568.70	1,568.70	1,568.70	1,568.70
E-1[5]	1,399.50																	

Figures in Step 8

BASIC PAY—EFFECTIVE JANUARY 1, 2010

Pay Grade	2 or less	Over 2	Over 3	Over 4	Over 6	Over 8	Over 10	Over 12	Over 14	Over 16	Over 18
O-10[2]											
O-9											
O-8	9399.00	9706.80	9911.10	9968.40	10223.40	10649.10	10748.40	11152.80	11268.60	11617.20	12121.20
O-7	7809.90	8172.90	8340.60	8474.10	8715.60	8954.40	9230.40	9505.50	9781.80	10649.10	11381.40
O-6	5788.50	6359.40	6776.70	6776.70	6802.50	7094.10	7132.50	7132.50	7537.80	8254.80	8675.40
O-5	4825.50	5436.00	5812.50	5883.30	6117.90	6258.60	6557.60	6794.10	7086.90	7535.10	7748.10
O-4	4163.70	4819.80	5141.40	5213.10	5511.60	5831.70	6230.10	6540.60	6756.60	6880.20	6951.90
O-3	3660.60	4149.90	4479.30	4883.40	5117.10	5373.90	5540.10	5813.40	5955.60	5955.60	5955.60
O-2	3162.90	3602.40	4149.00	4289.10	4377.30	4377.30	4377.30	4377.30	4377.30	4377.30	4377.30
O-1	2745.60	2857.50	3454.20	3454.20	3454.20	3454.20	3454.20	3454.20	3454.20	3454.20	3454.20
O-3[3]				4883.40	5117.10	5373.90	5540.10	5813.40	6043.50	6175.80	6355.80
O-2[3]				4289.10	4377.30	4516.80	4752.00	4933.80	5069.10	5069.10	5069.10
O-1[3]				3454.20	3688.80	3825.00	3964.80	4101.60	4289.10	4289.10	4289.10
W-5											
W-4	3783.00	4069.50	4186.50	4301.10	4499.10	4695.00	4893.00	5191.80	5453.40	5702.10	5905.50
W-3	3454.50	3598.50	3746.10	3794.70	3949.50	4254.00	4571.10	4720.20	4892.70	5070.90	5390.40
W-2	3057.00	3346.20	3435.30	3496.50	3694.80	4002.90	4155.30	4305.90	4489.50	4633.20	4763.40
W-1	2683.50	2971.80	3049.80	3213.90	3408.30	3694.20	3827.70	4014.30	4197.90	4342.20	4475.40
E-9[3]							4570.80	4674.30	4804.80	4958.40	5112.90
E-8						3741.60	3907.20	4009.50	4132.50	4265.40	4505.40
E-7	2601.00	2838.90	2947.50	3091.80	3204.00	3396.90	3505.50	3699.00	3859.50	3969.00	4085.70
E-6	2249.70	2475.30	2584.50	2690.70	2801.40	3051.00	3148.20	3336.00	3393.60	3435.60	3484.50
E-5	2061.30	2199.30	2305.50	2414.40	2583.90	2761.80	2906.70	2924.70	2924.70	2924.70	2924.70
E-4	1889.70	1986.30	2094.00	2199.90	2293.80	2293.80	2293.80	2293.80	2293.80	2293.80	2293.80
E-3	1705.80	1813.20	1923.00	1923.00	1923.00	1923.00	1923.00	1923.00	1923.00	1923.00	1923.00
E-2	1622.10	1622.10	1622.10	1622.10	1622.10	1622.10	1622.10	1622.10	1622.10	1622.10	1622.10
E-1[4]	1447.20										

(End Pay Charts)

Former Spouse Award Requirement

Retired Pay Application

Even if the divorce decree awards the former spouse a portion of retirement pay, additional action is needed. The former spouse must file an application to actually receive the retired pay award from the designated agent.

> "A former spouse may apply for payment anytime after the court has issued a court order enforceable under the USFSPA."[94]

The recommendation in this book is to apply within 90 days of divorce as is stated on the DD Form 2293, *Application for Former Spouse Payments from Retired Pay*, section 4a *(see* p. 175).

Ideally, lawyers should assist the former spouse through the entire application process until the lawyer receives a written acknowledgement of the pay division from the designated agent *(see* DFAS Acknowledgement Letter of Retired Pay, p. 136).

This is beneficial to the former spouse who may be easily overwhelmed with the intricacies of the process. It also ensures the lawyer has both informed and advised properly, and thus avoids any chance of malpractice allegations, state bar grievances, or negligent claims. Lawyers assisting former spouses should send a written notification to the former spouse stating the actions taken on his or her behalf with copies of all documentation attached. This way, both the lawyer and the former spouse have accurate records of all transactions.

---

94. DoD FMR Vol 7B Chapter 29, "When to Apply for USFSPA Payments," *Former Spouse Payments from Retired Pay*, Feb. 2009, 290404, http://comptroller.defense.gov/fmr/07b/07b_29.pdf.

Preparing a separate military retirement pay division order is advantageous because when copies are needed for the designated agent, one does not have to make a copy of the entire decree.

The following documents must be sent to the address on the Form 2293 to apply for payments under USFSPA:

1. DD Form 2293, *Application for Former Spouse Payments from Retired Pay*

2. Copy of the divorce decree or court order

3. Separate garnishment order (if applicable for any property division other than retired pay, such as alimony or child support)[95]

In addition, the following documents should be sent to assist the designated agent in determining eligibility and processing:

1. Copy of the marriage certificate

2. Letter stating the following

   a. The amount or percentage awarded to the former spouse (reiterating the decree).

   b. The former spouse and service member were married at least ten years during which there was ten years overlap of military service.

   c. The state court was a court of jurisdiction over the service member and the reason for this jurisdiction.

   d. The decree and military domestic relations order (if completed) are final judgments, and have not been appealed, amended, or superseded.

   e. A statement indicating desire for the order priority for payments *(see* Order Priority of Payments p.71).

   f. Request for written acknowledgment that the application has been processed.

---

95. DoD FMR Vol 7B Chapter 29, "Application by Former Spouse," *Former Spouse Payments from Retired Pay*, Feb. 2009, 2904, http://comptroller.defense.gov/fmr/07b/07b_29.pdf.

3. A Certificate of Finality of the Court Order (saying no appeal has been taken, nor has the decree been amended or suspended).
4. Certified Copy of a Domestic Relations Order for Military Retirement (if there is one).
5. FMS Form 2231, *Fast Start, Direct Deposit* with a voided check if direct deposit is desired upon receipt of retired pay.
6. Form W-4P, *Withholding Certificate for Pension or Annuity Payments*

Approval/Disapproval

The former spouse will receive notification of approval or disapproval within 30 days after the application is received by the designated agent.[96]

The service member also receives notification of the application and has 30 days to respond. Should the service member provide evidence to prevent payments, the designated agent will not start the payments and will in turn notify the former spouse (providing copies of the documented evidence).

---

96. DoD FMR Vol 7B Chapter 29, "Notification to Former Spouse of Approval or Disapproval," *Former Spouse Payments from Retired Pay*, Feb. 2009, 2905, http://comptroller.defense.gov/fmr/07b/07b_29.pdf.

DFAS Retired Pay Acknowledgement Letter

DEFENSE FINANCE AND ACCOUNTING SERVICE
GARNISHMENT OPERATIONS
PO BOX 998002
CLEVELAND, OH 44199-8002

(DFAS-DGG/CL)

(Date)

(Service Member's Name)

(Former Spouses Name
and
Address)

Dear (Former Spouse)

  We have received your application for payment of a portion of the retired/retainer pay of the above-named member under the Uniformed Services Former Spouses' Protection Act (10 U.S.C. § 1408). Prior to payment, Regulations require that we notify the member of your application and that he be given 30 days to provide information regarding the status of the court order.

  If the member does not provide an order which supercedes the order you submitted, payments should tentatively commence within 90 days after the member retires and begins to receive retired/retainer pay. Please keep this office advised of your current address. If you have a change of address, please send notification to the address at the top of this letter. Your correspondence must include the member's name and social security number, your name and social security number, and a notation that you are providing a change of address for future payments under the Uniformed Services Former Spouses' Protection Act.

  If your right to this payment is adjusted or terminated, it is your responsibility to notify this office immediately.

  If your divorce decree specifies that you are to be designated as a former spouse beneficiary for the Survivor Benefit Plan (SBP), you must make a 'deemed election' for SBP coverage within one year of the date of your divorce directly to the Retired Pay office; DFAS, US Military Retirement Pay, PO Box 7130, London, KY 40742-7130. If you have any questions regarding SBP coverage, you may call the Retired Pay office at 1-800-321-1080.

  You must include the member's social security number on all correspondence to this office. If you have any questions, you may contact us through the DFAS WEB page at www.dfas.mil/money/garnish or call the Customer Service Section at 1-866-859-1845.

          Sincerely,

          Paralegal Specialist

cc: (Former Spouse's Lawyer)

Retiree Account (Pay) Statements

Retiree Account Statement (RAS) Copies

Even if there is language in the decree waiving the privacy act (*see* Privacy Act p. 61), the former spouse will have limited access to the service member's financial records. Because of this, the divorce decree should require the service member to provide a copy of every Retiree Account Statement (RAS) to the former spouse.

By both the service member and the former spouse obtaining a copy of every RAS, errors can be discovered quickly, reasons for pay changes are readily available, and communication conflicts are reduced. Computations and explanations come from looking at the statement itself rather than relying on the interpretations or words of the opposing party.

Language requiring this in a decree might read:

> It is further ordered and decreed that service member shall, if, as, and when received by service member, deliver by first class mail to former spouse at (current address), or such other address as former spouse may hereafter specify in writing, a true and correct legible copy of each Retiree Account Statement received by service member from the designated agent within five (5) days of the receipt of the same.

Reading the RAS

The Front of the Retiree Account Statement:

myPay

View other RAS [ ] (Go)

RETIREE ACCOUNT STATEMENT		
STATEMENT EFFECTIVE DATE	NEW PAY DUE AS OF	SSN

PLEASE REMEMBER TO NOTIFY DFAS IF YOUR ADDRESS CHANGES

DFAS-CL POINTS OF CONTACT
DEFENSE FINANCE AND ACCOUNTING SERVICE
US MILITARY RETIREMENT PAY
PO BOX 7130
LONDON KY 40742-7130

Service Member's Name
Service Member's Mailing Address
are shown in this box

COMMERCIAL (216) 522-5955
TOLL FREE 1-800-321-1080
TOLL FREE FAX 1-800-469-6559

myPay
https://myPay.dfas.mil
1-877-363-3677

PAY ITEM DESCRIPTION

ITEM	OLD	NEW	ITEM	OLD	NEW
GROSS PAY			FITW		
VA WAIVER			SITW		
SBP COSTS			GARNISHMENT DED		
TAXABLE INCOME			FORMER SPOUSE DED		
			NET PAY		

PAYMENT ADDRESS | **YEAR TO DATE SUMMARY (FOR INFORMATION ONLY)**

DIRECT DEPOSIT

TAXABLE INCOME:
FEDERAL INCOME TAX WITHHELD:
STATE TAX WITHHELD FOR   Service member's state appears here

TAXES

FEDERAL WITHHOLDING STATUS:
TOTAL EXEMPTIONS:
FEDERAL INCOME TAX WITHHELD:

STATE CODE:
STATE INCOME TAX WITHHELD:

SURVIVOR BENEFIT PLAN (SBP) COVERAGE

SBP COVERAGE TYPE:	FORMER SPOUSE AND CHILD	ANNUITY BASE AMOUNT:	SBP Base amount appears here
SPOUSE COST:	SBP Amount for Spouse will show here	SPOUSE DOB:	Former Spouse's Date of Birth appears here
CHILD COST:	SBP Amount for Child will show here	CHILD DOB:	Date of birth of youngest child appears here

THE ANNUITY PAYABLE IS 55% OF YOUR ANNUITY BASE AMOUNT WHICH IS
YOU HAVE PAID   MONTHS TOWARD YOUR 360 MONTHS OF PAID UP RC/SBP COVERAGE. ONCE YOU
HAVE PAID AT LEAST 360 MONTHS TOWARD YOUR COVERAGE AND TURN AGE 70, YOUR COSTS WILL BE
TERMINATED BUT YOUR COVERAGE WILL REMAIN ACTIVE.

DFAS-CL 7220/148 (Rev 03-01)

The RAS image here is a statement provided online from http://www.mypay.gov. Hard copy forms may have a different appearance but will contain the same information. The RAS is similar to a Leave and Earnings Statement (LES) in that it shows all transactions concerning the service member's pay.

Retiree Account Statements are only issued when a change in pay occurs. The statement has an "old" and a "new" column to show what is changing effective with the new pay date (the date shown in the *New Pay Due As of* box).

The *Pay Item Description* area contains all pay information for the service member, including the former spouse payment (the Former Spouse Ded).

> *Left Side:* contains items affecting the taxable income. In the sample image, this service member has Gross Pay, a VA Waiver election, and a SBP election (SBP Costs).

> *Right Side:* contains all the deductions that are subtracted from the retiree's income to determine the *Net Pay* (the service member's take-home pay). In the sample this service member has the following deductions:

> — FITW: Federal Income Tax Withheld

> — SITW: State Income Tax Withheld

> — Garnishment: (such as for alimony or child support)

> — Former Spouse Ded: An amount deducted to pay the former spouse the retirement division award.

The *Payment Address* refers to the service member and usually states Direct Deposit.

The *Year to Date Summary* area is similar to a Form W-2 in that it provides figures as of current date and lists the taxable state for the service member.

The *Taxes* area also relates only to the service member's federal and state tax information; there is no former spouse tax information (withholdings, state, etc.) shown on the RAS.

The last area on the front of the RAS is the *Survivor Benefit Plan (SBP) Coverage*. In the sample, the former spouse and child have been elected; the cost for each will be listed separately and if summed together, would equal the *SBP Costs* figure (premium amount) stated above in the *Pay Item Description* area.

The Reverse of the Retiree Account Statement

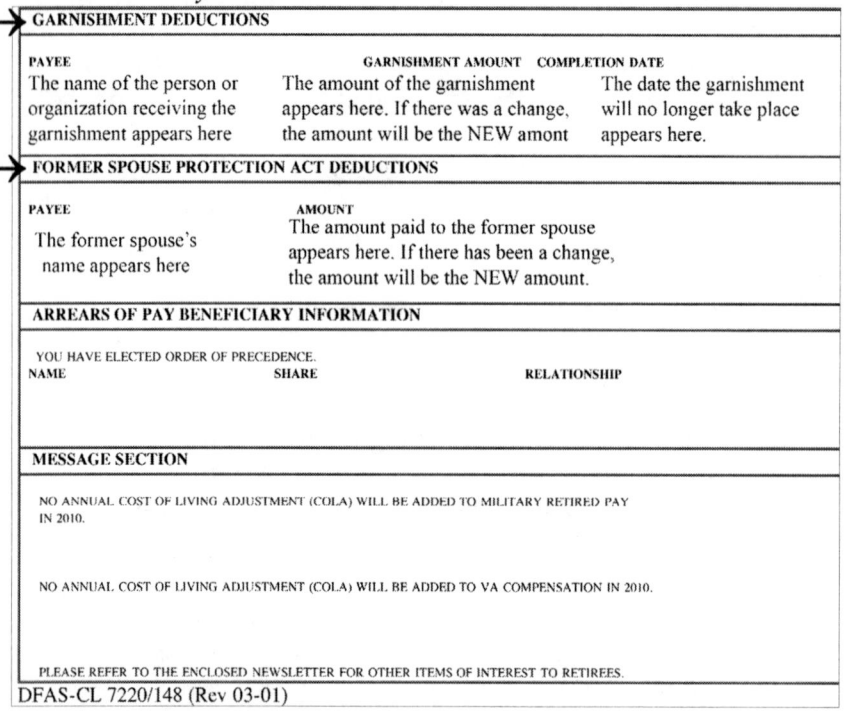

GARNISHMENT DEDUCTIONS

PAYEE	GARNISHMENT AMOUNT	COMPLETION DATE
The name of the person or organization receiving the garnishment appears here	The amount of the garnishment appears here. If there was a change, the amount will be the NEW amont	The date the garnishment will no longer take place appears here.

FORMER SPOUSE PROTECTION ACT DEDUCTIONS

PAYEE	AMOUNT
The former spouse's name appears here	The amount paid to the former spouse appears here. If there has been a change, the amount will be the NEW amount.

ARREARS OF PAY BENEFICIARY INFORMATION

YOU HAVE ELECTED ORDER OF PRECEDENCE.

NAME	SHARE	RELATIONSHIP

MESSAGE SECTION

NO ANNUAL COST OF LIVING ADJUSTMENT (COLA) WILL BE ADDED TO MILITARY RETIRED PAY IN 2010.

NO ANNUAL COST OF LIVING ADJUSTMENT (COLA) WILL BE ADDED TO VA COMPENSATION IN 2010.

PLEASE REFER TO THE ENCLOSED NEWSLETTER FOR OTHER ITEMS OF INTEREST TO RETIREES.

DFAS-CL 7220/148 (Rev 03-01)

Garnishment Deductions might show a child support agency as the Payee. The *Former Spouse Protection Act Deductions* shows the former spouse and the current amount paid. The *Message Section* contains updates, such as no COLA increase for 2010.

MYPAY.Gov for the Former Spouse

Former Spouses receiving a retired pay award have access to http://www.mypay.gov to view payments, set up direct deposit, add an email, and process a change of address. The legal office will help obtain access. The former spouse's online statement includes the *Disposable Pay Amount,* but is otherwise limited in detailed information, emphasizing further the need to receive RAS copies.

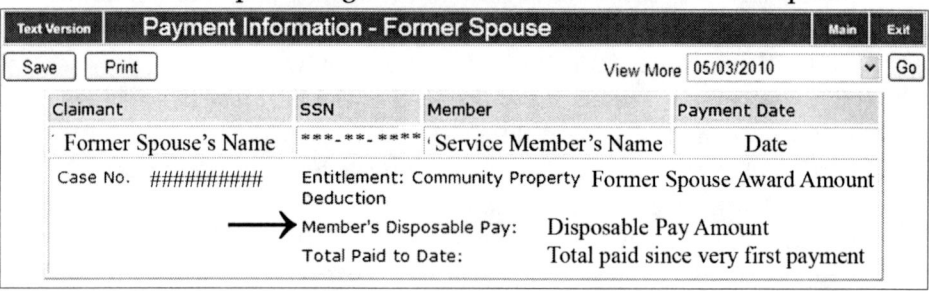

Payment Information - Former Spouse

View More 05/03/2010

Claimant	SSN	Member	Payment Date
Former Spouse's Name	***-**-****	Service Member's Name	Date
Case No. ##########	Entitlement: Community Property Deduction	Former Spouse Award Amount	
	Member's Disposable Pay:	Disposable Pay Amount	
	Total Paid to Date:	Total paid since very first payment	

Survivor Benefit Plan (SBP) & The Reserve Component (RCSBP)

Any portion of retirement pay awarded a former spouse will cease upon the service member's death.

The Survivor Benefit Plan (SBP) and the Reserve Component Survivor Benefit Plan (RCSBP) are inflation adjusted annuity payment plans following essentially the same concepts. The reserve component has some unique issues (discussed later).

SBP is often viewed as an insurance plan because it guarantees that upon the service member's death, the former spouse portion of retirement pay will continue *in the form of an annuity* receiving all future Cost of Living Adjustments.

SBP allows a former spouse to begin receiving annuity payments (as opposed to *retired pay* payments) after the service member has passed away. If elected "with children," then in the case of the former spouse's death or remarriage prior to age 55, dependent children will receive the annuity.

Survivor Benefit Plan (SBP) information can be found in:

1. The Department of Defense (DoD) Financial Management Regulation, Vol 7B, Chapter 43, Survivor Benefit Plan Elections and Election Changes.[97]

2. U.S. Code Title 10, Subtitle A, Part II, Chapter 73, Subchapter II, Survivor Benefit Plan[98]

---

97. DoD FMR Vol 7B Chapter 43, *Survivor Benefit Plan - Elections and Election Changes*, Jun. 2008, http://comptroller.defense.gov/fmr/07b/07b_43.pdf.

98. Title 10 > Subtitle A > Part II > Chapter 73 > Subchapter II, *Survivor Benefit Plan,* http://www.law.cornell.edu/uscode/html/uscode10/usc_sup_01_10_10_A_20_II_30_73_40_II.html.

SBP Comprehension Checklist

The next section provides explanations of the following Survivor Benefit Plan issues:

1. What are the SBP eligibility requirements?
2. How does remarriage affect SBP?
3. How is the annuity computed?
4. How is the SBP premium calculated?
5. What are the concerns when waiving SBP and choosing life insurance?
6. What are the viewpoints to consider when deciding who should pay for the SBP premiums?
7. What are the choices for handling reimbursement of SBP premiums?
8. What should be known about the Reserve Component Survivor Benefit Plan (RCSBP)?
9. What language is used to award SBP in a decree?
10. How and when must the former spouse make a deemed election for SBP?
11. How and when does the service member elect SBP?
12. What actions should be taken when the SBP is processed incorrectly?
13. When is SBP paid-up?

SBP Eligibility Requirements

If the service member was married to the former spouse while earning years of creditable service toward retirement pay, then there is no duration of marriage requirement. If the service member married the former spouse after becoming eligible for retired pay, in order for the former spouse to be eligible for SBP, the marriage must have lasted one year or there must be dependent children born from this marriage.[99]

Thus, if a retired service member decided to marry and this marriage lasted less than a year with no children, the former spouse *would not be* entitled to SBP. If this same marriage lasted less than a year and a child was conceived during the marriage (even if born after divorce) then this former spouse *would be* entitled to SBP.

SBP and Remarriage

Former Spouse: If a former spouse remarries before age 55, SBP premiums are suspended but eligibility is not lost. If this marriage ends due to divorce, annulment, or death of the new spouse, premiums resume.[100] Annuity payments follow the same rules.[101] The designated agent must receive a marriage certificate, death certificate, or divorce decree to make changes to an account.

Service Member: A service member may make only one SBP election. When the divorce decree awards SBP to the former spouse, the service member loses the opportunity to name a future spouse, as well as any new children, as SBP beneficiaries. A new spouse cannot be covered by SBP and thus, receives no military death benefits until there is a new court order modifying the divorce decree or a death certificate for the former spouse.

---

99. DoD FMR Vol 7B Chapter 43, "Election Coverage - Former Spouse and Children," *Survivor Benefit Plan - Elections and Election Changes*, Jun. 2008, 430503B, Following Retirement, http://comptroller.defense.gov/fmr/07b/07b_43.pdf.

100. "Former-Spouses SBP Coverage," Air Force Retiree Services, http://www.retirees.af.mil/factsheets/factsheet.asp?id=11579

101. DoD FMR Vol 7B Chapter 46, "Survivor Benefit Plan (SBP) Annuities," *Survivor Benefit Plan (SBP) Annuities*, Dec. 2009, 460902B, Reasons for Termination, http://comptroller.defense.gov/fmr/07b/07b_46.pdf.

SBP Base and Annuity Amounts

The Survivor Benefit Plan (SBP) pays spouses an annuity of 55 percent of the *Base Amount* selected when SBP is chosen.[102]

Retiring service members automatically participate in SBP at the maximum level unless they choose to decline (which requires the consent of their current spouse) or a court orders an election for a former spouse beneficiary. The SBP Base Amount ranges from $300 to a maximum of *Full Gross Pay* and adjusts with inflation.[103]

There used to be a Social Security offset, reducing the SBP annuity when the former spouse became eligible at age 62 for Social Security. This should no longer be considered when making SBP decisions because the offset policy was eliminated in 2008.[104]

The Base Amount is a negotiable item in a divorce. It effects:

1. The amount of the annuity
2. The amount of the premium

The minimum acceptable Base Amount for a former spouse should result in an annuity equivalent to the portion of retired pay the former spouse was receiving prior to the service member's death. By using this figure, when the service member passes away, the former spouse will notice no difference in *take-home* pay.

> **Example:** For a former spouse receiving $400 a month in retirement pay, the minimum Base Amount is $727.27.

Base Amount × 55% = Annuity Paid to Former Spouse

Base Amount × 55% = $400
Base Amount = $400/55%
Base Amount = $400/0.55
Base Amount = $727.27

---

102. Title 10 > Subtitle A > Part II > Chapter 73 > Subchapter II > § 1451, *Amount of Annuity,* http://www2.law.cornell.edu/uscode/uscode10/usc_sec_10_00001451----000-.html.

103. DoD FMR Vol 7B Chapter 43, "Election Option - Base Amount," *Survivor Benefit Plan - Elections and Election Changes,* Jun. 2008, 430201, Following Retirement, http://comptroller.defense.gov/fmr/07b/07b_43.pdf.

104. Defense Finance and Accounting Service, "Social Security Offset," *Retired Pay Newsletter,* April 2008, http://www.dfas.mil/rna-news/apr2008/socialsecurityoffset.html

The best outcome for the former spouse, however, is to negotiate for a Base Amount equal to *Full Gross Pay* or 100 percent of the retired pay currently being received at the time of the service member's death.

When this option is chosen, sometimes a former spouse will actually receive more upon the service member's death than was received when the service member was alive.

> **Example:** A former spouse was awarded 20 percent of the service member's disposable retired pay. SBP was awarded and elected at *Full Gross Pay*. The service member's *Full Gross Pay* at retirement is $2,000, the SBP premium is $130, so the disposable retired pay equals $1,870 ($2,000 less the $130 premium).
>
> The designated agent pays the former spouse $374 (20% × $1,870) while the service member is alive. When the service member passes away, the former spouse will receive $1,100 per month (55% × $2,000).

This situation will occur in cases where the retirement percentage awarded to the former spouse is less than 55 percent *and* the SBP Base Amount is set at *Full Gross Pay*.

A service member may feel there is no justification for the former spouse to benefit (receive more) upon the service member's death. The service member, however, also benefits (receives more) upon the death of the former spouse since the service member's retired pay will then revert back to the full amount. When negotiating the Base Amount figure, the service member and former spouse should have an understanding of the cost of premiums, how they will be paid, and how any reimbursements will be calculated (all discussed next).

SBP Premium Cost

There are two methods for determining SBP premiums:

1. For service members who came on active duty after 28 Feb 1990, the premium is 6.5 percent of the Base Amount.
2. For service members on active duty prior to 28 Feb. 1990, the cost of the SBP premium will be the lesser of:

    A. 6.5 percent of the elected Base Amount or

    B. A computation based on a threshold amount, which varies each year. The premium is equal to:

> Premium = 2.5% × Threshold + 10%(Base Amt. - Threshold)

For 2010, the turning point occurs at a Base Amount of $1,553. For an amount above this, Option A results in the lower premium and below this, Option B results in the lower premium.[105]

Using Option A, the calculation is 6.5% x $1,553 = $100.94

Using Option B, the calculation can also be computed using the table method for the threshold formula, as shown below. (A base amount of $1,553 is used to illustrate the turning point.)

1. Enter Base Amount	$1,553.00
2. Subtract the current threshold	$ 725.00
3. Remaining Amount	$ 828.00
4. Multiply the threshold (2) by .025	$ 18.13
5. Multiply remaining amount (3) by .10	$ 82.80
6. Cost per month (add 4 + 5)	$ 100.93

Dependent children can also be added to the plan. Dependent children under age 18 (or age 22, if a full-time student) will equally split the annuity should the former spouse either remarry prior to age 55 or pass away. Since children are only covered while they are dependents, the additional cost of adding them to the plan is usually minimal. Also, since computation depends on the age of the parents and the age of the youngest child, the designated agent must be contacted to determine the exact additional amount.

---

105. Air Force Retiree Services, "Factsheets: SBP Coverage Costs," *Spouse Costs*, http://www.retirees.af.mil/factsheets/factsheet.asp?id=11654

The premium cost is not a fixed amount for life. Cost of Living Adjustments (COLAs) affect all aspects of retired pay. This means COLAs will increase not only the retired pay, but also, any premiums currently being paid. Premiums are "paid-up" after 360 payments and reaching age 70.[106]

SBP Tax Benefit

The SBP premium is taken "off the top" (deducted) from the service member's pay prior to calculating taxable income, therefore, the true cost of the premium is less than the computed figure.

> **Basic (Married) Concept Example:** A married retiree's monthly pay is $1,502. The SBP election is *Full Gross Pay*, so the premium is $97.63 (6.5% × $1,502). The member's monthly taxable income reduces to $1,404.37 ($1,502 - $97.63). On an annual basis, the retiree will save the taxes owed on $1,171.56 ($97.63 x 12 months). The exact amount saved depends on the member's tax bracket.

Note: When there is a former spouse award, the service member's tax savings will be reduced proportionately.

> **Former Spouse Example:** A decree awards 40 percent to the former spouse. The retiree's monthly pay is $1,502, with an SBP election at *Full Gross Pay*, and SBP premium of $97.63. Before the premium deduction, member's monthly taxable pay is $901.20 (60% × $1,502). After the SBP deduction, the taxable amount is reduced to $842.62 (60% × ($1,502 - $97.63)). On an annual basis, the retiree saves the taxes he or she would have owed on $702.94 ((60% × $97.63) x12 months). The exact amount saved will depend on the service member's tax bracket.

Due to the tax savings, the true cost of the SBP premium is actually less than 6.5 percent of the base amount. Tax savings will vary depending on the member's tax bracket. The higher the tax bracket, the more the service member saves.

---

106. DoD FMR Vol 7B Chapter 45, "Paid Up Premiums After 30 years and age 70," *Survivor Benefit Plan - Premiums*, Jun. 2008, 4508, http://comptroller.defense.gov/fmr/07b/07b_45.pdf.

SBP or Life Insurance

Some consider SBP to be extremely expensive and recommend purchasing a life insurance policy instead. When considering waiving SBP for Life Insurance, consider the following:

- SBP is a final decision in the sense that service members cannot cancel it and only occasionally, has there been an *open enrollment* period (allowing a service member who previously declined, to choose to re-enroll by paying catch-up premiums)
- Whether the former spouse is likely to outlive the service member, noting that there is no possible cash value build-up or a premium refund should the former spouse die first
- The health expectations of the service member and former spouse (including considerations of family health histories)
- Employment or income opportunities of the former spouse
- The future needs of the former spouse
- The effects of either party remarrying
- The cost of SBP premiums and who will pay them
- The tax benefits of SBP premiums
- SBP premiums are "paid-up" after 360 payments and reaching age 70
- The inflation adjusted lifetime payments provided by SBP
- There is no medical exam required for SBP eligibility
- The role SBP plays in unlimited health care

The former spouse should not accept use of Servicemember's Group Life Insurance (SGLI) declaring the former spouse as the beneficiary, as an alternative to SBP because the member owns the policy. When life insurance is used to protect the former spouse award, the former spouse should own the policy (as a security control to ensure there are no changes).

Life insurance produces a fixed lump sum. This set figure could pose a problem because this amount can drop significantly when proceeds are invested poorly (as in the stock market in the fall of 2008) and thus the figure could possibly even run out. The alternative choice of participating in SBP provides the former spouse with a sure thing, a lifetime guaranteed source of inflation adjusted income.

In 2009 an article, *Too Many Retirees Turn Down SBP*, the net present value of SBP was emphasized to be worth $50,100 for a retiring officer and $22,300 for a retiring enlisted member. Net present value was defined and a mathematical example illustrating the value was provided:

> "Net present value is the dollar amount a new retiree would have to invest at time of retirement so that, when combined with monthly premiums, it would build an annuity for the surviving spouse of equal in value to SBP."

> "A 40-year-old retiree with a 38-year-old wife who elects full SBP coverage on a $2,000 monthly retirement could expect to pay $62,000 in total premiums if he died at age 65. If his widow were to live just seven more years, until she reaches 70, she would receive $401,897 in SBP." [107]

Health Care

There is also another benefit of SBP. The Survivor Benefit Plan plays an essential role in enabling the former spouse to qualify for unlimited health care.

One requirement for the former spouse to transfer from the 36 month health care plan into the unlimited plan is for the former spouse to be receiving (or entitled to receive) either retired pay or an annuity based on the retired pay. When the retiree passes away, all retired pay ceases, so if the former spouse has declined to participate in SBP, no annuity will be received and the former spouse will become ineligible for the unlimited health care plan (*see* Extending to Unlimited CHCBP Coverage p. 23).

---

107. Tom Philpott, "Too Many Retirees Turn Down SBP," *Today in the Military*, Oct. 29, 2009 http://www.military.com/opinion/0,15202,204849,00. html?wh=benefits&ESRC=retirees.nl

SBP Premium Responsibility

By federal law, the designated agent must deduct the Survivor Benefit Plan premium "off the top" of the member's pay. States cannot use a court order to direct the designated agent to deduct the premium in any other manner. This ensures the designated agent pays the premiums timely, regardless of any litigation tied up in the state's court system.

States can, however, direct either the service member or the former spouse to be responsible for all or a part of the premium. In such cases the divorce decree will order one party to reimburse the other by means of a check or allotment *(see* Calculating SBP Premium Reimbursement p.153).

Deciding who will be responsible to pay the SBP premium is a negotiable item in a military divorce.

Former Spouse Pays 100 Percent of SBP Premiums

An argument might be presented for the former spouse to pay 100 percent of the cost since the former spouse benefits from SBP. If negotiations do result in the former spouse paying 100 percent of the cost, then there should be no objections to set the SBP Base Amount at *Full Gross Pay* to maximize former spouse's interest in the retirement pay *(see* SBP Base and Annuity Amounts p. 144).

Service Member Pays 100 Percent of SBP Premiums

An argument can be made for the service member to pay 100 percent of the premium. This viewpoint holds that the Survivor Benefit Plan itself is not a divisible asset, but instead a means of ensuring the retirement pay will continue (in the form of an annuity). This reasoning argues the service member should pay 100 percent of the cost since SBP is a means of preserving the retirement pay, a means of ensuring the decree award will be carried out in full. Just as non-custodial parents must purchase life insurance to ensure child support payments continue in the case of their death, the argument here is the service member must purchase SBP to ensure the division of retirement pay will continue in the case of the service member's death.

Another argument in favor of the service member paying premiums concerns the legal right to retirement pay. The service member automatically has the right to his or her share of the retirement pay, but the former spouse will only have this same right if elected the SBP beneficiary. Having the service member pay for the premiums is the only way to pass this right to the former spouse. If the premiums are not paid, the former spouse award would terminate upon the service member's death, which means the right to the retirement pay was not truly given in full.

By this same reasoning, but from the viewpoint of the former spouse, if the former spouse were to pay for the SBP premiums, the former spouse would be "purchasing" the right to his or her share of retirement pay when in fact, he or she was entitled to receive it in the first place.

Share the Cost of SBP Premiums

Sharing premium costs is also an option. As a matter of fact, if no actions are taken to negotiate a reimbursement, then the service member and former spouse will each automatically pay a proportional share of the premiums when they are taken "off the top" of the service member's pay.

> **Example:** If a premium is $97.63 and the former spouse award is 40 percent of the disposable retired pay, the former spouse automatically pays $39.05 (40% × $97.63) of the premium and the service member automatically pays $58.58 (60% × $97.63).

Lawyers negotiating to share the cost might first discuss the previously mentioned rationale to hold both parties individually accountable, and then reason, as a compromise, the cost be shared.

Further arguments state that if the service member does not share in the cost, the service member will be *receiving* a *free* death benefit, whereas, the former spouse, paying 100 percent of the premium, would be *purchasing* a similar death benefit. A scenario (next page) will help explain this position further.

Consider the scenarios when either party passes away:

• When the former spouse passes away, the service member benefits because the retirement pay is restored to the full amount (no longer reduced by the former spouse award).

• When the service member passes away, the former spouse benefits through receipt of the annuity. This might even be an increase in pay if SBP was elected at *Full Gross Pay (see SBP Base and Annuity Amounts p. 144).*

It would be unfair for the former spouse to have to purchase a benefit that the service member receives for free. Only by sharing in the premium costs, will both sides contribute toward the benefit received upon the death of the other party.

> **Example:** A service member receives $2,000 retirement pay. The court awarded a division of 80 percent to the service member and 20 percent to the former spouse, with SBP awarded at a Base Amount equal to *Full Gross Pay*. While both parties are alive, the service member receives $1,600 and the former spouse receives $400.
>
> * Should the former spouse die first, the retiree's pay will increase to $2,000 (instead of $1,600 a month) since the former spouse award is no longer paid.
>
> * Should the service member die first, the former spouse will receive an increase from $400 to $1,100 (55% × $2,000, the Base Amount set at *Full Gross Pay*).

Thus, a case can be made to share in the SBP premium since both parties benefit upon the other's death, and neither party should receive this benefit for free. A case can also be made for the former spouse to bear responsibility for a larger percentage of the monthly premium, since the former spouse increase is $700 (due to the *Full Gross Pay*) and the service member's increase is only $400.

How well these lines of reasoning are argued and upheld will depend upon the skills of the lawyers involved and the local state laws view concerning division of military benefits. The premium responsibility is a negotiable item decided by the state, not by the codes and regulations, nor by the designated agent.

The final reason to consider accepting a proportionate share in the responsibility of SBP premiums is both parties will avoid having to deal with reimbursement calculations (discussed next).

Calculating SBP Premium Reimbursement

When responsibility for the SBP premium is shared, each party pays a portion of the premium at the same percentages used for their division of retirement pay. This happens automatically by the designated agent deducting the SBP premium first, "off the top" of the retirement pay.

The Air Force Retiree Services explains the proportions well:

> "It is important to understand that in cases in which a former spouse is awarded a percentage of a military retiree's retired pay, and SBP coverage is elected for the former spouse (either voluntarily or involuntarily), the former spouse, in effect, pays a portion of the SBP premiums in an amount proportionate to the division of retired pay. This happens automatically because divisions of retired pay are based upon disposable retired pay, which has already been reduced because of the SBP premium."[108]

When negotiations result in one party accepting full responsibility for the SBP premium, there are two ways to handle this:

- Have the responsible party write the other a check, or
- Adjust the division percentages within the divorce decree.

Understanding how the premium payment is proportioned is essential to calculating the correct reimbursement or percentage adjustment. The following scenario will be used to illustrate both methods:

> **Example, SBP Reimbursement:** A service member's gross retirement pay equals $2,000. The court awarded a division of disposable retired pay of 80 percent to the service member and 20 percent to the former spouse. SBP was awarded at a Base Amount of *Full Gross Pay*, and the former spouse was ordered to pay 100 percent of the premium cost. The monthly premium is $130 (6.5% × $2,000).

---

108. A.F. Retiree Services, "SBP Costs," *Former Spouse and Child Coverage Fact Sheet*, http://www.retirees.af.mil/factsheets/factsheet.asp?id=11580

Check Reimbursement

For personal reimbursements, the decree will include an order for the responsible party to reimburse the other, as in:

> It is further ordered and decreed that former spouse shall pay one hundred percent (100 percent) of the cost of that portion of the SBP monthly premiums paid by service member (that is the premiums that are withheld out of his/her portion of the retired pay), by former spouse reimbursing the service member within thirty days of the date the premium is withheld out of service member's retired pay.

In the example, the designated agent deducts the $130 premium "off the top" of the service member's pay, sends the former spouse $374 and sends the service member $1,496. The SBP premium on the Retiree Account Statement (RAS) will sate: SBP Costs: $130.

Example Computations:

$2,000 Retirement Pay
-$ 130 SBP Premium (calculated from 6.5% × $2,000)
$1,870 Disposable Pay

$1,870 Disposable Pay	$1,870 Disposable Pay
× 80% for Service Member	× 20% for Former Spouse
$1,496 to the Service Member	$ 374 to the Former Spouse

The service member and former spouse might think the reimbursement amount is the $130 listed on the RAS, but this would be would be an overpayment.

The former spouse has already paid a portion of the $130 premium when it was taken "off the top." (The service member paid part too.) The decree statement, *that portion of SBP monthly premiums paid by the service member* does not refer to the figure on the RAS. The service member is due $1,600 (80% × $2,000). If the service member receives $1,496 from the designated agent, plus $130 from the former spouse, the total of $1,626 is an overpayment.

To compute the correct reimbursement, multiply the SBP Costs listed on the service members RAS by (100% - the percentage of pay awarded the party responsible for reimbursement).

SBP Reimbursement Amount	= SBP Premium	×	(100% - the Percent Awarded the Party Responsible for Reimbursement)

Applying the formula to the previous example where the former spouse was to pay for 100 percent of the premiums results in:

SBP Reimbursement Amount = $130 × (100% - 20%)

SBP Reimbursement Amount = $130 × 80%

SBP Reimbursement Amount = $104

The former spouse will reimburse the service member $104 each month. This amount was automatically paid by the service member when the premium was taken "off the top." The former spouse likewise, automatically paid $26 in premiums (20 percent awarded the former spouse multiplied by the $130 premium).

> *Note:* If the service member had been ordered to pay 100 percent of the costs, the result would have been a check in the amount of $26 (from $130 × (100% - 80%)) to be paid by the service member to the former spouse.

Per the decree, the former spouse was due $400 ($2,000 × 20% award), but also, responsible for 100 percent of the SBP premium of $130, thus the former spouse should receive $270 ($400-$130). This is the amount the former spouse now receives $270 ($374 from the designated agent - $104 reimbursed to the service member).

The reimbursement amount must be recalculated every time there is a Cost of Living Adjustment. This additional hassle might be enough reason for the parties to decide to either share in the SBP costs or to make an adjustment to the decree percentage to account for reimbursement.

Adjust the Decree Award Percentage for Reimbursement

The premium reimbursement can be handled by adjusting the percentage awarded in the decree itself. This method removes all reimbursement language from the decree, eliminates the need for calculations, and reduces communication between the parties as there is no need for reimbursement checks.

If a service member is not yet retired and the Marital Share is defined using *a denominator of total years in service*, this method cannot be used. Since the total years in service would be unknown, the percentage is also unknown and thus, cannot be adjusted.

If the service member is retired or the hypothetical language uses the *date of divorce variation* of the Marital Share (which uses a denominator of Months of Service *up to Divorce*) the adjustment can be accomplished.

Suppose the proposed language choice for a decree was to use a *Fixed Percentage*, as in:

> "The former spouse is awarded **20 percent** of the member's disposable military retired pay"

This draft language will now be adjusted to account for the SBP premium reimbursement. In the example, since the former spouse is to be held responsible for the premium, the expectation is for the percentage to be reduced. (This formula can also be used if the service member were to be responsible for 100 percent of the costs. In such case, the service member's percentage would be reduced, increasing the percentage for the former spouse award.)

The full formula to adjust the responsible party percentage is:

$$\text{Responsible Party Award Percentage} = \frac{\text{Responsible Party Pay Award - SBP Premium}}{\text{Service Member's Gross Pay - SBP Premium}}$$

$$\text{Responsible Party Award Percentage} = \frac{(\text{Pay} \times \text{Responsible Party \%}) - (\text{Pay} \times 6.5\%)}{(\text{Pay} \times 100\%) - (\text{Pay} \times 6.5\%)}$$

The simplified formula is:

$$\text{Responsible Party Award Percentage} = \frac{\text{Responsible Party \% - 6.5\%}}{93.5\%}$$

The SBP reimbursement example (p. 153), where the former spouse receives 20 percent of the $2,000 retired pay and the former spouse was responsible for reimbursement, the percentage reduces to 14.4385.

$$\frac{\text{Responsible Party}}{\text{Award Percentage}} = \frac{\text{Responsible Party \% - 6.5\%}}{93.5\%}$$

$$\frac{\text{Responsible Party}}{\text{Award Percentage}} = \frac{20\% - 6.5\%}{93.5\%}$$

$$\frac{\text{Responsible Party}}{\text{Award Percentage}} = 14.4385\%$$

After the adjustment, there is no need for a SBP reimbursement statement and the decree award language would instead read:

> "The former spouse is awarded **14.4385 percent** of the member's disposable military retired pay"

The designated agent still deducts the $130 premium "off the top" but now, using the new percentage, pays the former spouse $270 and the service member $1,600. The SBP premium on the Retiree Account Statement will still state: SBP Costs: $130. Proper payment occurs without any reimbursement required.

Example Computations (compare with those on p. 154):

$2,000 Retirement Pay
-$ 130 SBP Premium (calculated from 6.5% × $2,000)
$1,870 Disposable Pay

$1,870 Disposable Pay	$1,870 Disposable Pay
× 85.5615% Service Member	× 14.4385% Former Spouse
$1,600 to the Service Member	$ 270 to the Former Spouse

Final Decision

Accurate computations are essential to avoid long term confusion over reimbursement. When other factors affect retired pay (such as disability indemnification) more calculations will be necessary. This percentage adjustment only adjusted for SBP costs.

Extra care must be taken when adjusting percentages since errors can be costly and require judicial modification. Using an indemnification statement with check reimbursement provides more flexibility, especially with unknown future military pay changes.

Reserve Component Survivor Benefit Plan (RCSBP)

Reservists are unique because they are not able to begin drawing retirement pay until age 60, yet they may become retirement eligible prior to this date. Reservists receive an official notification, often referred to as the "twenty year letter," when they have enough points equivalent to the twenty years required for retirement. The term "gray area reservist" is often used to describe this time frame, between receipt of the letter and age 60.

Reservists have three SBP options upon eligibility notification:

A. "Decline to make an election until age 60 - You will remain eligible to elect Survivor Benefit Plan (SBP) coverage at age 60. An annuity will *not* be payable to your beneficiaries if you die before age 60.

B. Deferred annuity - Provide coverage for an annuity to begin on the 60th anniversary of your birth, if you die before age 60, or to begin immediately if you die after age 60.

C. Immediate annuity - Provide coverage for an annuity to begin immediately, whether you die before or after age 60."[109]

Two Different Premium Possibilities

Premiums are not paid until the service member actually receives retired pay. Reservists who choose Option A will follow the same premium rules previously discussed. This is because coverage and premium payments begin at age 60.

Reservists who choose Option B or Option C will have a slightly higher premium than the general rules of 6.5 percent of the Base Amount. This is because these reservists were covered during the "gray" years, but never paid a premium at that time. In a sense, they are catching up. The amount varies because it is based upon the age of the reservist and the age of the beneficiary, when the election (Option B or C) was made. These reservists should use reimbursement by check when premiums are not shared.

---

109. "Reserve Component Survivor Benefit Plan," RCSBP Fact Sheet, Election Options, Jan. 2010, http://www.armyg1.army.mil/rso/docs/sbp/fact/RCSBPforHomepage.doc

Awarding the Former Spouse SBP

The language of the divorce decree should specifically award the right of the former spouse to be named as the beneficiary. Such language, including children, might read:

> The court further finds that former spouse and the parties' children should be named as "former spouse beneficiary and/with children" under the Armed Services Survivor Benefit Plan (SBP) and service member should be ordered to elect/designate former spouse as a "former spouse beneficiary and/with children" by completing DoD Form 2656, Section IX, Survivor Benefit Plan Election, Number 26, Beneficiary Categories, Box b, "I elect coverage for former spouse and children."

Former Spouse Deemed Election

When a divorce occurs while the service member is still on active duty and expected to retire at some future date, a deemed election must be made. Deemed elections can be made by either the former spouse or the former spouse's lawyer on behalf of the former spouse, and they must be made within one year of the date of the court order.[110]

In the summer of 2008, completing the DD Form 2656-10 became the only way for a former spouse or authorized agent to request a valid deemed election.[111]

Paperwork should be sent immediately to the designated agent. The former spouse needs to follow up until the deemed election is confirmed in writing *(see* DFAS Deemed Election Acknowledgement p. 163).

---

110. DoD FMR Vol 7B Chapter 43, "Election Coverage -Former Spouse or Former Spouse and Children," *Survivor Benefit Plan - Elections and Election Changes,* Jun. 2008, 430503C, Deemed Elections, http://comptroller.defense.gov/fmr/07b/07b_43.pdf.

111. Office of the Under Secretary of Defense, "DD Form 2656-10, SBP/RC SBP Request for Deemed Election," *Memorandum for the Assistant Secretary of the Army, Navy, Air Force and DFAS,* http://www.hcmmlaw.com/files/blogMilitaryDeemed_Election.pdf

The decree language should be as detailed as possible when ordering the former spouse to make a deemed election, as in:

> Former spouse is herby directed to apply for Former Spouse's entitlement to be deemed a "former spouse beneficiary" of Service Member's Armed Forces SBP by contacting the designated agent Legal Department, notifying it of this Court's deemed election pursuant to 10 U.S.C. 1447 et. Seq., by completing and sending DoD Form 2656-10, Survivor Benefit Plan (SBP)/Reserve Component (RC) SBP Request for Deemed Election along with a certified copy of this order to: [the designated agent's address on the Form 2656-10] by certified mail.

Ideally lawyers should insist on aiding former spouses through to completion. This will not only be beneficial to the former spouse, who may be overwhelmed with the intricacies of the process, but it will also ensure the lawyer has both informed and advised properly, and thus avoid any chance of malpractice allegations, state bar grievances, or negligence claims.

In the case of deemed elections, lawyers are not usually involved when the actual retirement takes place, so the former spouse should maintain a file with copies of all documents, forms, and letters for any required follow-up or actions needed.

The following should be sent to the designated agent no later than *one year* (preferably in the first month) following the divorce:

- Certified copy of the divorce decree

- Completed DoD Form 2656-10, *Survivor Benefit Plan (SBP)/Reserve Component (RC) SBP Request for Deemed Election*

- Certified copy of a Domestic Relations Order for Military Retirement (if accomplished)

- A letter, signed by the former spouse, deeming election and requesting written confirmation of receipt *(see* Former Spouse Written Deemed Election, p. 162)

The real purpose behind sending a letter repeating the deemed election is to obtain written acknowledgement. The Form 2656-10 *(see* Form p. 182-183) does not require the designated agent to provide any written confirmation.

Since the former spouse must make the SBP deemed election within one year of divorce, it follows that within one year of divorce, the former spouse should have a written confirmation from the designated agent, acknowledging this election. Patient and consistent follow-up might be needed to obtain this written confirmation.

Retirement Time

At retirement time, the former spouse may be contacted, (usually by the service member's SBP counselor) as part of the service member's retirement transition. The SBP counselor may send the former spouse a DD Form 2656-1, Survivor Benefit Plan Election Statement for Former Spouse Coverage. This form should be carefully reviewed for accuracy, especially the coverage in Block 1, *Due to Divorce Change My SBP Coverage to,* including the election "with children," if so ordered in the decree *(see* form p. 180-181).

At this time, the former spouse should also request a copy of the service member's completed DD Form 2656, *Data for Payment of Retired Personnel,* to ensure all election choices concerning the Base Amount *(see* form p. 179) have been completed in accordance with the divorce decree. This is the best time to catch any errors or disagreements, prior to the paperwork being processed by the designated agent.

Only under certain circumstances can SBP be changed *(see* SBP Processed Incorrectly p.166).

Former Spouse Written Deemed Election

Date:_____

To:
DFAS U.S. Military Retirement Pay
P.O. Box 7130
London, KY 40742-7130

Re: Deemed Election for SBP Coverage
Retiree Name: _____
Retiree SSN:_____
Retiree DOB:_____

I deem my election as a former spouse in the SBP program of retiree (name) _____, SSN _____, Rank _____ .

My name is _____, SSN _____, at address _____, and phone number _____. My former spouse and I were divorced on _____. I am enclosing a copy of the divorce decree.

I qualify due to my previous marriage on _____ (date of marriage) to _____ (service member's name), SSN _____ whom I divorced on _____.

Please confirm in writing that I am listed as the former spouse for the Survivor Benefit Plan, SBP.

(signature)

Printed former spouse's name
Address
Phone

cc: Att.
(Former spouse's lawyer's name)   Divorce decree

DFAS Deemed Election Acknowledgement Letter

DEFENSE FINANCE AND ACCOUNTING SERVICE
Retired and Annuity Pay

(Former Spouses Name
and
Address)

(Date)

To whom it may concern:

    Our records reflect that the military retired pay account of (Service Member's Name) (Service)(Ret.) indicates former spouse Survivor Benefit Plan (SBP) coverage for (Former Spouse) The referenced retiree has not retired at this time. When his retired account is established, (Former Spouse) will be placed as the former spouse Survivor Benefit Plan (SBP) beneficiary per divorce decree and court order.

    Should you have any further questions, please contact us at Defense Finance and Accounting Service; U.S. Military Retired Pay; P.O. Box 7130; London, KY 40742-7130; or call toll free 1-800-321-1080, commercial (216) 522-5955 (M-F from 7:00 a.m. to 7:30 p.m. ET). You may also send us a fax to, toll free 1-800-469-6559.

Sincerely,

Contact Representative
Retired and Annuity Pay

Service Member SBP Election

If the retired service member listed the spouse as the SBP beneficiary prior to divorce, an election must still be made after divorce. The change from spouse to former spouse does not happen automatically.

If required in the divorce decree, the service member will elect the former spouse as the SBP beneficiary sending the designated agent the following forms:

1. DD Form 2656, *Data for Payment of Retired Personnel*
2. DD Form 2656-1 *Survivor Benefit Plan Election Statement for Former Spouse Coverage*
3. Certified Copy of the Divorce Decree[112]

The SBP counselor will assist the service member in completion of the DD Form 2656. If SBP was not awarded at the Base Amount of *Full Gross Pay* or stated as a specific amount in the decree, the SBP counselor and the service member will decide the figure for the Base Amount to be entered on the Form 2656.

The language of the decree should order the service member to make the election for SBP, possibly with children, as in:

> It is therefore ordered and decreed that service member be and is herby ordered to elect to designate former spouse as "former spouse beneficiary and/with children" of service member's SBP. It is further ordered and decreed that, pursuant to this Order, former spouse be and is herby deemed designated, to the extent permitted by law, as a "former spouse beneficiary and/with children" of service member's SBP to receive an annuity resulting from a Base Amount of [specific amount or *Full Gross Pay*]. It is further ordered and decreed that the service member shall provide a copy of the signed DD Form 2656, *Data for Payment of Retire Personnel* to the former spouse prior to submission to the designated agent.

---

112. *See* "Instructions," *DD Form 2656, Data for Payment of Retired Personnel,* Apr. 2009, *Instructions,* Apr. 2009, para. 26e and 26f.

Sending a copy of the DD Form 2656 to the former spouse is necessary because this form declares the Base Amount *(see* form p. 176-179). Without a copy of this form, the former spouse will have no notification that the Base Amount to be set in the military pay system by the designated agent will match that required by the decree. The designated agent will not release this information to the former spouse due to the privacy act rules. The decree must order the service member to provide this form; the justification being, the former spouse requires such knowledge to ensure accurate timely processing.

Without receiving a copy of this form, the former spouse could conceivably calculate the Base Amount from the Retiree Account Statement (RAS), but this would be after the election has been declared and processed. Finding errors at this time might require an appeal to the Board of Corrections which is time consuming and may also create a debt on the service member's account.

Lawyers can assist their clients, transition personnel, and the designated agent itself, by considering even further detailed language than the example above. The language could clearly order the service member to check specific boxes on the DD Form 2656. In such a case, the order should also state in words, what is expected since forms often change with updates.

Along with the DD Form 2656, the service member sends the designated agent a completed DD Form 2656-1, *Survivor Benefit Plan Election Statement for Former Spouse Coverage* and a certified copy of the final decree.

The DD Form 2656-1 requires the former spouse's signature. As explained in the prior section, Former Spouse Deemed Election, at retirement time the service member's SBP counselor will contact the former spouse by letter and if ordered, provide both the Form 2656 and the Form 2656-1 for review and signature, as needed. This grants the former spouse the opportunity to bring to light any concerns or questions prior to final processing.

The former spouse actually makes the election twice, once through the deemed election procedures and once upon the service member's retirement.

SBP Processed Incorrectly

Even when negotiations have concluded, the divorce decree finalized, and all documents sent to the designated agent in a timely manner, sometimes paperwork is processed incorrectly.

There are certain circumstances where changes can be made after the SBP election. One example is called a Correction of Administrative Error.[113] The following example illustrates the importance of receiving advance copies of the Form 2656, as well as receiving copies of the Retiree Account Statement (RAS).

> **Example, SBP processed incorrectly:** A service member's gross pay is $2,000 and the court awarded division was 80 percent to the service member and 20 percent to the former spouse. The decree awarded SBP based on the maximum amount allowed by law.
>
> Upon retirement, the SBP counselor and service member misinterpreted the Base Amount to be $400, (from 20% ×$2,000). The Form 2656 was completed by checking 27b, I elect coverage with a *reduced* Base Amount of $400. No *advance copy* was sent to the former spouse.
>
> *Note:* The maximum SBP amount allowed by law would be based on *Full Gross Pay*. If left uncorrected and the service member should pass away, the former spouse would receive an annuity of only $220 (55 percent of $400), instead of $1,100 (55 percent of $2,000).
>
> Since no advance Form 2656 copy was provided, the first opportunity for the former spouse to catch the error occurs upon receipt of the RAS. The SBP premium will be only $26 (6.5% × $400) when it was expected to be $130 ($2,000 x 6.5%). To correct this, an appeal must be made to the military Board of Corrections.

---

113. DoD FMR Vol 7B Chapter 43, "Changes in Election and Coverage - Correction of Administrative Error," *Survivor Benefit Plan - Elections and Election Changes,* Jun. 2008, 430707, http://comptroller.defense.gov/fmr/07b/07b_43.pdf.

Family members and former spouse may request changes to a service member's military records by appealing to the appropriate military Board of Corrections within three years of the error discovery (although exceptions may occur) and after all other avenues for change have been exhausted (*see* DD Form 149 *Application for Correction of Military Record Under the Provisions of Title 10, U.S. Code Section 1552*, Instructions p. 173).

A Board of Correction appeal is very time consuming:

1. Allow one month for the request packet to process through the Board of Corrections

2. Allow an additional month for the Board of Corrections to send the packet to the SBP office at Randolph for an advisory review and recommendation.

3. Allow time for Randolph to provide both the service member and former spouse with a copy of the final recommendation, requesting comments within 30 days.

4. If one party responds with additional information or non-concurrence, this will delay the process further as the packet will again loop through steps 2 and 3 above (requiring an additional review, recommendation, and 30 days allowance for responses).

5. The final packet will be sent to the Board of Corrections for a final decision, at which time each party also has the option of appearing at the final ruling. Notification of the outcome is sent to the designated agent, service member, and former spouse.

6. The former spouse should fax a copy of this notification to the designated agent to ensure timely receipt and expedite processing.

7. The designated agent will immediately set up any debts, so the service member and former spouse must be prepared for the possibility of reduced paychecks.

This process is expedited by proper preparation of a complete packet that both parties would readily concur on. The entire packet is sent to the applicable address on the DD Form 149, which should reply with a written acknowledgement of receipt.

The former spouse should include the following in the packet:

- DD Form 149, *Application for Correction of Military Record Under the Provisions of Title 10, U.S. Code Section 1552,*
- A statement that the former spouse has not remarried
- A statement explaining the reason for the request
- An *entire copy* of the divorce decree with all attachments, court orders etc. (It does not have to have a raised seal.)

Decree Language Awarding SBP

The language of the decree should clearly order:

1. The award of SBP to the former spouse
2. The level of coverage awarded for the former spouse, specifically describing the Base Amount as either a figure or *Full Gross Pay*
3. The former spouse to make a SBP deemed election by sending Form 2656-10 to the designated agent within one year
4. The service member to make the SBP election on DoD Form 2656,
   - Section IX 26, *Beneficiary Categories,* specifically stating which category former spouse (with or without children) will be chosen
   - Section IX 27, *Level of Coverage,* specifically stating the level of coverage to be chosen (*Full Gross Pay* or other amount)
5. The service member to complete Form 2656-1, specifically stating which box to check (Former Spouse or Former Spouse and Children)
6. Premium reimbursement language if applicable
7. The service member to provide the former spouse with the Form 2656 and Form 2656-1, prior to processing

Including this type of language will assist all parties (the service member, former spouse, and designated agent) when completing forms accurately and timely at retirement.

Taxes *Incident to Divorce* and IRS Form 1099-R

Every January, the service member and former spouse each receive a Form 1099-R, *Distributions From Pensions, Annuities, Retirement or Profit-Sharing Plans, IRAs, Insurance Contracts, etc.,* reporting the taxable income and withholdings for the prior year.

The service member and former spouse should have each submitted a Form W-4P, *Withholding Certificate for Pension or Annuity Payments* to the designated agent, declaring the amount of taxes to withhold based on their filing status.

Disability Pay and the Survivor Benefit Plan are two pay items that reduce taxable income. The result is a win-win situation for both parties. The U.S. Code § 1041, *Transfers of Property between Spouses or Incident to Divorce* states no gain or loss shall be recognized on a transfer of property from an individual to a former spouse if the transfer is incident to divorce, defined as:

> "A transfer of property is incident to the divorce if such transfer—
>
> (1) occurs within one year after the date on which the marriage ceases, or
>
> (2) is related to the cessation of the marriage."[114]

Example: A retiree receives $2,000 in retired pay, has a 10 percent disability, an indemnification clause, and a 25 percent former spouse award (with SBP elected at *Full Gross Pay*). The former spouse is responsibility for 100 percent of the SBP premiums, to be reimbursed by check to the retiree.

---

114. Title 26 > Subtitle A > Chapter 1 > Subchapter O > PART III > § 1041, "Transfers of property between spouses or incident to divorce," http://www.law.cornell.edu/uscode/uscode26/usc_sec_26_00001041----000-.html.

Example Computations:
  $2,000 Retirement Pay
  -$ 200 Disability Pay (calculated from 10% × $2,000)
  -$ 130 SBP Costs (premium of 6.5% × $2,000)
  $1,670 Disposable Pay

  $1,670 Disposable Pay $1,670 Disposable Pay
  × 75% for Service Member   × 25% for Former Spouse
  $1,252.50 to Service Member $ 417.50 to Former Spouse

Disability Indemnification and SBP reimbursement requires:
-The service member to send the former spouse $50 (25% × 200)
-The former spouse to send the service member $97.50 (75% × $130)

Summary: The decree award totals match:

* The service member was awarded 75 percent of $2,000 which is $1,500 and received $1,500 ($1,252.50 + 97.50).

* The former spouse was awarded $500 (25 percent of $2,000) less the SBP costs of $130, which equals $370 and in this case, the former spouse did receive $370 ($417.50 - $97.50 + $50).

Both parties save 16.5 percent (10% + 6.5%) on their taxable income. The Forms 1099-R will show the following taxable pay received (multiplied by 12 months):
  $1,252.50 for the service member ($1,500 reduced by $247.50)
  $ 417.50 for the former spouse ($500 was reduced by $82.50)

DFAS Form 1099-R

Control Number		☐ CORRECTED (if checked)		12/11/09	
PAYER'S name, street address, city, state, and ZIP code DEFENSE FINANCE AND ACCOUNTING SERVICE US MILITARY RETIREMENT PAY PO BOX 7130 LONDON KY 40742-7130		1 Gross distribution $ Amount 2a Taxable amount $ Amount	OMB No. 1545-0119 20**09**	**Distributions From Pensions, Annuities, Retirement, or Profit-Sharing Plans, IRAs, Insurance Contracts, etc.**	
PAYER'S Federal identification number 34-0727612	RECIPIENT'S identification number Social Security Number	2b Total distribution ☐		Form **1099-R**	
RECIPIENT'S name, street address, city, state, and ZIP code ǁıǁıǁıııǁıǁıǁıǁıııǁıııǁıǁıǁıǁıǁıǁıǁıǁıı 00043512 Name and Address		4 Federal income tax withheld May have $ an amount 9 Your percentage of total distribution % 10 State tax withheld $	7 Distribution code 7 11 State/Payer's state no.	**Copy 2** File this copy with your state, city, or local income tax return, when required.	
Form **1099-R**				Department of the Treasury - Internal Revenue Service	

Forms

Form W-4P Withholding Certificate for Pension or Annuity Payments

Form **W-4P** Department of the Treasury Internal Revenue Service	**Withholding Certificate for Pension or Annuity Payments**	OMB No. 1545-0074 **2010**

Purpose. Form W-4P is for U.S. citizens, resident aliens, or their estates who are recipients of pensions, annuities (including commercial annuities), and certain other deferred compensation. Use Form W-4P to tell payers the correct amount of federal income tax to withhold from your payment(s). You also may use Form W-4P to choose (a) not to have any federal income tax withheld from the payment (except for eligible rollover distributions, or payments to U.S. citizens delivered outside the United States or its possessions) or (b) to have an additional amount of tax withheld.

Your options depend on whether the payment is periodic, nonperiodic, or an eligible rollover distribution, as explained on pages 3 and 4. Your previously filed Form W-4P will remain in effect if you do not file a Form W-4P for 2010.

What do I need to do? Complete lines **A** through **G** of the **Personal Allowances Worksheet.** Use the additional worksheets on page 2 to further adjust your withholding allowances for itemized deductions, adjustments to income, any additional standard deduction, certain credits, or multiple pensions/more-than-one-income situations. If you do not want any federal income tax withheld (see *Purpose* above), you can skip the worksheets and go directly to the Form W-4P below.

Sign this form. Form W-4P is not valid unless you sign it.

Personal Allowances Worksheet (Keep for your records.)

- **A** Enter "1" for **yourself** if no one else can claim you as a dependent . . . . **A** _____
- **B** Enter "1" if:
  - You are single and have only one pension; or
  - You are married, have only one pension, and your spouse has no income subject to withholding; or
  - Your income from a second pension or a job, or your spouse's pension or wages (or the total of all) is $1,500 or less.

  . . . . **B** _____
- **C** Enter "1" for your **spouse**. But, you may choose to enter "-0-" if you are married and have either a spouse who has no income subject to withholding or you have more than one source of income subject to withholding. (Entering "-0-" may help you avoid having too little tax withheld.) . . . . **C** _____
- **D** Enter number of **dependents** (other than your spouse or yourself) you will claim on your tax return . . . . **D** _____
- **E** Enter "1" if you will file as **head of household** on your tax return . . . . **E** _____
- **F** **Child Tax Credit** (including additional child tax credit). See Pub. 972, Child Tax Credit, for more information.
  - If your total income will be less than $61,000 ($90,000 if married), enter "2" for each eligible child; then **less** "1" if you have three or more eligible children.
  - If your total income will be between $61,000 and $84,000 ($90,000 and $119,000 if married), enter "1" for each eligible child plus "1" **additional** if you have six or more eligible children . . . . **F** _____
- **G** Add lines A through F and enter total here. (**Note.** *This may be different from the number of exemptions you claim on your tax return.*) . . . . ▶ **G** _____

For accuracy, complete all worksheets that apply.
- If you plan to **itemize** or claim **adjustments to income** and want to reduce your withholding, see the Deductions and Adjustments Worksheet on page 2.
- If you have more than one source of income subject to withholding or a spouse with income subject to withholding **and** your combined income from all sources exceeds $18,000 ($32,000 if married), see the **Multiple Pensions/More-Than-One-Income Worksheet** on page 2 to avoid having too little tax withheld.
- If **neither** of the above situations applies, **stop here** and enter the number from line G on line 2 of Form W-4P below.

------- Cut here and give Form W-4P to the payer of your pension or annuity. Keep the top part for your records. -------

Form **W-4P** Department of the Treasury Internal Revenue Service	**Withholding Certificate for Pension or Annuity Payments** ▶ For Privacy Act and Paperwork Reduction Act Notice, see page 4.	OMB No. 1545-0074 **2010**

Type or print your first name and middle initial	Last name	Your social security number

Home address (number and street or rural route)	Claim or identification number (if any) of your pension or annuity contract
City or town, state, and ZIP code	

Complete the following applicable lines.

1. Check here if you **do not want any** federal income tax withheld from your pension or annuity. (Do not complete lines 2 or 3.) ▶ ☐
2. Total number of allowances and marital status you are claiming for withholding from each **periodic** pension or annuity payment. (You may also designate an additional dollar amount on line 3.) . . . . ▶ _____ (Enter number of allowances.)
   Marital status: ☐ Single ☐ Married ☐ Married, but withhold at higher "Single" rate
3. Additional amount, if any, you want withheld from each pension or annuity payment. (**Note.** *For periodic payments, you cannot enter an amount here without entering the number (including zero) of allowances on line 2.*) . . . ▶ $ _____

Your signature ▶ _____ Date ▶ _____

Cat. No. 10225T   Form **W-4P** (2010)

DD Form 149, Application for Correction of Military Record under the Provisions of Title 10

APPLICATION FOR CORRECTION OF MILITARY RECORD UNDER THE PROVISIONS OF TITLE 10, U.S. CODE, SECTION 1552
(Please read instructions on reverse side BEFORE completing this application.)

OMB No. 0704-0003
OMB approval expires
Jun 30, 2009

The public reporting burden for this collection of information is estimated to average 30 minutes per response, including the time for reviewing instructions, searching existing data sources, gathering and maintaining the data needed, and completing and reviewing the collection of information. Send comments regarding this burden estimate or any other aspect of this collection of information, including suggestions for reducing the burden, to the Department of Defense, Executive Services Directorate, Information Management Division, 1155 Defense Pentagon, Washington, DC 20301-1155 (0704-0003). Respondents should be aware that notwithstanding any other provision of law, no person shall be subject to any penalty for failing to comply with a collection of information if it does not display a currently valid OMB control number.

PLEASE DO NOT RETURN YOUR COMPLETED FORM TO THE ABOVE ORGANIZATION. RETURN COMPLETED FORM TO THE APPROPRIATE ADDRESS ON THE BACK OF THIS PAGE.

PRIVACY ACT STATEMENT

AUTHORITY: Title 10 US Code 1552, EO 9397.

ROUTINE USE(S): None.

PRINCIPAL PURPOSE: To initiate an application for correction of military record. The form is used by Board members for review of pertinent information in making a determination of relief through correction of a military record.

DISCLOSURE: Voluntary; however, failure to provide identifying information may impede processing of this application. The request for Social Security number is strictly to assure proper identification of the individual and appropriate records.

1. APPLICANT DATA *(The person whose record you are requesting to be corrected.)*

a. BRANCH OF SERVICE *(X one)* | ARMY | NAVY | AIR FORCE | MARINE CORPS | COAST GUARD

b. NAME *(Print - Last, First, Middle Initial)* | c. PRESENT OR LAST PAY GRADE | d. SERVICE NUMBER *(If applicable)* | e. SSN

2. PRESENT STATUS WITH RESPECT TO THE ARMED SERVICES *(Active Duty, Reserve, National Guard, Retired, Discharged, Deceased)*

3. TYPE OF DISCHARGE *(If by court-martial, state the type of court.)*

4. DATE OF DISCHARGE OR RELEASE FROM ACTIVE DUTY *(YYYYMMDD)*

5. I REQUEST THE FOLLOWING ERROR OR INJUSTICE IN THE RECORD BE CORRECTED: *(Entry required)*

6. I BELIEVE THE RECORD TO BE IN ERROR OR UNJUST FOR THE FOLLOWING REASONS: *(Entry required)*

7. ORGANIZATION AND APPROXIMATE DATE *(YYYYMMDD)* **AT THE TIME THE ALLEGED ERROR OR INJUSTICE IN THE RECORD OCCURRED** *(Entry required)*

8. DISCOVERY OF ALLEGED ERROR OR INJUSTICE

a. DATE OF DISCOVERY *(YYYYMMDD)* | b. IF MORE THAN THREE YEARS SINCE THE ALLEGED ERROR OR INJUSTICE WAS DISCOVERED, STATE WHY THE BOARD SHOULD FIND IT IN THE INTEREST OF JUSTICE TO CONSIDER THE APPLICATION.

9. IN SUPPORT OF THIS APPLICATION, I SUBMIT AS EVIDENCE THE FOLLOWING ATTACHED DOCUMENTS: *(If military documents or medical records are pertinent to your case, please send copies. If Veterans Affairs records are pertinent, give regional office location and claim number.)*

10. I DESIRE TO APPEAR BEFORE THE BOARD IN WASHINGTON, D.C. *(At no expense to the Government) (X one)* | YES. THE BOARD WILL DETERMINE IF WARRANTED. | NO. CONSIDER MY APPLICATION BASED ON RECORDS AND EVIDENCE.

11. a. COUNSEL *(If any)* NAME *(Last, First, Middle Initial)* and ADDRESS *(Include ZIP Code)*
b. TELEPHONE *(Include Area Code)*
c. E-MAIL ADDRESS
d. FAX NUMBER *(Include Area Code)*

12. APPLICANT MUST SIGN IN ITEM 15 BELOW. If the record in question is that of a deceased or incompetent person, **LEGAL PROOF OF DEATH OR INCOMPETENCY MUST ACCOMPANY THE APPLICATION.** If the application is signed by other than the applicant, indicate the name *(print)* _____ and relationship by marking one box below.

SPOUSE | WIDOW | WIDOWER | NEXT OF KIN | LEGAL REPRESENTATIVE | OTHER *(Specify)*

13. a. COMPLETE CURRENT ADDRESS *(Include ZIP Code)* OF APPLICANT OR PERSON IN ITEM 12 ABOVE *(Forward notification of all changes of address.)*
b. TELEPHONE *(Include Area Code)*
c. E-MAIL ADDRESS
d. FAX NUMBER *(Include Area Code)*

14. I MAKE THE FOREGOING STATEMENTS, AS PART OF MY CLAIM, WITH FULL KNOWLEDGE OF THE PENALTIES INVOLVED FOR WILLFULLY MAKING A FALSE STATEMENT OR CLAIM. *(U.S. Code, Title 18, Sections 287 and 1001, provide that an individual shall be fined under this title or imprisoned not more than 5 years, or both.)*

CASE NUMBER *(Do not write in this space.)*

15. SIGNATURE *(Applicant must sign here.)*

16. DATE SIGNED *(YYYYMMDD)*

DD FORM 149, SEP 2007   PREVIOUS EDITION IS OBSOLETE.   Adobe Designer 7.0

DD Form 149, Application for Correction of Military Record under the Provisions of Title 10 (back)

INSTRUCTIONS

1. All information should be typed or printed. Complete all applicable items. If the item is not applicable, enter "None."

2. If space is insufficient on the front of the form, use the "Remarks" box below for additional information or attach an additional sheet.

3. List all attachments and enclosures in item 9. Do not send original documents. Send clear, legible copies. Send copies of military documents and orders related to your request, if you have them available. Do not assume that they are all in your military record.

4. The applicant must exhaust all administrative remedies, such as corrective procedures and appeals provided in regulations, before applying to the Board of Corrections.

5. ITEM 5. State the specific correction of record desired. If possible, identify exactly what document or information in your record you believe to be erroneous or unjust and indicate what correction you want made to the document or information.

6. ITEM 6. In order to justify correction of a military record, it is necessary for you to show to the satisfaction of the Board by the evidence that you supply, or it must otherwise satisfactorily appear in the record, that the alleged entry or omission in the record was in error or unjust. Evidence, in addition to documents, may include affidavits or signed testimony of witnesses, executed under oath, and a brief of arguments supporting the application. All evidence not already included in your record must be submitted by you. The responsibility of securing evidence rests with you.

7. ITEM 8. U.S. Code, Title 10, Section 1552b, provides that no correction may be made unless a request is made within three years after the discovery of the error or injustice, but that the Board may excuse failure to file within three years after discovery if it finds it to be in the interest of justice.

8. ITEM 10. Personal appearance before the Board by you and your witnesses or representation by counsel is not required to ensure full and impartial consideration of your application. If the Board determines that a personal appearance is warranted and grants approval, appearance and representation are permitted before the Board at no expense to the government.

9. ITEM 11. Various veterans and service organizations furnish counsel without charge. These organizations prefer that arrangements for representation be made through local posts or chapters.

10. ITEM 12. The person whose record correction is being requested must sign the application. If that person is deceased or incompetent to sign, the application may be signed by a spouse, widow, widower, next of kin (son, daughter, mother, father, brother, or sister), or a legal representative that has been given power of attorney. Other persons may be authorized to sign for the applicant. Proof of death, incompetency, or power of attorney must accompany the application. Former spouses may apply in cases of Survivor Benefit Plan (SBP) issues.

11. For detailed information on application and Board procedures, see: Army Regulation 15-185 and www.arba.army.pentagon.mil; Navy - SECNAVINST.5420.193 and www.hq.navy.mil/bcnr/bcnr.htm; Air Force Instruction 36-2603, Air Force Pamphlet 36-2607, and www.afpc.randolph.af.mil/safmrbr; Coast Guard - Code of Federal Regulations, Title 33, Part 52.

MAIL COMPLETED APPLICATIONS TO APPROPRIATE ADDRESS BELOW

ARMY	NAVY AND MARINE CORPS
(For Active Duty Personnel) Army Board for Correction of Military Records 1901 South Bell Street, 2nd Floor Arlington, VA 22202-4508 **(For Other than Active Duty Personnel)** Army Review Boards Agency Support Division, St. Louis 9700 Page Avenue St. Louis, MO 63132-5200	Board for Correction of Naval Records 2 Navy Annex Washington, DC 20370-5100
AIR FORCE	**COAST GUARD**
Board for Correction of Air Force Records SAF/MRBR 550-C Street West, Suite 40 Randolph AFB, TX 78150-4742	Board for Correction of Military Records 245 Murray Lane Room 5126, Mail Stop #0900 Washington, DC 20528

17. REMARKS

DD FORM 149 (BACK), SEP 2007

DD Form 2293, Application for Former Spouse Payments from Retired Pay

APPLICATION FOR FORMER SPOUSE PAYMENTS FROM RETIRED PAY
(Please read instructions on back and the Privacy Act Statement before completing this form.)

OMB No. 0730-0008
OMB approval expires
Jan 31, 2011

FOR OFFICIAL USE

The public reporting burden for this collection of information is estimated to average 15 minutes per response, including the time for reviewing instructions, searching existing data sources, gathering and maintaining the data needed, and completing and reviewing the collection of information. Send comments regarding this burden estimate or any other aspect of this collection of information, including suggestions for reducing the burden, to the Department of Defense, Washington Headquarters Services, Executive Services Directorate, Information Management Division, 1155 Defense Pentagon, Washington, DC 20301-1155 (0704-0008). Respondents should be aware that notwithstanding any other provision of law, no person shall be subject to any penalty for failing to comply with a collection of information if it does not display a currently valid OMB control number.

PLEASE DO NOT RETURN YOUR FORM TO THE ABOVE ORGANIZATION. RETURN COMPLETED FORM TO THE APPROPRIATE SERVICE ADDRESS LISTED ON BACK.

PRIVACY ACT STATEMENT

AUTHORITY: Title 10 USC 1408; DoD 7000.14, Vol. 7B, Chapter 29; and EO 9397.

PRINCIPAL PURPOSE(S): To request direct payment through a Uniformed Service designated agent of court ordered child support, alimony, or division of property to a former spouse from the retired pay of a Uniformed Service member.

ROUTINE USE(S): In addition to those disclosures generally permitted under 5 U.S.C. Section 552a(b) of the Privacy Act, these records or information contained therein may specifically be disclosed outside the DoD as a routine use pursuant to 5 U.S.C. Section 552a(b)(3) as follows: Records are provided to the Internal Revenue Service for normal wage and tax withholding purposes. The "Blanket Routine Uses" published at the beginning of the DoD compilation of systems of records notices also apply.

DISCLOSURE: Voluntary; however, failure to provide requested information may delay or make impossible processing this direct payment request.

1. APPLICANT IDENTIFICATION	2. SERVICE MEMBER IDENTIFICATION
a. NAME *(As appears on court order) (Last, First, Middle Initial)*	a. NAME *(Last, First, Middle Initial)*
b. CURRENT NAME *(Last, First, Middle Initial)*	b. BRANCH OF SERVICE
c. SOCIAL SECURITY NUMBER	c. SOCIAL SECURITY NUMBER
d. TELEPHONE NUMBER *(Include Area Code)*	d. TELEPHONE NUMBER *(Include Area Code) (If known)*
e. EMAIL ADDRESS	e. EMAIL ADDRESS *(If known)*
f. ADDRESS *(Street, City, State, ZIP Code)*	f. ADDRESS *(Street, City, State, ZIP Code) (If known)*

3. REQUEST STATEMENT

I request direct payment from the retired pay for one or more of the following categories of the above named Uniformed Service member based on the enclosed court order. I acknowledge that the payment priority will be (1) division of property; (2) child support; and (3) alimony unless I designate otherwise in Item 4.e.

I request payment of:

(1) A division of property in the amount of $ _____ , or _____ percent of disposable retired pay per month.

(2) Child support in the amount of $ _____ per month.

(3) Alimony, spousal support or maintenance in the amount of $ _____ , or _____ percent of disposable retired pay per month.

I certify that any request for current child and/or spousal support is not being collected under any other wage withholding or garnishment procedure authorized by statute. Furthermore, I certify that the court order has not been amended, superseded or set aside and is not subject to appeal. As a condition precedent to payment, I agree to refund all overpayments and that they are otherwise recoverable and subject to involuntary collection from me or my estate, and I will notify the appropriate agent (as listed on back) if the operative court order, upon which payment is based, is vacated, modified, or set aside. I also agree to notify the appropriate agent (as listed on back) of a change in eligibility for payments. This includes notice of my remarriage, if under the terms of the court order or the laws of the jurisdiction where it was issued, remarriage causes the payments to be reduced or terminated; or notice of a change in eligibility for child support payments by reason of the death, emancipation, adoption, or attainment of majority of a child whose support is provided through direct payments from retired pay. I hereby acknowledge that any payment to me must be paid from disposable retired pay as defined by the statute and implementing regulations.

DD FORM 2293, FEB 2008   PREVIOUS EDITION IS OBSOLETE.   Adobe Professional 7.0

DD Form 2293, Application for Former Spouse Payments from Retired Pay (back)

90 Day Limit

4. I HAVE ENCLOSED ALL PERTINENT DOCUMENTATION TO INCLUDE: *(X as applicable)*

a. A copy of the operative court order and other accompanying documents that provide for payment of child support, alimony or a division of retired pay as property, containing a certification dated by the clerk of the court within 90 days preceding the date the application is received by the designated agent.

b. Evidence of the date(s) of my marriage to the member if the application is for the direct payment of a division of the member's disposable retired pay as property.

c. If payment request includes child support, give name(s) and birth date(s) of child(ren):

(1) NAME OF CHILD *(Last, First, Middle Initial)*	(2) DATE OF BIRTH *(YYYYMMDD)*

d. If applying under Title 10 U.S.C. 1408(h), Dependent Victims of Abuse provision, in addition to 4.a. above, enclose both a copy of the member's court martial order and the member's statement of service.

e. Other information *(please identify)* or remarks.

5a. APPLICANT'S SIGNATURE	b. DATE SIGNED *(YYYYMMDD)*

INSTRUCTIONS FOR COMPLETION OF DD FORM 2293

GENERAL. These instructions govern an application for direct payment from retired pay of a Uniformed Service member in response to court ordered child support, alimony, or a division of property, under the authority of 10 USC 1408.

SERVICE OF APPLICATION. You may serve the application by mail on the appropriate Uniformed Service designated agent. The Uniformed Services' designated agents are:

(1) **ARMY, NAVY, AIR FORCE, AND MARINE CORPS:** Attn: DFAS-HGA/CL, Assistant General Counsel for Garnishment Operations, P.O. Box 998002, Cleveland, OH 44199-8002. Application may also be served by fax to 877-622-5930 (toll-free) or (216) 522-6960.

(2) **COAST GUARD:** Commanding Officer (1GL), United States Coast Guard, Personnel Service Center, 444 S.E. Quincy Street, Topeka, KS 66683-3591. Application may also be served by fax to 785-339-3788.

(3) **PUBLIC HEALTH SERVICE:** Attn: Retired Pay Section, CB, Division of Commissioned Personnel, PUBLIC HEALTH SERVICE, Room 4-50, 5600 Fishers Lane, Rockville, MD 20857-0001.

(4) **NATIONAL OCEANIC AND ATMOSPHERIC ADMINISTRATION:** Same as U.S. Coast Guard.

IMPORTANT NOTE: Making a false statement or claim against the United States Government is punishable. The penalty for willfully making a false claim or false statement is a maximum fine of $10,000 or maximum imprisonment of 5 years or both (18 USC 287 and 1001).

ITEM 1.
a. Enter full name as it appears on the court order. Applicant's signature required; the form may not be signed by a member or attorney.
b. Enter current name if different than it appears on court order.
c. Enter Social Security Number.
d. Enter telephone number.
e. Enter email address, if applicable.
f. Enter current address. Failure to apprise DFAS of address changes may result in the suspension of payments.

ITEM 2.
a. Enter member's full name as it appears on the court order.
b. Enter member's branch of service.
c. Enter member's Social Security Number.
d. Enter member's telephone number, if known.
e. Enter member's email address, if known.
f. Enter member's current address, if known.

ITEM 3. Read the Request Statement carefully.

ITEM 4. A certified copy of a court order can be obtained from the court that issued the court order. Other documents include, but are not limited to, final divorce decree, property settlement order, and any appellate court orders. If the court order does not state that the former spouse was married to the member for ten years or more while the member performed ten years creditable service and the request is for payment of a division of property, the applicant must provide evidence to substantiate the ten years' marriage condition. Additional evidence must show that the ten years' requirement has been met, including: Uniformed Service orders, marriage certificate, and other documents that establish the period of marriage. Other information or documents included with the request should be clearly identified by the document's title and date. Remarks may be provided to clarify specific points.

DD FORM 2293 (BACK), FEB 2008

DD Form 2656, Data for Payment of Retired Personnel

DATA FOR PAYMENT OF RETIRED PERSONNEL

PRIVACY ACT STATEMENT

AUTHORITY: 10 U.S.C. Chapter 73, subchapters II and III; DoD Instruction 1332.42, Survivor Annuity Program Administration, DoD Financial Management Regulation, Volume 7B, Chapter 42; and E.O. 9397 (SSN).

PRINCIPAL PURPOSE(S): To collect information needed to establish a retired/retainer pay account, including designation of beneficiaries for unpaid retired pay, state tax withholding election, information on dependents, and to establish a Survivor Benefit Plan election.

ROUTINE USE(S): Disclosures are made to the Department of Veterans Affairs (DVA) regarding establishments, changes and discontinuing of DVA compensation to retirees and annuitants.

To former spouses for purposes of providing information, consistent with the requirements of 10 U.S.C. Section 1450(f)(3), regarding Survivor Benefit Plan coverage.

To spouses for purposes of providing information, consistent with the requirements of 10 U.S.C. Section 1448(a), regarding Survivor Benefit Plan coverage.

DISCLOSURE: Voluntary; however, failure to provide requested information will result in delays in initiating retired/retainer pay.

INSTRUCTIONS

GENERAL.

1. Read these instructions and Privacy Act Statement carefully before completing the data form.

2. The Defense Finance and Accounting Service (DFAS) - Cleveland will establish your retired/retainer pay account based on the data provided on the form and your retirement/transfer orders. Your personnel office, disbursing/finance office, and SBP Counselor will assist you in the proper completion and submission of this form. You should maintain these instructions along with a copy of the form as a permanent record of your pay data. Please complete the form by typing or printing in ink.

3. Ensure that you promptly advise DFAS - Cleveland of changes to your marital/family status and any changes to your correspondence address and direct deposit information (or your Reserve Component if a gray area retiree).

SECTION I - PAY IDENTIFICATION.

ITEMS 1 and 2. Self-explanatory.

ITEM 3. If you are retiring from active duty, enter the date you transfer to the Fleet Reserve or date of retirement. If you are a Reserve member qualified to retire under 10 U.S. Code, Chapter 1223, enter either the date of your 60th birthday or, a later date on which you desire to begin receiving retired pay.

ITEMS 4 and 5. Self-explanatory.

ITEM 6. Enter the address and telephone number (include area code) where you can be contacted.

SECTION II - DIRECT DEPOSIT/ELECTRONIC FUND TRANSFER INFORMATION.

This section must be completed. Your net retired/retainer pay must be sent to your financial institution by direct deposit/electronic fund transfer (DD/EFT).

ITEMS 7 through 10. If you are directing your retired pay to the same account number and financial institution to which you directed your active duty pay, annotate Items 7 through 10 "SAME AS ACTIVE DUTY". If you have a copy of the Direct Deposit Authorization form used to establish your DD/EFT for your active duty pay, attach a copy to this form.

If you are not currently on DD/EFT or are a Reservist, you must complete Items 7 through 10. Provide the nine digit Routing Transit Number (RTN) of your financial institution in Item 7. The RTN is the nine digit number located in the lower left-hand corner of either your checks or check deposit tickets. If you still are unable to obtain the RTN, you will have to contact your financial institution to which you want your retired/retainer pay directed and request the RTN. Also, indicate whether your account is (S) for Savings or (C) for Checking account in Item 8, your account number in Item 9, and your financial institution name and address in Item 10.

SECTION III - SEPARATION PAYMENT INFORMATION.

ITEM 11. Complete if you are retiring from active duty or a member/former member of the Reserve Component not on active duty retiring at age 60.

11.a. through 11.c. Complete if you received any type of separation bonus. In Item 11.a, enter an X in the YES block. In Item 11.b., enter "SE" for Severance Pay, "SP" for Separation Pay, "VSI" for Voluntary Separation Incentive, and "SSB" for Special Separation Bonus. In Item 11.c., enter the lump-sum gross amount for Severance, Separation and Special Separation Bonus payments and the annual installment gross amount for Voluntary Separation Incentive payments. Be sure to attach a copy of the orders that authorized the payment and a copy of your DD Form 214.

SECTION IV - MEMBER OF THE RESERVE COMPONENT.

ITEM 12. Complete if you are a member/former member of a Reserve Component, not on active duty, retiring at age 60.

SECTION V - DESIGNATION OF BENEFICIARIES FOR UNPAID RETIRED PAY.

ITEM 13. Upon your death, 10 U.S. Code Section 2771 provides that any pay due and unpaid will be paid to the surviving person highest on the following list: (1) beneficiary(ies) designated in writing; (2) your spouse; (3) your children and their descendants, by representation; (4) your parents in equal parts, or if either is dead, the survivor; (5) the legal representative of your estate, and (6) person(s) entitled under the law of your domicile. Therefore, if you choose to designate a beneficiary or beneficiaries, you must complete Items 13.a. through 13.e. If you designate multiple beneficiaries, you can either provide a SHARE percentage to be paid to each person or leave the SHARE percentage blank. If you leave the SHARE percentage blank, any retired pay you are owed when you die will be divided equally among your designated beneficiaries. If you list more than one person with a 100% SHARE, the beneficiaries will be paid in the order as you list them on the form. If, for example, you designate two beneficiaries, then the SHARE percentage must either be 100% for each beneficiary, or the SHARE percentages when added together must equal 100%. If you designate more than one person, and the total percentage designated is greater than 100%, the person listed first is considered the primary beneficiary. Use the Remarks section for additional beneficiary information.

If you do not designate a beneficiary or beneficiaries in Item 13, or all designated beneficiaries have died before the date of your death, any unpaid retired pay will be paid to the living person or persons in the highest category of beneficiary listed above, as required by law.

SECTION VI - FEDERAL INCOME TAX WITHHOLDING INFORMATION.

Complete this section after determining your allowed exemptions with the aid of your disbursing/finance office, or from the instructions available on IRS Form W-4, or other available IRS publications. Leave Items 14 through 16 blank if completing Item 17.

ITEM 14. Mark the status you desire to claim.

ITEM 15. Enter the number of exemptions claimed.

ITEM 16. Enter the dollar amount of additional Federal income tax you desire withheld from each month's pay. Leave blank if you do not desire additional withholding.

ITEM 17. Enter the word "EXEMPT" in this item only if you meet all the following criteria: (1) you had no Federal income tax liability in the prior year; (2) you anticipate no Federal income tax liability this year; and (3) you therefore desire no Federal income tax to be withheld from your retired/retainer pay.

NOTE: You must file a new exemption claim form with DFAS - Cleveland by February 15th of each year for which you claim exemption from withholding.

DD FORM 2656 INSTRUCTIONS, APR 2009   PREVIOUS EDITION IS OBSOLETE   Adobe Professional 8.0

DD Form 2656, Data for Payment of Retired Personnel (back)

INSTRUCTIONS (Continued)

SECTION VI (Continued)

ITEM 18. If you are not a U.S. citizen, provide, on an additional sheet, a list of all periods of ACTIVE DUTY served in the continental U.S., Alaska, and Hawaii. Indicate periods of service by year and month only. List only service at shore activities; do not report service aboard a ship.
For example:
FROM (Year/Month)   DUTY STATION   TO (Year/Month)
1994/02   NAVSTA, Norfolk, VA   1995/01

NOTE: This information may affect the determination as to that portion of retired/retainer pay which is taxable in accordance with the Internal Revenue Code, if you will maintain your permanent residence outside the U.S., Alaska, or Hawaii.

SECTION VII - VOLUNTARY STATE TAX WITHHOLDING.

NOTE: Complete this section only if you want monthly state tax withholding. If you choose not to have a monthly deduction, you remain liable for state taxes, if applicable.

ITEM 19. Enter the name of the state for which you desire state tax withheld.

ITEM 20. Enter the dollar amount you want deducted from your monthly retired/retainer pay. This amount must not be less than $10.00 and must be in whole dollars (Example: $50.00, not $50.25).

ITEM 21. Enter only if different from the address in Item 6.

SECTION VIII - DEPENDENCY INFORMATION.

This information is needed by DFAS to determine SBP costs, annuities and options, and to maintain your account in special circumstances at the time of death.

ITEM 22.a. Provide your spouse's name. If none, enter "N/A" and proceed to Item 25.

ITEMS 22.b. through 24. Provide the requested information about your spouse. In Item 24, if marriage occurred outside the United States, include city, province, and name of country.

ITEM 25. If you do not have dependent children, enter "N/A" in this item. If you do have dependent children, provide the requested information. Designate which children resulted from marriage to former spouse, if any, by indicating (FS) after the relationship in column d.

25.e. A disabled child is an **unmarried** child who meets one of the following conditions: a child who has become incapable of self support before the age of 18, or, a child who has become incapable of self support after the age of 18 but before age 22 while a full time student. Attach documentation. Enter Yes or No as appropriate.

SECTION IX - SURVIVOR BENEFIT PLAN (SBP) ELECTION.

It is very important that you are counseled and are fully aware of your options under SBP. You may discontinue your SBP participation within one year after the second anniversary of the commencement of retired/retainer pay. Termination of SBP is effective the first of the month after DFAS-Cleveland receives the SBP disenrollment request. There will be no refund of SBP costs paid for the period before the SBP disenrollment. If you make no election, maximum coverage will be established for all eligible family members (spouse and/or children). It is highly advisable to complete this part in the presence of your SBP counselor.
Members qualified to retire under 10 U.S. Code 1223 after 20 qualifying years of service, who either elected Reserve Component Survivor Benefit Plan (RCSBP) or who received automatic coverage under RCSBP must attach a copy of the RCSBP election or the notification of coverage to this form. Do not complete Items 26 through 28 as that election is permanent. However, Reserve members who declined SBP until age 60 must complete Items 26 through 28 (and Items 32 and 33 if applicable). If you elected either Immediate (Option C) or Deferred (Option B) RCSBP coverage and the elected beneficiary is no longer eligible, annotate this in the Remarks section and provide supporting documentation with this form.

ITEM 26. Complete if you are retiring from active duty or if you are a reservist (retiring under 10 U.S. Code, Chapter 1223) who declined RCSBP. You may only select one item.

SECTION IX (Continued)

26.a. through 26.c. Mark the applicable item that indicates the beneficiaries you desire to cover under SBP. In Items a. and c., you MUST indicate whether you do or do not have eligible dependents.

ITEM 26.d. Mark if you are not married and desire coverage for a person with an insurable interest in you, and provide the requested information about that person in Item 28. An election of this type must be based on your full gross retired/retainer pay. If the person is a non-relative or as distantly related as a cousin, attach evidence that the person has a financial interest in the continuance of your life. Under provisions of Public Law 103-337, you are permitted to withdraw from insurable interest coverage at any time. Such a withdrawal will be effective on the first day of the month following the month the request is received by DFAS - Cleveland. Therefore, no refund of SBP costs collected before the effective date of the withdrawal will be paid.

26.e. and 26.f. Mark Item 26.e. if you desire coverage for a former spouse. Mark Item 26.f. if you desire coverage for a former spouse and dependent child(ren) of that marriage, and provide the requested information about these children in Item 25 as appropriate. Provide a certified photocopy of final decree that includes separation agreement or property settlement which discusses SBP for former spouse coverage. The DD Form 2656-1, "Survivor Benefit Plan (SBP) Election Statement for Former Spouse Coverage," must also be completed and accompany the completed DD Form 2656 to DFAS - Cleveland.

26.g. Mark if you do not desire coverage under SBP. If married and declining coverage, Items 32 and 33 of Section XII must be completed.

ITEM 27.a. Mark if you desire the coverage to be based on your full gross retired/retainer pay.

27.b. Mark if you desire the coverage to be based on a reduced portion of your retired/retainer pay. This reduced amount may not be less than $300.00. If your gross retired/retainer pay is less than $300.00, the full gross pay is automatically used as the base amount. Enter the desired amount in the space provided to the right of this item. Proceed to Section XII, if married.

27.c. Used by a REDUX member who wants coverage based on actual retired pay received under REDUX. If this option is selected, proceed to Section XII, if married.

27.d. Mark if you desire the higher threshold amount in effect on the date of your retirement.

ITEM 28. Enter the information for insurable interest beneficiary.

SECTION X - REMARKS.

ITEM 29. Reference each entry by item number. Continue on separate sheets of paper if more space is needed.

SECTION XI - CERTIFICATION.

Read the statement carefully, then sign your name and indicate the date of signature. For your SBP election to be valid, you must sign and date the form prior to the effective date of your retirement/transfer. A witness cannot be named as beneficiary in Sections V, VIII, or IX.

SECTION XII - SURVIVOR BENEFIT PLAN SPOUSE CONCURRENCE.

Title 10 U.S. Code, Section 1448 requires that an otherwise eligible spouse concur if the member declines to elect SBP coverage, elects less than maximum coverage, or elects child only coverage. Therefore, a member with an eligible spouse upon retirement, who elects any combination other than items 26.a. or 26.b. **and** 27.a., must obtain the spouse's concurrence in Section XII. A Notary Public must be the witness. In addition, the witness cannot be named beneficiary in Section V, VIII, or IX. Spouse's concurrence must be obtained and dated on or after the date of the member's election, but before the retirement/transfer date. If concurrence is not obtained when required, maximum coverage will be established for your spouse and child(ren) if appropriate.

DD FORM 2656 INSTRUCTIONS (BACK), APR 2009

DD Form 2656, Data for Payment of Retired Personnel

DATA FOR PAYMENT OF RETIRED PERSONNEL
(Please read Instructions and Privacy Act Statement before completing form.)

SECTION I - PAY IDENTIFICATION

1. NAME *(LAST, First, Middle Initial)*	2. SSN	3. RETIREMENT/ TRANSFER DATE *(YYYYMMDD)*	4. RANK/PAY GRADE/ BRANCH OF SERVICE	5. DATE OF BIRTH *(YYYYMMDD)*

6. CORRESPONDENCE ADDRESS *(Ensure DFAS - Cleveland Center is advised whenever your correspondence address changes.)*

a. STREET *(Include apartment number)*	b. CITY	c. STATE	d. ZIP CODE	e. TELEPHONE *(Incl. area code)*

SECTION II - DIRECT DEPOSIT/ELECTRONIC FUND TRANSFER (DD/EFT) INFORMATION *(See Instructions)*

7. ROUTING NUMBER *(See Instructions)*	8. TYPE OF ACCOUNT *(Savings (S) or Checking (C))*	9. ACCOUNT NUMBER *(See Instructions)*

10. FINANCIAL INSTITUTION

a. NAME	b. STREET ADDRESS	c. CITY	d. STATE	e. ZIP CODE

SECTION III - SEPARATION PAYMENT INFORMATION

11. Complete if you have received any one of the payment types listed in 11.a.

a. DID YOU RECEIVE SEVERANCE PAY (SE), READJUSTMENT PAY (RP), SEPARATION PAY (SP), VOLUNTARY SEPARATION INCENTIVE (VSI), OR SPECIAL SEPARATION BONUS (SSB)? *(X one. If "Yes," attach a copy of the orders which authorized the payment, and a copy of the DD Form 214.)* YES ☐ NO ☐	b. TYPE OF PAYMENT	c. GROSS AMOUNT

SECTION IV - MEMBER OF THE RESERVE COMPONENT

12. Complete only if a member or former member of the reserve component not on active duty retiring at age 60.

a. DO YOU RECEIVE OR WERE YOU RECEIVING ON THE DATE OF RETIREMENT ANY VA COMPENSATION FOR DISABILITY? *(X one)* YES ☐ NO ☐	b. EFFECTIVE DATE OF PAYMENT *(YYYYMMDD)*	c. MONTHLY AMOUNT OF PAYMENT

SECTION V - DESIGNATION OF BENEFICIARIES FOR UNPAID RETIRED PAY *(See INSTRUCTIONS)*

13. Complete this section if you wish to designate a beneficiary or beneficiaries to receive any unpaid retired pay you are due at death. *(Continue in Section X, "Remarks," if necessary.)*

a. NAME *(Last, First, Middle Initial)*	b. SSN	c. ADDRESS *(Street, City, State, ZIP Code)*	d. RELATIONSHIP	e. SHARE
				%
				%
				%
				%
				%

SECTION VI - FEDERAL INCOME TAX WITHHOLDING INFORMATION *(Submit information in Items 14 - 17 in lieu of IRS Form W-4 for tax purposes.)*

14. MARITAL STATUS *(X one)* ☐ SINGLE ☐ MARRIED ☐ MARRIED BUT WITHHOLD AT HIGHER SINGLE RATE	15. TOTAL NUMBER OF EXEMPTIONS CLAIMED	16. ADDITIONAL WITHHOLDING *(Optional)*	17. I CLAIM EXEMPTION FROM WITHHOLDING *(Enter "EXEMPT")*	18. ARE YOU A UNITED STATES CITIZEN? *(X one)* YES ☐ NO ☐ *(See Instructions)*

SECTION VII - VOLUNTARY STATE TAX WITHHOLDING INFORMATION *(Complete only if monthly withholding is desired.)*

19. STATE DESIGNATED TO RECEIVE TAX	20. MONTHLY AMOUNT *(Whole dollar amount not less than $10.00)*	21. RESIDENCE ADDRESS *(If different from address listed in Item 6)*			
		a. STREET *(Include apartment number)*	b. CITY	c. STATE	d. ZIP CODE

SECTION VIII - DEPENDENCY INFORMATION *(This section must be completed regardless of SBP Election.)*

22. SPOUSE

a. NAME *(Last, First, Middle Initial)*	b. SSN	c. DATE OF BIRTH *(YYYYMMDD)*	23. DATE OF MARRIAGE *(YYYYMMDD)*	24. PLACE OF MARRIAGE *(See Instructions)*

25. DEPENDENT CHILDREN *(Indicate which child(ren) resulted from marriage to former spouse by entering (FS) after relationship in column d. Continue in Section X, "Remarks," if necessary.)*

a. NAME *(Last, First, Middle Initial)*	b. DATE OF BIRTH *(YYYYMMDD)*	c. SSN	d. RELATIONSHIP *(Son, daughter, stepson, etc.)*	e. DISABLED? *(Yes/No)*

DD FORM 2656, APR 2009

DD Form 2656, Data for Payment of Retired Personnel (back)

MEMBER NAME *(LAST, First, Middle Initial)* **SSN**

SECTION IX - SURVIVOR BENEFIT PLAN (SBP) ELECTION
(It is recommended that you see your Survivor Benefit Plan counselor before making an election.)

26. BENEFICIARY CATEGORY(IES) *(X only one item) (See Instructions and Section XI.)*

- a. I ELECT COVERAGE FOR SPOUSE ONLY.   I (X) ☐   DO ☐   DO NOT HAVE DEPENDENT CHILD(REN).
- b. I ELECT COVERAGE FOR SPOUSE AND CHILD(REN).
- c. I ELECT COVERAGE FOR CHILD(REN) ONLY.   I (X) ☐   DO ☐   DO NOT HAVE A SPOUSE.
- d. I ELECT COVERAGE FOR THE PERSON NAMED IN ITEM 28 WHO HAS AN INSURABLE INTEREST IN ME *(See Instructions).*
- e. I ELECT COVERAGE FOR MY FORMER SPOUSE *(See Instructions and complete DD 2656-1, "Survivor Benefit Plan (SBP) Election Statement for Former Spouse Coverage").*
- f. I ELECT COVERAGE FOR MY FORMER SPOUSE AND DEPENDENT CHILD(REN) OF THAT MARRIAGE *(See Instructions and complete DD 2656-1, "Survivor Benefit Plan (SBP) Election Statement for Former Spouse Coverage").*
- g. I ELECT NOT TO PARTICIPATE IN SBP.   I (X) ☐   DO ☐   DO NOT HAVE ELIGIBLE DEPENDENTS UNDER THE PLAN.

27. LEVEL OF COVERAGE *(X one. Complete UNLESS 26.d. or 26.g. was selected above. See Instructions.)*

- a. I ELECT COVERAGE BASED ON FULL GROSS PAY. *(If I elected the Career Status Bonus and REDUX, full gross pay is the amount of retired pay I would have received had I NOT elected the Career Status Bonus.)*
- b. I ELECT COVERAGE WITH A REDUCED BASE AMOUNT OF $_____   *(See Instructions).*
- c. REDUX MEMBERS ONLY: I ELECT COVERAGE BASED ON MY FULL GROSS PAY UNDER REDUX. I UNDERSTAND THAT THIS REPRESENTS A REDUCED BASE AMOUNT AND REQUIRES SPOUSE CONCURRENCE. *(See Instructions).*
- d. I ELECT COVERAGE BASED ON THE THRESHOLD AMOUNT IN EFFECT ON THE DATE OF RETIREMENT.

28. INSURABLE INTEREST BENEFICIARY

a. NAME *(Last, First, Middle Initial)*	b. SSN	c. RELATIONSHIP	d. DATE OF BIRTH *(YYYYMMDD)*
e. STREET ADDRESS *(Include apartment number)*		f. CITY	g. STATE	h. ZIP CODE

SECTION X - REMARKS
29. Use this section to continue an item or make additional comments. Attach separate sheets if more space is needed.

SECTION XI - CERTIFICATION
30. MEMBER.
Under penalties of perjury, I certify that the number of withholding exemptions claimed does not exceed the number to which I am entitled, and that all statements on this form are made with full knowledge of the penalties for making false statements *(18 U.S. Code 287 and 1001 provide for a penalty of not more than $10,000 fine, or 5 years in prison, or both).*
Also, I have been counseled that I can terminate SBP participation, with my spouse's written concurrence, within one year after the second anniversary of commencement of retired pay. However, if I exercise my option to terminate the SBP, future participation is barred.

a. SIGNATURE	b. DATE SIGNED *(YYYYMMDD)*

31.a. WITNESS NAME *(Last, First, Middle Initial)*	b. SIGNATURE	c. DATE SIGNED *(YYYYMMDD)*
d. UNIT OR ORGANIZATION ADDRESS *(Include room number)*	e. CITY/BASE OR POST	f. STATE	g. ZIP CODE

SECTION XII - SBP SPOUSE CONCURRENCE
(Required when member is married and elects child(ren) only coverage, does not elect full spouse coverage, or declines coverage. The date of the spouse's signature in item 32.b MUST NOT be before the date of the member's signature in item 30.b, above.) The spouse's signature MUST be notarized.

32. SPOUSE. I hereby concur with the Survivor Benefit Plan election made by my spouse. I have received information that explains the options available and the effects of those options. I know that retired pay stops on the day the retiree dies. I have signed this statement of my free will.

a. SIGNATURE	b. DATE SIGNED *(YYYYMMDD)*

33. NOTARY WITNESS.
On this _____ day of _____, 20 _____, before me, the undersigned notary public,

personally appeared *(Name of spouse (block 32.a.)* _____, provided to me through

satisfactory evidence of identification, which were _____, to be

the person whose name is signed in block 32.a. of this document in my presence.

(Signature of Notary) _____   My commission expires: _____

NOTARY SEAL

DD FORM 2656 (BACK), APR 2009

DD Form 2656-1, Survivor Benefit Plan Election Statement for Former Spouse Coverage

SURVIVOR BENEFIT PLAN (SBP) ELECTION STATEMENT FOR FORMER SPOUSE COVERAGE
(Please read Privacy Act Statement and Instructions on back BEFORE completing form.)

SECTION I - ELECTION OF COVERAGE - RETIRED MEMBERS ONLY
RETIRED MEMBERS changing from spouse or spouse and child(ren) coverage to former spouse or former spouse and child(ren) coverage.
RETIRING MEMBERS must complete required section of DD Form 2656 to elect coverage for former spouse or former spouse and child(ren).

1. DUE TO DIVORCE, CHANGE MY SBP COVERAGE TO *(X one)*
   - FORMER SPOUSE
   - FORMER SPOUSE AND CHILD(REN)*

   *NOTE: If an election included child(ren), list in Item 10 ONLY the child(ren) resulting from the marriage of the member and the former spouse. Include the date of birth and SSN for each child.

SECTION II - RETIRED AND RETIRING MEMBERS | YES | NO

2. ARE YOU CURRENTLY MARRIED? *(X one)*

3. IS THIS ELECTION BEING MADE PURSUANT TO THE REQUIREMENTS OF A COURT ORDER? *(X one)*

4. IS THIS ELECTION BEING MADE PURSUANT TO A WRITTEN AGREEMENT PREVIOUSLY ENTERED INTO VOLUNTARILY AS PART OF OR INCIDENT TO A PROCEEDING OF DIVORCE, DISSOLUTION OR ANNULMENT? *(X one)*

5. IF "YES" TO ITEM 4, WAS SUCH A VOLUNTARY WRITTEN AGREEMENT INCORPORATED IN, RATIFIED, OR APPROVED BY A COURT ORDER? *(X one)*

6. DATE OF BIRTH OF FORMER SPOUSE *(YYYYMMDD)*
7. DATE MARRIED TO FORMER SPOUSE *(YYYYMMDD)*
8. DATE DIVORCED FROM FORMER SPOUSE *(YYYYMMDD)*
9. HAS FORMER SPOUSE REMARRIED? *(If "YES", give date - YYYYMMDD)* NO | YES

10. DEPENDENT CHILDREN *(To be completed only by retired members electing former spouse and child(ren) coverage. Continue in Item 11, "Remarks," if necessary.)*

a. NAME *(Last, First, Middle Initial)*	b. DATE OF BIRTH *(YYYYMMDD)*	c. SSN	d. RELATIONSHIP *(Son, daughter, etc.)*	e. DISABLED? *(Yes/No)*

11. REMARKS

SECTION III - CERTIFICATIONS - RETIRED AND RETIRING MEMBERS AND FORMER SPOUSES

12. MEMBER		13. FORMER SPOUSE TO BE COVERED	
a. NAME *(Last, First, Middle Initial)*	b. SSN	a. NAME *(Last, First, Middle Initial)*	b. SSN
c. SIGNATURE		c. SIGNATURE	
d. ADDRESS (1) Street *(Include apartment number)*		d. ADDRESS (1) Street *(Include apartment number)*	
(2) City	(3) State	(4) ZIP Code	(2) City	(3) State	(4) ZIP Code

14. MEMBER'S WITNESS				15. FORMER SPOUSE'S WITNESS			
a. NAME *(Last, First, Middle Initial)*				a. NAME *(Last, First, Middle Initial)*			
b. SIGNATURE		c. DATE SIGNED		b. SIGNATURE		c. DATE SIGNED	
d. ADDRESS (1) Street *(Include apartment number)*				d. ADDRESS (1) Street *(Include apartment number)*			
(2) City	(3) State	(4) ZIP Code		(2) City	(3) State	(4) ZIP Code	

DD FORM 2656-1, APR 2009 — PREVIOUS EDITION IS OBSOLETE. — Adobe Professional 8.0

DD Form 2656-1, Survivor Benefit Plan Election Statement for Former Spouse Coverage (back)

PRIVACY ACT STATEMENT

AUTHORITY: 10 U.S.C. Chapter 73, subchapter II; DoD Instruction 1332-42, Survivor Annuity Program Administration; DoD Financial Management Regulation, Volume 7B; and E.O. 9397 (SSN).

PRINCIPAL PURPOSE(S): To establish a Survivor Benefit Plan election for the eligible former spouse of a servicemember.

ROUTINE USE(S): To former spouses for purposes of providing information, consistent with the requirements of 10 U.S.Code, Section 1450(f)(3), regarding Survivor Benefit Plan coverage.

To spouses for purposes of providing information, consistent with the requirements of 10 U.S.Code, Section 1448(a), regarding Survivor Benefit Plan coverage.

DISCLOSURE: Voluntary; however, failure to furnish requested information may result in delay in initiating Survivor Benefit Plan coverage for a former spouse.

INSTRUCTIONS

GENERAL.

Type or print all information in ink.

RETIRED MEMBERS: Complete Sections I, II, and III. If electing former spouse and child(ren) coverage, provide information pertaining to eligible child(ren) in Item 10, "Dependent Children."

RETIRING MEMBERS: Complete Sections II and III, but make the election on DD Form 2656, "Data for Payment of Retired Personnel."

ALL MEMBERS AND FORMER SPOUSES must complete Section III.

When the form has been completed (ensure it is signed by both member and former spouse, and is properly witnessed), submit it to:

DFAS - US Military Retirement Pay
PO Box 7130
London, KY 40742-7130

Attach a certified copy of the divorce decree, amendment, or other documentation as described in Items 3, 4, and 5. If not received by DFAS within the first year following the date of divorce, the election will be invalid.

SECTION I.

ITEM 1. Retired member places an X in the appropriate block to indicate whether election is for former spouse, or former spouse with child(ren) coverage.

SECTION II.

ITEM 2. Indicate member's marital status by marking appropriate block.

ITEMS 3, 4, and 5. Mark the block that reflects legal basis for coverage.

ITEMS 6 and 7. Self-explanatory.

ITEM 8. Enter date of divorce decree, or amendment requiring SBP.

ITEM 9. Mark the appropriate block. If "Yes," provide the date that member's former spouse remarried. Former spouse may remarry after age 55 and eligibility will not be affected. If former spouse remarries before age 55, coverage is suspended and premiums are not deducted from member's retired pay for the duration of that marriage. If former spouse's marriage ends by death, divorce, or annulment, coverage will resume. Retiree or former spouse must notify DFAS of any changes in former spouse's marital status, providing appropriate documentation.

ITEM 10. Retired members electing former spouse and child(ren) must list eligible children in this section. Only children resulting from the marriage of the member and the former spouse are covered in a former spouse and child(ren) election. The former spouse is the primary beneficiary; children receive an annuity only if the former spouse remarries before age 55 or dies. Indicate in block 10.e. if the child is incapable of self support and attach substantiating documentation, if available. Eligible children of retiring members should be listed in Block 25 of DD Form 2656.

ITEM 11. This block may be used for comments or additional information not covered in the form.

SECTION III.

ITEMS 12 through 15. Self-explanatory.

DD FORM 2656-1 (BACK), APR 2009

DD Form 2656-10, Survivor Benefit Plan (SBP)/Reserve Component (RC) SBP Request for Deemed Election

SURVIVOR BENEFIT PLAN (SBP)/RESERVE COMPONENT (RC) SBP REQUEST FOR DEEMED ELECTION

OMB No. 0704-0448
OMB approval expires Apr 30, 2011

The public reporting burden for this collection of information is estimated to average 20 minutes per response, including the time for reviewing instructions, searching existing data sources, gathering and maintaining the data needed, and completing and reviewing the collection of information. Send comments regarding this burden estimate or any other aspect of this collection of information, including suggestions for reducing the burden, to the Department of Defense, Washington Headquarters Services, Executive Services Directorate, Information Management Division, 1155 Defense Pentagon, Washington, DC 20301-1155 (0704-0448). Respondents should be aware that notwithstanding any other provision of law, no person shall be subject to any penalty for failing to comply with a collection of information if it does not display a currently valid OMB control number.

PRIVACY ACT STATEMENT

AUTHORITY: 10 U.S.C. Chapter 73, subchapters II and III; DoD Instruction 1332.42, Survivor Annuity Program Administration; DoD Financial Management Regulation, Volume 7B, Chapter 43; and E.O. 9397 (SSN).

PRINCIPAL PURPOSE(S): Used by a former spouse to deem an election for Former Spouse SBP coverage.

ROUTINE USE(S): To former spouses for purposes of providing information, consistent with the requirements of 10 U.S.C. Section 1450(f)(2), regarding Survivor Benefit Plan coverage.

DISCLOSURE: Voluntary; however, failure to provide requested information within the first year following filing of the court order or filing which requires former spouse SBP coverage will result in delays in initiating, or denial of, former spouse SBP coverage.

INSTRUCTIONS

GENERAL.

1. Read these instructions carefully before completing the form. Please print legibly.

2. Ensure that you advise the finance center (see Item 3 below for address) of your marital status, correspondence and check address changes, at all times. Reserve Component former spouses must notify their personnel center (see Item 4 below for address) of their marital status and correspondence address at all times.

3. For those who are deeming an SBP election against a member who is currently serving on active duty or receiving retired pay, mail your election (certified or registered mail with return receipt requested is strongly recommended) to the appropriate Uniformed Service designated agent. The Uniformed Services' designated agents are:

(a) ARMY, NAVY, AIR FORCE and MARINE CORPS: Defense Finance and Accounting Service, U.S. Military Retirement Pay, P.O. Box 7130, London, KY 40742-7130;

(b) COAST GUARD: Commanding Officer (LGL), USCG Personnel Service Center, 444 S.E. Quincy Street, Topeka, KS 66683-3591;

(c) PUBLIC HEALTH SERVICE: Office of Commissioned Corps Support Services, Compensation Branch, 5600 Fishers Lane, Room 4-50, Rockville, MD 20857;

(d) NATIONAL OCEANIC AND ATMOSPHERIC ADMINISTRATION: Same as U.S. Coast Guard.

4. For those who are deeming an SBP election against a Reserve Component member who is not yet receiving retired pay (under age 60), mail your election (certified or registered mail with return receipt attached is strongly recommended) to the appropriate Branch of Service as follows:

(a) ARMY: Commander, Human Resources Command - St. Louis, ATTN: AHRC-PAP-T, 1 Reserve Way, St. Louis, MO 63132-5200;

(b) NAVY: Navy Reserve Personnel Center (PERS 912), 5722 Integrity Drive, Millington, TN 38054;

(c) AIR FORCE: Headquarters, ARPC/DPSSE, 6760 E. Irvington Place, Denver, CO 80250-4020;

(d) MARINE CORPS: Headquarters, U.S. Marine Corps, Separation & Retirement Branch (MMSR-6), 3280 Russell Road, Quantico, VA 22134-5103;

(e) COAST GUARD: Commanding Officer (LGL), USCG Personnel Service Center, 444 S.E. Quincy Street, Topeka, KS 66683-3591.

SECTION I - MEMBER IDENTIFICATION

1. MEMBER NAME *(Last, First, Middle Initial)*	2. SSN	3.a. BRANCH OF SERVICE	b. *(X one)* ACTIVE / RESERVE / NATIONAL GUARD
4. IS MEMBER RETIRED? YES / NO		5. IF YES, DATE OF RETIREMENT *(YYYYMMDD)*	

SECTION II - FORMER SPOUSE IDENTIFICATION

6. FORMER SPOUSE NAME *(Last, First, Middle Initial)*	7. SSN	8. ADDRESS *(Include ZIP Code)*	9. DATE OF BIRTH *(YYYYMMDD)*

10. MARRIAGE HISTORY

a. DATE MARRIED TO MEMBER *(Listed in Item 1 above) (YYYYMMDD)*	b. DATE OF DIVORCE *(YYYYMMDD)*	c. ARE YOU CURRENTLY MARRIED? YES / NO	d. IF YES, DATE OF CURRENT MARRIAGE *(YYYYMMDD)*

DD FORM 2656-10, APR 2009 PREVIOUS EDITION IS OBSOLETE. Adobe Professional 8.0

DD Form 2656-10, Survivor Benefit Plan (SBP)/ Reserve Component (RC) SBP Request for Deemed Election p.2

MEMBER NAME (Last, First, Middle Initial)	SSN

SECTION III - AUTHORITY TO REQUEST DEEMED SBP ELECTION

11. IS ELECTION MADE PURSUANT TO REQUIREMENTS OF COURT ORDER? *(If "Yes", attach a copy of the document.)* ☐ YES ☐ NO

12. IS ELECTION BEING MADE PURSUANT TO WRITTEN AGREEMENT PREVIOUSLY ENTERED INTO VOLUNTARILY AS PART OF OR INCIDENT TO A PROCEEDING OF DIVORCE, DISSOLUTION OR ANNULMENT? ☐ YES ☐ NO

NOTE: If you answered "No" to both 11 and 12, above, STOP. You are NOT eligible to request a Deemed SBP election.

13. IF "YES" TO QUESTION 12, WAS SUCH VOLUNTARY WRITTEN AGREEMENT INCORPORATED IN, RATIFIED, OR APPROVED BY A COURT ORDER? *(If "Yes, attach a copy of the document.)* ☐ YES ☐ NO

SECTION IV - DEPENDENT CHILDREN INFORMATION

14. LIST DEPENDENT CHILDREN *(If required to be covered under court order/agreement) (List only children resulting from the parties' marriage to each other.)*

a. NAME (Last, First, Middle Initial)	b. DATE OF BIRTH (YYYYMMDD)	c. SSN	d. RELATIONSHIP (Son, daughter, stepson, etc.)	e. DISABLED? (Yes/No)

15. REMARKS *(Use this space to further explain any item if necessary. Reference by item number.)*

SECTION V - FORMER SPOUSE SIGNATURE

16. SIGNATURE	17. DATE SIGNED (YYYYMMDD)

DD FORM 2656-10 (BACK), APR 2009

Contacts

CHCBP through TRICARE
Humana Military Health Services
Attn: CHCBP
PO Box 740072
Louisville, KY 40201
Phone: (800) 444-5445

DEERS
Defense Manpower Data Center (DMDC) Support Office
400 Gigling Road
Seaside, CA 93955-6771
Phone: (800) 538-9552

Legal Garnishment Dept
DFAS-GAG-CL,
PO Box 998002,
Cleveland, OH 44199
Phone: (216) 522-5096 or (888) 332-7411
Fax: (216) 522-6960 or (877) 622-5930

Military Pay
DFAS U.S. Military Retired Pay
PO Box 7130,
London KY 40742-7130
Phone (7am-7.30pm ET):
(800) 321-1080 or (216) 522-5977
Fax: (800) 469-6559 or (216) 522-6496

DFAS U.S. Military Annuitant Pay
Po Box 7131,
London KY 40742-7130
Phone: (800) 321-1080
Fax: (800) 982-8459

USAA
Divorce Specialist
Phone: (800) 531-8722 ext. 75007

Veterans Affairs
VA Benefits: (800) 827-1000
GI Bill: (888) 442-4551
Health Care: (877) 222-8387

Further Reading

Divorce and the Military II: A Comprehensive Guide for Service Members, Spouses and Attorneys, Marsha L. Thole and Frank W. Ault, CA: The American Retirees Association, 2003

The Military Divorce Handbook, A Practical Guide to Representing Military Personnel and Their Families, by Mark E. Sullivan, IL: American Bar Association, 2006

Internet Resources

As new information is released internet addresses often change. Please notify us if an internet Uniform Resource Locator (URL) referenced in this book is no longer found.

For additional current recommended sites visit:
http://www.militarydivorcetips.com/links.html

Index

A

abused spouses, 8, 70
accountants, x, 17
age 18
  GI Bill transfer, 53
  SBP, 146
  USAA transfer, 49
age 55, remarriage
  health care rules, 24–27
  SBP suspension, 146
age 60
  reservist health care, 16
  reservist SBP election, 158
age 70 for paid up SBP, 147–148
alimony, 4, 7–8, 41, 50–51, 65, 67
annuity. *See* Survivor Benefit Plan
Armed Forces Benefit Association, 52
arrears, 65

B

back pay. *See* retroactive pay
Basic Allowance for Housing (BAH), 51
Basic Allowance Subsistence (BAS), 51
beneficiary
  life insurance, 1, 52
  retirement pay (SBP/RCSBP), 6, 8, 25, 40, 66, 158–161, 164
Board of Corrections, 165, 167
bonus, 5, 6
BX. *See* exchange benefits

C

Career Status Bonus, 76–77, 114
car registration, 42, 49
Certificate of Creditable Coverage (CoCC), 19–20, 25, 28–29, 39
Certificate of Eligibility (VA loan), 56
checklists
  delay divorce, 5
  designated agent, 60
  discovery, 7
  divorce decree, 8
  divorce notification, 1
  divorce process, 6
  lawyer interview, 2
  remarriage, 8
  retirement award steps, 104, 122
  SBP comprehension, 142
  state comparison, 41
children. *See* dependent children
child support
  account set up, 72
  back pay, 65
  calculations, 51
  garnishment for, 8, 50–51, 140
  obligation and life insurance, 150
  priority of payments, 71
  state comparison, 4, 41
  USFSPA, 67
college (GI Bill), 55
commissary, 5, 8, 46, 101
community property, 89
Concurrent Retirement Disability Pay (CRDP), 87
confirmation letters
  retired pay, 133
  SBP, 160–163
  VA health care, 14
consent, 42–43, 144
Consumer Price Index (CPI), 76–77
Continued Health Care Benefit Program (CHCBP), 9–39
  18 month coverage, 11, 18
  18 month period prior, 23–24
  36 month coverage, 7–8, 12, 17–23, 149
  60 day application, 6, 17, 19–23, 30–32
  missed, 20
  unlimited coverage, 8, 12, 17–18, 23–27, 39, 51, 148–149
Continuing Exclusive Jurisdiction, 43
correction of administrative error, 166
Cost of Living Adjustment (COLA), 74–77
  hypothetical retired pay increase, 117
  language preventing, 74, 108
  table for past years, 77
Cost of Living Allowance (COLA), 74
court martial, 65
credit cards, 1
custodial parent ID cards, 10

D

date for division, 4, 41. *See also* rank at retirement; *See also* rank at divorce
date of divorce
  18 months prior for CHCBP, 24
  COLA increases after, 74–77
  hypothetical retired pay, 115–116
  marital share variation, 91, 97, 112
  reservist marital share, 92
  retired pay, 4, 41, 74, 83, 91–92, 94, 99–100, 105, 108, 110, 117
DD Forms. *See* forms
decimal rounding, 90
decree language. *See* language
deemed election for SBP, 142, 159–162, 168, 182–183
DEERS (Defense Enrollment Eligibility Reporting System), 10, 12, 55
delay divorce, 5
  for health care, 12, 16
  GI Bill, 55
  moving expenses, 45
  negotiated for benefits, 101
  promotions and line numbers, 102
dental, 10, 22
dependent children
  commissary, 46
  escort letter, 10
  health care, 10
  qualifying spouse for SBP, 143
  SBP beneficiaries, 141, 146
  TRICARE records access, 40
designated agent
  checklist for assistance, 60
DFAS (Defense Finance and Accounting Service), 59, 67, 184
direct deposit, 135, 139–140
disability pay, 8, 65, 78–87, 170
discovery process, 6–7
Dislocation Allowance (DLA), 45
disposable retired pay, x, 63, 65, 69, 74, 78. *See also* retired pay
domicile, 42–44

E

education, xi, 3. *See* GI Bill
eligibility (begin former spouse payments upon), 64, 113
employment, 10, 12–13, 148
  Civil Service, 8, 72
  Military Spouse Preference Program, 5, 47
escort letter, 10
examples
  50 percent limit rule, 69
  65 percent limit rule, 70
  COLA reduction, 76
  disability pay
    indemnification and taxes, 84
    waiving, 78
  disposable retired pay, 65, 145, 153
  divorce after retirement (former spouse percentage), 95
  language for division of pay, 104
  marital share, 90–92, 97
  priority of payments, 71
  reservist marital share, 92
  saving/losing retired pay division, 43
  SBP base amount, 145
  SBP processed incorrectly, 166
  SBP reimbursement, 153–157
  SBP tax benefit, 147
  service member not retired (former spouse percentage), 96
  tax benefits (disability and SBP), 169
exchange (BX/PX) benefits, 5, 8, 46, 101
exclusive jurisdiction. *See* Continuing Exclusive Jurisdiction (CEJ)

F

Federal Income Tax Withheld, 139
fixed amount, 73, 103, 108
fixed percentage, 73, 103, 108
former spouse
  defined, x
  percentage, 94, 105
  retired pay application, 133
  unmarried former spouse, 26
  unremarried former spouse, 26

forms
- DD Form 149, Application for Correction of Military Record, 168–169, 171
- DD Form 214, Certificate of Release or Discharge from Active Duty, 7, 14
- DD Form 1172, Application for Uniformed Services Identification Card DEERS Enrollment, 10
- DD Form 2293, Application for Former Spouse Payments from Retired Pay, 133, 134, 174–175
- DD Form 2656-1, Survivor Benefit Plan Election Statement for Former Spouse Coverage, 168, 180–181
- DD Form 2656-10, Survivor Benefit Plan (SBP)/Reserve Component (RC) SBP Request for Deemed Election, 168, 182–183
- DD Form 2656, Data for Payment of Retired Personnel, 159, 176–179
- DD Form 2837, CHCBP Application, 30–32
- Form 1099-R, Distributions From Pensions, Annuities, Retirement or Profit-Sharing Plans, IRAs, Insurance Contracts, etc., 68, 84, 169–170
- Form W-2, Wage and Tax Statement, 51
- Form W-4, Employee's Withholding Allowance Certificate, 7, 50
- Form W-4P, Withholding Certificate for Pension or Annuity Payments, 135, 169, 171
- VA Form 10-10EZ, Application for Health Benefits, 14

formula percentage language, 73, 109–110
formulas
- COLA adjustment (hypothetical retired pay), 117
- former spouse award
  - adjusting hypothetical
    - method A, 120
    - method B, 121
  - core formula for decree, 73
- former spouse percentage, 94
- High-3 Pay. *See herein* retired pay base
- marital share, 90
  - reservist, 92
- present value (converting hypothetical award), 117
- retired pay amount, 114
- retired pay base (High-3 Pay), 107
- retired pay multiplier, 114
- SBP base amount, 144
- SBP premium, 146
- SBP reimbursement amount
  - adjusting decree percentage, 156
  - by check, 155
- value of accrued leave, 46
full-time student and SBP, 146
future spouse, 55, 143

G

gap years (reservist), 16, 27, 158
garnishment, 50–51, 67, 184
- 10/10 rule, 68
- 60 days for set up, 72
- priority of payments, 71
GI Bill, 5, 53–55
gray area Reservist, 16, 158. *See also* reservist
gross retired pay, 65, 78, 82, 87, 139, 144, 145, 147, 150, 152–153, 156, 164, 166

H

health care, 27
- 20/20/15 rule, 17
- 20/20/20 rule, 16
- 36 month coverage, 18
- children, 10
- reservist, 16, 27
- retired pay or annuity required, 25
- unlimited coverage, 23–27, 51, 149
- valuing loss of, 17
High-3 retirement pay, 77, 106–107, 114, 119, 122
Humana Military Health Care Services (HMHS), 20, 26
- acceptance ID card, 34–35
- bill, 33
- expiration, 36–38

hypothetical formula, 73, 114
  converting to actual percent, 120
  language, 103, 111–113
hypothetical retired pay base, 106

I

ID card
  dependent, 10
  HMHS/CHCBP, 21, 25, 35
  Veterans Affairs, 15
income taxes, 42. *See also* taxes
indemnification
  catch all, 80
  Civil Service Employment, 72
  disability waiver, 79–87
Individual Retirement Account, 50
interview, 2–5
involuntary separation, 23–24

J

jurisdiction, 42

L

language (divorce decree)
  COLAs (preventing), 74, 108
  fixed amount or percentage, 108
  formula award, 109–110
  hypothetical award, 111–112
  indemnification
    Civil Service transfer, 72
    disability pay waiver, 79–80
  jurisdiction reasons, 42
  life insurance (required for both), 52
  privacy act waiver, 61
  RAS copies required, 137
  remarriage stopping former spouse award (order stating), 66
  retroactive payments (paid by service member), 65, 72
  SBP award, 159
  SBP deemed election order, 160
  SBP election by service member, 164
  SBP reimbursement, 154
  variations, 110
last will and testament, 1, 8, 47

Leave and Earnings Statement (LES), 4, 6, 7, 139
legal fees, 4
letters. *See* confirmation letters
life insurance, 6
  Armed Forces Benefit Association (AFBA), 52
  child support obligation, 51–52
  Servicemembers' Group Life Insurance (SGLI), 52, 148
  United Services Automobile Association (USAA), 52–53
  Veterans' Group Life Insurance (VGLI), 52
line numbers, 102

M

malpractice, 2, 133, 160
marital share (marital fraction), 90–92
marriage. *See also* remarriage
  15 years for health care, 17
  20 years for commissary/exchange, 46
  20 years for health care, 16
  limit for CHCBP, 19
  short term, 63, 68
Military Spouse Preference Program, 47
Military Spouses Residency Relief Act (MSRRA), 44
moving expenses, 45

N

net present value
  health care, 17
  retirement pay, x
  SBP, 149
non-custodial parent, 150

O

offset, x, 88, 144
open enrollment, 148

P

pay charts, 107, 123–132
pay entry date. *See* service entry date
pension. *See* retired/retainer pay or pension

Per Diem, 45
Permanent Change of Station, 45
permanent residence, 41
premium
    CHCBP, 18
    SBP, 146
    SBP responsibility, 150
present value
    adding COLAs to retired pay, 104, 120
    health care loss, 17
    offset for retired pay, x
    SBP worth, 149
priority group for VA, 14
priority of payments, 71
privacy act, 61
promotions, 102
PX. *See* exchange benefits

R

rank at divorce. *See* date of divorce
rank at retirement, 60, 98–99, 101
remarriage
    20/20/15 health care, 17
    20/20/20 health care, 16
    checklist, 8
    retirement pay, 66
    SBP, 143
    unlimited health care, 26
reservist, 7, 27. *See also* gray area
        Reservist
    fixed language, 108
    formula percentage language, 110
    hypothetical language, 113
    marital share, 92–93
    Reserve Component (RCSBP), 141, 142, 158
    retired pay multiplier, 114
retainer (attorney), 3
retired pay base, 104, 106–107, 111–112, 114–115, 119, 122. *See also* hypothetical retired pay base
retired pay figure (for core formula)
    negotiated, 101
    promotions, 102
    rank at date of divorce, 100
    rank at retirement, 101

retired pay multiplier, 104, 114–115, 118, 122
retired/retainer pay or pension
    10/10 rule. *See* rules
    20/20/15 rule. *See* rules
    20/20/20 rule. *See* rules
    50 percent pay limit, 69–70
    60 day account set up, 72
    application deadline, 133
    beneficiary (SBP/RCSBP), 158–159
    computation of final, 114–115, 118
    computing division, 73–101
    defined, x, 66
    language for decree, 103–115
    line numbers, 102
    paying prior to retirement, 64, 113
    stopping/saving/losing, 43, 66, 113
    vested, 64
Retiree Account Statement (RAS), 137–140
retroactive pay, 65, 72
rounding figures and months, 90, 107, 111, 115, 117, 119
rules
    10/10 rule, 63, 68
    20/20/15 rule, 8, 11, 13, 17, 19, 22, 26
    20/20/20 rule
        commissary and exchange, 46
        health care, 11, 13, 16–17, 26–27, 101

S

SBP. *See* Survivor Benefit Plan
service entry date, 60, 106, 111–112
Servicemembers Civil Relief Act (SCRA), 44
Servicemembers' Group Life Insurance (SGLI), 52
Social Security, 8, 21, 88, 144
Soldiers' and Sailors' Civil Relief Act (SSCRA), 44
State Income Tax Withheld (SITW), 139
state percentage, 73, 89
states (choosing for divorce), 41–42, 80, 113

Alabama, 64
Arizona, 64, 89
Arkansas, 64
California, 64, 89
Colorado, 89
Community Property States, 89
Florida, 86
Idaho, 89
Indiana, 64
Iowa, 86
Louisiana, 89
Missouri, 69
Nevada, 89
New Mexico, 64, 89
Puerto Rico, 64
Texas, 89, 102
Virginia, 80
Washington, 89
Wisconsin, 89
stay of proceedings, 44. *See also* delay divorce
story hour, 5
Survivor Benefit Plan (SBP)
    6.5 percent premium, 146
    55 percent annuity, 144–146
    age 55, remarriage, 143
    agee 70, paid up premiums, 148
    base amount, 144–154, 161, 164–167
    deemed election, 159–161
    eligibility, 143
    incorrect, 166
    language in decree, 159, 168
    level of coverage, 168
    life insurance alternative, 148
    net present value, 149
    one year for application, 6, 159–161
    one year marriage requirement, 143
        SBP exception for dependent children, 143
    premium reimbursement, 153–157
    premium responsibility, 150–152
    remarriage causing suspension, 146
    Reserve Component SBP (RCSBP). *See* reservist

T

taxes, 68, 84, 88
    alimony, 50
teacher (client), 5
Temporary Lodging Allowance (TLA), 45
Temporary Lodging Expense (TLE), 45
Thrift Savings Plan (TSP), 46
transfer of property, 169
Transition Assistance Program (TAP), xii
travel expenses, 41, 45. *See*
TRICARE, 9–14, 18–24

U

Uniformed Services Former Spouses' Protection Act (USFSPA), 63, 67, 98, 134
    disposable retired pay, 65
United Services Automobile Association (USAA), 48–49, 52
unmarried former spouse (UMFS), 26
unremarried former spouse (URFS), 19, 22–23, 26

V

VA (Department of Veterans Affairs)
    Certificate of Eligibility (home loan), 56
    home loan, 56
    Post 9/11 GI Bill, 53
    priority group, 14
vested retirement pay, 64
Veterans' Group Life Insurance (VGLI), 52
veteran spouse, 13, 58
voter registration, 42

W

waive
    disability pay, 65, 78–87
    privacy act, 61
    retired pay award, 68
    right to retirement pay, x, 25, 50, 68, 89
    SBP for life insurance, 148
will. *See* last will and testament
workforce (out of), 4, 89. *See also* employment

Review Request

If you would recommend this book to others, please consider writing a 5 star review on Amazon.com.

How to write a review in four easy steps:

1. On the Internet visit http://www.amazon.com
2. Enter 0-9814737-2-5 in the search box on Amazon
3. About half way down, click *Create Your Own Review*
4. Please tell others what you liked about this book

Reader Comments and Inquiries

Comments, inquiries, or documented updates should be emailed to militarydivorcetips@gmail.com. All remarks are considered for future editions and/or the website to further assist readers.

To view updates visit:
http://www.militarydivorcetips.com/updates.html

Easily Order this Book

- at your local bookstore
- from the publisher at www.militarydivorcetips.com
- online from Amazon at:
www.amazon.com/exec/obidos/ASIN/0981473725/tracytrends